What star is that?

What star is that?

PETER LANCASTER BROWN

A STUDIO BOOK

THE VIKING PRESS · NEW YORK

Published in 1971 by The Viking Press, Inc.
625 Madison Avenue, New York, N.Y. 10022

SBN: 670–75865–5
Library of Congress catalog card number: 73–149587

Printed and bound in Great Britain

Contents

	page
Preface	7
1 Origin of the constellations	9
2 Finding one's way about the sky	26
3 Observing aids	36
A note on abbreviations and conventions	51
4 The northern circumpolar stars	55
5 The Milky Way	67
6 Stars of spring	71
7 Stars of summer	89
8 Stars of autumn	117
9 Stars of winter	135
10 Stars of the southern hemisphere	162
11 What planet is that?	171
Table of planetary positions, 1971–1980	186
Charts	193
Northern stars	
Equatorial and Zodiacal stars	
Southern stars	
Variable stars	
Naked-eye variables	215
Index of stars	217
General index	219

Preface

Man has now landed on the Moon. In near space he knows no limitations and his probes are now reaching out to the nearer planets. But the stars remain aloof, too far away for man to visit save in thought. Yet from time immemorial man has known the stars well – long before he knew about the planets. He learned to use them to find his way, even on the blackest nights, across his territory; by their regular movement he was able to observe the passage of time and they later served him as his calendar to foretell the change of seasons.

Ancient man used the stars more than our immediate ancestors realized. It was not only the Chaldeans, the Mesopotamians and the Egyptians who orientated their temples by the stars. In north-west Europe there is good contemporary evidence to show that church sites – particularly British ones – are orientated to the risings of certain stars. Many of these church sites were originally pagan ones occupied by a Megalithic race who knew as much about astronomy as did many of the Middle Eastern civilizations contemporary to them. There is reason to believe that the Chiltern hills in southern England were used by these ancient men as a primitive celestial computer.

The movement of the stars and planets was the only stable phenomenon in the life of primitive man, and astrological prediction grew naturally out of the early farmers' attempts to relate the prospects for their crops to the only stable thing they knew.

In many books about stars little or nothing is written about the classical mythology associated with the constellations. But the stars and their influence have fascinated mankind since the earliest times, and experience with planetaria has shown quite conclusively that the general public are a good deal interested in the stories of the constellations.

Nowadays, the man in the street has no need of this star knowledge to help him in his daily living. And yet many still succumb to the fascination and beauty of the night sky. Modern man has also learnt, as did his forebears, that the coal-black night outdoors is not half such an unfriendly place if one can recognize the familiar patterns of a few 'old friends'. Familiarity with the pattern of the stars is not difficult to acquire. After preliminary study of the star maps, a few evenings outdoors will provide a working basis for a more leisurely and detailed examination of the constellations, using binoculars or small telescopes.

This book is designed as a manual of star identification for all levels of interest, be it a simple naked-eye recognition of the Great Bear or of Sirius, the Dog Star, or the major seasonal changes of the star sphere. There is also a section on planet recognition. Included in the text are hints and descriptions for observers who wish to see more of the night sky. Equipped with small inexpensive binoculars or telescopes, the observer is led into a new world of beauty just beyond the threshold of naked-eye visibility, which provides a never-ending source of pleasure and satisfaction. He will not be asking the question which Carlyle asked himself: 'Why did not somebody teach me the constellations, and make me at home in the starry heavens, which are always overhead?'

CHAPTER I

Origin of the constellations

Even a casual glance at the night sky shows the heavens strewn with stars that possess definite groupings, and with stars of greater brightness apparently isolated from the rest. These groups and individual stars have always been noticed, even by the most primitive, the Eskimos of the Greenland ice cap or the aborigines of Central Australia.

The early stargazers knew nothing of the nature of the stars and had no conception of the vast emptiness of the universe. Yet even our primitive ancestors were fired with mankind's fundamental and inborn urges: the urge to organize and the urge to measure. Living as they did, exposed to the canopy of open sky, they could not help but notice the various patterns in which the stars were grouped as they appeared to rotate round the heavens, hour by hour and season by season.

When the fundamental truth was discovered that the ever-changing patterns regularly repeated their configuration in the sky at precise intervals, the science of astronomy can be said to have been truly born. This happened so far in the past that no one knows which race or even which civilization first discovered it. Even the traditional star groupings – or constellations as they are called – date back to an age when man carried all his knowledge in his head and passed it on by word of mouth alone. Yet perhaps the truth is that each civilization invented, or adapted, its own system of star names and groupings to suit its own specific needs, each culture attaching names largely borrowed from their immediate terrestrial experience and from their own religions and mythologies.

Astronomy and astrology were born together, and in these early years were brother sciences, complementary to one another. Although astrology is now generally not reckoned as a science – except by the gullible – *early* astrology was considered quite respectable, especially that part of it which was connected with the vagaries of the weather, and which was really the foundation of the more modern science of meteorology. It foretold the weather purely by the passage of time measured by the movement of the stars. The seasons could be predicted very accurately by simply using the ever-changing star sphere as a clock. The Egyptians, observing the rising of the brilliant, blue-white star Sirius in the morning sky, could predict with certainty the flooding of the Nile, and it was likewise with the other stars. It was only when astrology was applied to the direct affairs of men that its decadence began – yet right up to the turn of the seventeenth century astrology was often more highly regarded than astronomy. History relates that the great astronomer Kepler worked for the latter in pursuit of truth, but earned his daily bread by the former, and even chose his second wife by casting horoscopes!

The constellation patterns as we know them today have come down to us direct from Ptolemy's great catalogue, the *Almagest*, dated about AD 137. Ptolemy, one of the greatest astronomers that the world has ever known, lived in Alexandria and was the author of several important astronomical works. The *Almagest* was by far the most famous, and astonishingly survived as a practical everyday work until at least the middle of the fifteenth century. However, this work – or rather catalogue, containing the positions of over one thousand stars in forty-eight groups or constellations – was only a copy of the *Catalogue* of Hipparchus, compiled some 250 years earlier and consisting of 1,080 stars. This original work, now unfortunately lost, is supposed to have contained forty-nine constellations. No manuscript of Ptolemy's *Almagest* is now in existence; the oldest copy is a Greek retranslation dated about the ninth century AD.

But for the unexpected appearance of a new star, a nova or exploding star, in the constellation of Scorpio, the Scorpion, in the year 134 BC, we might know a good deal less about the ancients' knowledge of the constellations. This new star, which could be seen in full daylight, convinced Hipparchus that the heavens and the stars were not immutable, as had long been thought, and that therefore it might be a good idea to catalogue the brighter ones for future reference.

The constellations themselves had been described in the *Phenomena*, a poem by Aratus of Soli dated about 280 BC. This poem is known to have been a versification of an astronomical work by Eudoxus dated 370 BC, and he again had borrowed freely from still more ancient sources which in some instances dated thousands of years earlier. These sources can be inferred from definite clues referring to the place of the equator and the rising and setting of identifiable stars. There are good reasons to suppose that the traditional forty-eight constellations were not defined piecemeal at different times by different races, but represent a premeditated attempt, at an early age, by one man or group of men, to document the stars in a sophisticated and definitive manner.

Many authorities attribute the definition – or formation, as it is properly termed – of the constellations to the period of the early Chaldean civilization, others to the Akkadian culture. But we possess no complete records of their astronomies – only glimpses given by the Babylonians who followed them in the period beginning about 2000 B C, and who borrowed all their culture from their predecessors. Whatever race it may have been, they had already made advances in agriculture. The constellations through which the Sun passes in the spring are named after useful livestock such as lambs, calves and rams: hence Aries, the Ram; Taurus, the Bull; Gemini, the Twins (or goats, which give birth to twins). The other seasons are also recognized in symbolic fashion: summer, with Leo, the Lion, probably signifying the fierceness of the heat in July; there is Virgo, the Virgin, in the autumn when young girls were sent to glean the crops; in the winter there are the constellations concerning the weather, such as Aquarius, the Water Bearer, signifying a period of rains, and Pisces, the Fishes, for the season when the fish were at their best. Perhaps these deductive reasons are too glib or simply coincidental, yet to the ancients, animals of all kinds were very significant, and Herodotus says of the Egyptians, 'in Egypt all sorts of beasts, whether wild or tame, were sacred, and received divine honours.'

Later civilizations, which borrowed the forty-eight constellations from their Middle Eastern source, adapted them to their own imaginations and they bespattered the celestial sky with bedsteads, dogs' tails, ear-rings, couches, elephants' teeth, cats' claws, lions' tails, festoons, razors, pieces of coral, pearls and other whimsical objects equally inappropriate.

Some modern astronomical detectives have traced back the forty-eight constellations of Ptolemy far beyond the previously authenticated history of over 2,300 years. When these forty-eight constellations are plotted on a globe, a large portion of the sky remains uncovered. It can be deduced that those stars not included in the forty-eight constellations did not rise above the horizon where the earliest constellation designer, or designers, lived, so they could not be observed or be included in any scheme of the heavens.

Were it not for the phenomenon known as precession, the astronomical detectives would not have the use of this important research tool to assist them. This precession is simply a wobbling of the Earth on its axis, reminiscent of the wobbling one sees in a spinning top. The main difference in the analogy is that the spinning top will complete its wobble in a matter of seconds while the Earth takes almost 26,000 years to complete one motion. The immediate effect is that over a period of time the stars near the pole may gradually be seen to shift – just observable to the naked eye in the span of a man's lifetime, but it would be centuries before an appreciable shift was readily apparent. However, the movement is a continuous one and it can be measured over a very short period of time.

The shifting of the apparent position of the stars implies that the present Pole Star is not eternally in that position. This is true, and in the period of the Earth's wobble of 26,000 years, many stars come and go in the role of Polaris, as can be seen from fig. 1,

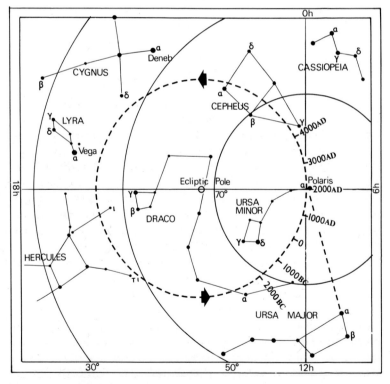

1 *Precessional shift of the north celestial pole.*

which shows the track made by the Earth's north pole in its precessional wobble through different constellations, during the period 2000 BC–AD 4000. It must, however, be borne in mind that with this movement the stars are not shifted in relation to each other – they are only shifted relatively to an observer from the surface of the Earth. The motion which moves the stars relatively to each other is known as proper motion and is due to the rotation of our galaxy, the Milky Way; this can be ignored in considering the origins of the constellations.

Returning to the problem of the actual date when man arbitrarily formed the first groups, it can be assumed that the area of the globe not covered with any stars must logically have been the south celestial pole *at the date when the constellations were fixed.* We know that the location of the observer, or observers, must have been in the northern hemisphere – so stars located in the extreme southern regions could not possibly be visible.

The problem for the astronomical detectives was to find a date when the barren area on the globe was in the position of the south celestial pole – a fairly simple matter once the principles are established. Their subsequent deductions indicated a date of approximately 5000 BC, and from considerations of the probable latitude at which the observers were located, they were led to an area in Asia Minor and Armenia, the birthplace of the great civilizations at the head of the Euphrates Valley.

The constellation detectives also have other valuable clues such as the orientations of the mythical figures depicting the various traditional star groupings. In particular, the important constellations that form the Zodiac can be traced with certainty to the Babylonian system of astronomy. These so-called zodiacal stars and constellations have always held more significance than the rest, for it is through these stars that the wandering 'stars' or planets, including the Sun and the Moon, appeared to travel at precise and regular intervals. There is considerable archeological evidence that, quite independently of each other, many ancient civilizations were able to develop their own astronomies and to map out the apparent journey of the Sun during the annual rotation of the star sphere by adopting twelve (or in some cases ten) signs in what we know as the zodiacal zone. However, there is also evidence to show that the apparently isolated astronomers of the ancient worlds of Egypt, Arabia, Babylon, Persia and India all used, with only minor differences, the basic pattern of twelve signs – which suggests that perhaps the zodiacal groups themselves originated from an earlier, common source.

One question remaining open is whether the constellations, as a whole, were delineated for purely astronomical purposes, or were there other motives? For although the constellations were beautifully mapped out, they often (to modern eyes and reasoning) ignore astronomical convenience in their presentation, and many of the traditional figures are positioned in unnatural attitudes. Also the symbols that the figures represent raise many problems, since often the ancient description of a constellation form is only a terse literary one, handed down by word of mouth or known only from translations of original texts now lost. Star maps and planispheres with the figures actually depicted in a realistic cartographical style are relatively modern productions and were drawn up from literal descriptions – although there are numerous archeological artefacts in existence which depict them in symbolic terms.

2 The Dendera planisphere, 1790 BC (opposite), shows the twelve signs of the Zodiac.

3 Right: the Atlante Farnese. This Roman sculpture of about 200 BC is the first complete picture of the heavens.

    One of the most remarkable of these artefacts is the famous planisphere of Dendera which was found by one of Napoleon's officers in 1798, set in the roof of a secret chamber in the ruins of the temple of Isis at Tentyra where the modern Arab village of Dendera lies. It depicts the twelve signs of the Zodiac with other figures corresponding to Egyptian gods. It has been dated to 1790 BC, and it now stands in the entrance hall of the National Library in Paris.

    The earliest complete 'picture' of the heavens, as against the fragmentary earlier works, is the sculptured Roman marble globe known as the Atlante Farnese, dated about 200 BC (fig. 3), which many suppose to be a copy of a globe constructed by Eudoxus of Cnidos (409–356 BC). This globe is now in the Royal Museum of Naples and is borne by the mythical Atlas resting on one knee.

Depicted on its surface are forty-two constellations, and five others are known to be obliterated by the ravages of time. The earliest known map is the planisphere of Geruvigus, again showing mythical figures, contained in the *Phenomena* of Aratus, of the second century AD, and now in the British Museum Library (fig. 4). The earliest map that depicted actual stars located within the mythical figures, in planisphere form, is that produced by Peter Apian, and dated 5 August 1536; he made it in order to teach his pupils the basic forty-eight constellations.

In earlier times, the zodiacal constellation groups which marked the beginnings of the four seasons were: spring, Taurus, the Bull; summer, Leo, the Lion; autumn, Scorpio, the Scorpion; and winter, Aquarius, the Water Bearer. The principal constellations were often used on banners and coins. In biblical times the Israelites made much use of these sky pictures in their mythology. We can be sure that many of the earlier figures have suffered alterations through the ages and even many well-known groups can represent different forms. In most instances, no stretch of the imagination can reconcile the natural configurations of the stars with the mythical figures that have been draped around them.

It is known that even Ptolemy made his own changes, and it may be concluded that the actual present-day figures are at best only inspired guesses. Confusion sometimes arose because the Asian astronomers often drew their constellations by straight lines connecting prominent stars (as in the modern charts in this book). The object (animal, artefact, etc.) chosen to represent the constellation would then be placed within the geometrical pattern in the form of hieroglyphics. Later, Greek astronomers attempted to actually draw in the representative figures to fit the natural star groups – with obvious difficulties and failures. In some instances, we do know fairly certainly how the constellations were changed. In the case of Virgo, the Virgin, some stars were depicted by Hipparchus in the shoulder of the mythical figure; Ptolemy re-positioned the figure so that these stars appeared in its sides.

Ptolemy's catalogue, apart from one by the Persian astronomer Al-Sufi (AD 903–986) which was copied for the most part from Ptolemy's, remained the only comprehensive catalogue of stars until Tycho Brahe, the last great pre-telescopic astronomer, was inspired to construct a new one – for exactly the same reasons that had induced Hipparchus many centuries before. In 1572, a new star, or nova, burst forth in the constellation of Cassiopeia – and again it was so brilliant that it could be easily seen at midday.

4 *The Geruvigus planisphere, second century AD.*

Tycho's catalogue, consisting of 1,005 stars (and planetary observations), was infinitely more accurate than any done previously – so accurate in fact were his observations of the planet Mars that they enabled his pupil, the great Kepler, to formulate the laws of motion of the planets, whose precise movements had perplexed astronomers from early times. From this work of Tycho, Kepler constructed the Rudolphine Tables, which were to form a basis for all calculations in the solar system for more than a century

5 In 1536 Peter Apian produced this planisphere, the first to show not only the mythological constellation figures but also stars within them.

18

following. History relates that they became a best-seller of the age, being eagerly snatched up by calendar makers, by astronomers to test their theories, by charlatans to cast horoscopes, and by the new generation of seamen who were making the great exploratory voyages around the world.

The first truly scientific star atlas with the likeness to present-day work was the *Uranometria* of Dr Johann Bayer, published in 1603. This important work, a milestone in the history of celestial cartography, contained fifty-one maps etched on copper by Alexander Mair. Bayer was the first to adopt the present-day method of using letters of the Greek alphabet to denote the brighter stars in each constellation. Previous to his time, the individual stars were identified by the position that they occupied in the constellation; the brighter ones received special names to denote their position accurately, as for example, 'in the upper head Castor Apollo'. With Bayer's new system it was merely α Geminorum,* and one was not required even to know its classical name. Before Bayer, it was even more confusing and cumbersome with the unnamed stars; for example a 5th-magnitude star taken from the same constellation of Gemini could be identified as 'in the left hand of the former twin'. One can appreciate that the observer had to know his classical figures extremely well and also be sure he was using the correct version! Nowadays this same star is simply known as θ Geminorum.

Another of Bayer's innovations was to depict stars on charts and globes which represented the *inside* of the celestial sphere; prior to this they were always represented as looking inwards towards the Earth, and were therefore extremely confusing since by this former method they are reversed from what the observer actually sees when he looks up at the sky. It is surprising to read that this innovation was viewed with much disfavour by the other contemporary astronomers, yet in spite of this the more convenient method was quickly adopted by others.

However, Bayer is still much criticized by astronomers for his lack of care in affixing the Greek letters in strict order of brightness – or magnitude, as it is now called. Quite often a star with the Alpha (α) designation is observed to be fainter than the Beta (β) star. Astronomers have argued as to whether some of these reversals are real ones, or simply Bayer was blatantly careless, or his

* Note that in the Bayer system the correct usage is not α Gemini (Alpha the Twins) but the Latin genitive α Geminorum (Alpha *of* the Twins) and similarly with all other constellations.

observing technique was defective. The nineteenth-century German astronomer Argelander, who studied the problem, concluded that Bayer was influenced in his choice of placing the Greek letters simply by the form and direction of the constellations. However, he appears to have followed Ptolemy's brightness estimates to a great extent and it is reasonable to suppose that *some* of the changes are real ones.

Bayer's *Atlas* shows a total number of sixty constellations. The old forty-eight of Ptolemy had been increased by two which Tycho Brahe had formed, and a further twelve new southern circumpolar ones of which Bayer had obtained particulars from the contemporary Dutch navigators Petrus Theodori (Pieter Dirckszoon Keyser), and Friedrick Houtmann. The latter had visited the coast of Western Australia, but had probably plagiarized much of the former's work, publishing it as a catalogue in 1603, the same year as the *Uranometria*.

Although 1,706 individually depicted stars were shown in both hemispheres, Bayer wreathed them in their traditional mythological figures, and from their general appearance it would seem that for the most part they were taken directly from the Geruvigus planisphere. Some, however, are a great departure and are garbed in dress of the late sixteenth century. This practice of Bayer's was not unusual, for at the British Museum there is a copy of an Anglo-Saxon manuscript version of Aratus which depicts Perseus attired as a Saxon noble!

Fig. 6 shows a typical contemporary hand-coloured planisphere of both hemispheres, on the authority of the French astronomer Philippe de la Hire, dated 1702, which forms part of the author's collection. Also from this collection (see fig. 7) is a Zodiac attributed to Backer, 1690. These are typical of the beautifully hand-coloured celestial maps of the period, but both ignore the Greek designations introduced by Bayer. It will be noticed that the planisphere, at least, uses Bayer's idea of representing the constellations by stars as seen from the surface of the Earth, while the Zodiac uses the former method. Nevertheless, eventually all Bayer's innovations became accepted as standard practice, and most, but not all, of the famous names of the seventeenth century adopted them. In his wake followed Flamsteed, Hévelius, Halley,

6 Opposite, upper: planisphere by the French astronomer Philippe de la Hire, 1702.

7 Opposite, lower: zodiac by Remmet Jevnisse Backer, 1690.

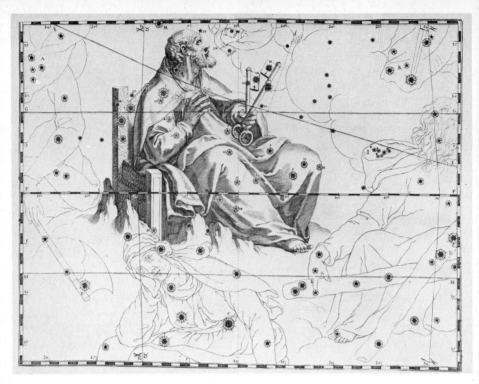

8 Above: Aries depicted as St Peter, by Julius Schiller, 1627.

9 Opposite: 'Caelum Heraldicum' – the 'heraldic' constellations of Erhard Weigel.

Royer, Pardies, Blaeu, Hond and Cellarius; all produced first-class atlases and planispheres and also introduced new constellations – especially in the star maps of the southern skies, which were now being explored systematically by scientific expeditions dispatched specially for the purpose to southern latitudes.

One of the more interesting mapmakers was Julius Schiller, who published in 1627 what he called a major revision of Bayer's *Uranometria*. In the place of the latter's traditional mythological figures he enshrined among the stars numerous Christian saints and biblical figures to replace the heathen ones. The constellation of Aries, the Ram, is drawn as St Peter (see fig. 8); Taurus, the Bull, as St Andrew; and Lyra, the Harp, as the Manger of the Child Christ. Yet Schiller had not been the first in attempts to christianize the pagan constellations, for, as long ago as the eighth century, the Venerable Bede had deposed the Olympian gods for biblical figures, and there were further attempts by other and lesser scholars right up to the time of the Reformation.

Another curious attempt at celestial reform in the seventeenth century was made by Erhard Weigel, a professor of mathematics at the University of Jena – a scholar of great learning who was supposed to have written some 104 books, most of which are now lost or destroyed. Weigel published a star atlas called *Caelum Heraldicum* in which the stars were adorned with the coats of arms of many of the more influential princes of Europe. On the maps in this atlas, Ursa Major, the Great Bear, became 'the Elephant of Denmark', and Cygnus, the Swan, or Northern Crow, 'The Ruta and swords of Saxony'. In more modern times, too, there have been serious attempts to change or rationalize the ancient constellation figures, and even to change the traditional Arabic star names. The English writer A. P. Herbert published a work entitled *A Better Sky*, showing the stars named after contemporary politicians, and the constellations after countries and nations. Needless to say, it created considerable amusement – but fortunately that is all.

23

Our consideration of the history of the constellations has so far been confined to the cradle of Western civilization. In China, the science of astronomy appears to have begun in earnest during the reign of Hoangti Yuchi, at the time when a 'large' star lay near the pole of the heavens (a Draconis). In many cultures we find that the heavens were regarded as the father and the Earth the mother of things. The Australian aborigines considered that when they died, they automatically went up among the stars to enter a further period of life.

The Polynesian races had a well-developed star lore which they had developed in a similar fashion to the Phoenicians, primarily as a navigation tool for sea voyaging. They discovered that by using the azimuth of certain stars, at setting or rising, they could make predictable landfalls when sailing between the scattered islands of the Pacific. The idea behind Polynesian astronomy has attracted great interest in recent years since attempts have been made to use it in the general problem of the origin of these Pacific people. Did they originate from South America or Eastern Asia? Some of their astronomy certainly resembles the Babylonian or later Egyptian ideas, but this may easily have arrived via India and the South-East Asian folk-lore route. On the other hand, Mayan astronomy shows similar connections, but at the present time these astronomical clues tend to complicate the problems rather than solve them.

Outside the Western cradle of civilization, only the ancient Chinese astronomy had a comparable sophistication, and one which in many ways outrivalled that of the West. The oldest Chinese star maps are ascribed to two writers who lived about 350 B C, but they are thought to be only transcriptions of a much earlier work – for they are crudely drawn by unskilled copyists. There is some evidence to indicate that they were based on charts which had infiltrated from the West.

Chinese observations of comets and new stars are particularly well documented, and more comprehensive than those of the West. It is of considerable interest that in the case of Hipparchus' new star in Scorpio in 134 B C, the reality of which was treated with much scepticism by some modern authorities, the Chinese chronicles record it in very precise terms. These 'guest stars', as the Chinese knew them, are now known to be associated with those new, very puzzling deep-sky objects called pulsars. In A D 1054, the Chinese chronicles record that a 'guest star' appeared in a position where in modern times we observe an object called the Crab nebula (see page 160 and fig. 38). In 1969, near its centre, the radio signals from a pulsating star were identified and a little later it was seen visually – the very first pulsar to be observed in such a manner.

These records of the heavens collected by our ancient forebears, although at first glance they appear far removed from modern times, can be seen to provide highly valuable historical data for contemporary astronomical research. In the case of Halley's comet, these records span over 2,000 years and document every instance when the comet, during its 75- to 76-year round-trip to the frontiers of the solar system, had returned to the vicinity of the Sun.

Modern astronomy has come a long way from its mythical and astrological antecedents in its understanding of some of the physical mechanisms that govern natural phenomena. The modern astronomer need not know the mythical constellation figures as his predecessors were required to, to find their way among the stars (although often he does!). He no longer consults richly ornamented, painstakingly hand-coloured star maps – instead, he might have them hanging on his study wall if he is fortunate and wealthy, for they are now rare collectors' items and in much demand. His contemporary chart will more likely be some such photographic masterpiece as the *Palomar Sky Atlas*, which took many years to produce, and which requires a complete cabinet system to house, recording stars in numbers that are simply uncountable in a normal life-span.

Yet, in spite of it all, when new objects are discovered there is often a hurried recourse to the old maps and old records, for the modern astronomer is highly conscious of his great heritage, of the painstaking work of those who have gone before him, and of the ancient myths and folk-lore.

CHAPTER 2

Finding one's way about the sky

Unlike the ancient watchers of the sky, the modern professional astronomer is entirely divorced from the night sky by the protective hemispherical dome above him, and in addition he is often totally submerged within the cage of the telescope, through which he is exposing his photographic plates rather than looking at the stars directly. The spectacle of the night sky can only be fleetingly glimpsed through the narrow shutter, and he is unable to see the constellation at which his telescope is directed. If he wishes to observe a particular star, he will merely consult his modern catalogue for its precise location and then feed in its celestial co-ordinates to the fully automated controls of his great telescope. To complete his night's work he need never leave his observatory building for the chill night air, and he will be totally unaware of what is happening as the invisible stars glide silently across the heavens.

It cannot be so for those who wish to learn the stars, to count them among intimate friends, to make them even recognizable at an instant through a narrow gap in the clouds. The business of learning the stars, although it requires the occasional braving of the elements, is one of the most enjoyable and *free* experiences left to modern man (or woman!). For the beginner there is no need to rush outdoors in attempts to survey the entire heavens in one clear evening. This is not truly possible in any case, since the star sphere is continually and gradually changing its appearance to the observer throughout the year. It is best for the beginner to start in easy stages and absorb the various sky patterns in a methodical step-by-step approach; building from a foundation of elementary facts about the stars and their apparent movements, learnt even before taking the initial step outdoors to attempt the first recognitions.

Outdoors, on a clear night, the heavens give the appearance of a large bowl, or the *inside* of a vast hemispherical dome, with the observer located at the centre looking outwards and upwards. If one lives in a town or city – or if the Moon is above the horizon –

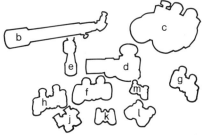

10 *Small instruments suitable for deep-sky observations by amateurs:* a (right), 25 × 105 *binocular telescope, field* 3° *(ex military reconnaissance);* b, 2-*in. refracting telescope* (× 25, × 50, × 75); c, 10 × 80 *binocular telescope, field* 7½° *(ex military reconnaissance);* d, e, 7 × 50 *monocular, field* 7½° (d, *ex military predictor 'scope);* f, 7 × 35 *binoculars, wide-field* 11½°; g, 8 × 30 *binoculars, medium wide-field* 8½°; h, 6 × 30 *binoculars, medium field* 9°; j, 7 × 25 *miniature sport binoculars, wide-field* 11°; k, 6 × 24 *miniature sport binoculars, wide-field* 9°; l, *Galilean field glasses, wide-field* 14°; m, 2 × 25 *Galilean opera glasses, wide-field* 9°.

Note contrast in size (above) between a *and* m.

only the brighter stars will be visible; but in many ways this is no disadvantage to the beginner since he will only be able to see those brighter members of each constellation which go to form the distinctive shapes, or groups, and his eyes will not be distracted by the myriads of fainter stars that spawn into view when the Moon is absent and the atmosphere crystal-transparent.

On these clear, moonless nights, the observer can see approximately 3,000 stars with the naked eye if he possesses normal vision. At his first view of the night sky, a beginner will quite often remark that the stars he or she can see are so numerous as to be uncountable. However, the effect is purely a psychological one; nevertheless, even with the simplest optical assistance such as a pair of opera glasses (fig. 10*m*) the number of visible stars increases enormously, and if he had sufficient time to count them with such an instrument, the number would be over 100,000. With a more powerful instrument such as modern prismatic binoculars (fig. 10*c*), the number could easily be doubled.

As a first step to make recognition easier, the beginner is recommended to concentrate on learning only the brighter stars that form the constellation shapes, which are shown on the seasonal star maps in this book. After thus gaining a working familiarity with the principal groups, he will be equipped to inspect each constellation in more detail, with the assistance of the individual maps and descriptive text detailing all the bright and interesting objects contained within the boundaries of the constellations.

It has already been remarked in the previous chapter that *almost* all the brighter stars and constellations had special names given to them by astronomers in the past when they were first mapped. It will also be remembered that when Bayer produced his star atlas in 1603, he gave the stars designations signified by letters of the Greek alphabet. Although one can learn the stars without even knowing the Greek designations, they are an invaluable guide – especially for locating those which were not given names by the older astronomers – and they are easy to memorize.

α Alpha	ι Iota	ρ Rho
β Beta	κ Kappa	σ Sigma
γ Gamma	λ Lambda	τ Tau
δ Delta	μ Mu	υ Upsilon
ε Epsilon	ν Nu	φ Phi
ζ Zeta	ξ Xi	χ Chi
η Eta	o Omicron	ψ Psi
θ Theta	π Pi	ω Omega

On the detailed maps will also be found other ways of designating stars, since the Greek letters are limited by their number. The first Astronomer Royal, Flamsteed, like Bayer, introduced his own system of identifying stars, this time simply by the number in his catalogue. Later observers, who discovered the double and variable stars, clusters and nebulae, also introduced designations from their own lists and catalogues. Although it may sound a highly complicated business, it is not really so, for all the well-used numbers, letters and symbols quickly become familiar. A brighter star can be identified in many ways: for example, *Aldebaran* (Arabic name), α (Alpha) Tauri (Bayer method), 87 (Flamsteed's number), 1420 BAC (British Association Catalogue number) and 8639 LI (the number in the catalogue of the French astronomer Lalande). There are many more, but I shall not encumber the reader with further ones since knowledge of them is beyond the scope of this book. A list of the abbreviations which are used is given on p. 51.

Star positions

Although all the brighter stars are designated to various constellations with names, Greek letters, numbers etc., the method is too imprecise to locate accurately in the sky the position of all celestial objects, particularly the fainter ones only rendered visible by optical means. It may be remembered that on a clear night upward of 3,000 individual stars can be seen with the naked eye alone, and with binoculars at least 100,000. It would be useless to state that such and such an unnamed star belonged to a particular constellation – since finding it again would be like looking for the proverbial needle in a haystack.

Just as with terrestrial maps one can easily locate the position of a city or large town simply by inspecting the map without further reference if one knows the county or district, so with a brighter star. But with an obscure village or geographical name, one would consult a gazetteer to find its latitude and longitude, and the same is true of obscure stars, which are located by a similar method known as Right Ascension and Declination. These celestial angular co-ordinates were invented in the dim and distant past as an imaginary fixed grid to measure against. One of the earliest instruments to measure star angles was found in the tomb of Tutankhamen.

The sky co-ordinates right ascension and declination (RA and Dec) are then the exact equivalent to the more familiar longitude and latitude. The minor difference is that right ascension can be

expressed in *both* angular measure – degrees (°), minutes ('),
seconds (″) – and also in time – hours, minutes and seconds. However, it is more usual to use the latter, because right ascension is
also directly related to sidereal time or star time. Using time
intervals is more convenient for astronomers, who are for ever
having to take into account the different kinds of time, the subject
of which is outside our considerations in simple star recognition.

All co-ordinates have to have reference points, just as longitude on earth is referred to the Greenwich meridian, and latitude to
the equator. Now if the Earth's axis were not inclined, the path that
the Sun, Moon and planets appear to make in the sky, called the
ecliptic, would coincide with an imaginary line (like its earthly
imaginary line) called the celestial equator. But the Earth's axis is
tilted at $23\frac{1}{2}°$, so that the ecliptic and the equator are separate
planes (fig. 11). However, it can be seen that they must, at some
point, intersect each other, and these cross-points are known as the
spring and autumnal equinoxes, or in other words, simply the
apparent location points of the Sun on 21 March and 22 September
each year.

The ancients hit upon the idea of using the position of the
spring equinox as their zero point for measuring right ascension,
which is then carried round the sky in an eastwards, or counter-
clockwise, direction until it comes back to the zero point. As
stated earlier, right ascension is another way of expressing sidereal time; and is star time for any particular observer, as the heavens
revolve across another imaginary line – called the meridian –
running north and south and cutting the vertical (the zenith)
above the observer's head. For example, when the spring equinox
point (zero) is on an observer's north-south line (the meridian),
the right ascension of any star on that line is also zero.

All professional observatories, and many amateur ones, are
equipped with a clock which runs at sidereal time. Knowing
sidereal time, and with a star catalogue showing right ascension
and declination, it is possible to position a telescope precisely on
the star to be observed, without any direct reference to the sky –
simply by using the graduated circles attached to the telescope's
mounting. Declination is always measured as a plus (+) or minus
(−) angle, north and south respectively of the celestial equator.
Now, although it is useful for the observer to understand how
objects are located by using celestial co-ordinates, the method will
not be used to locate the deep-sky objects described in subsequent
chapters. Since the book is designed for observers using the naked
eye and small instruments, we shall be using the direct method

which will give the observer a more intimate knowledge of the sky, firstly by locating the brighter, more prominent members of the constellations, and then by using them as reference points to find the fainter ones. Although some small telescopes are equipped with graduated circles, the amateur sky observer rarely uses them – except perhaps for locating a planet during daylight when it cannot be seen directly with the naked eye. The larger telescopes have very small angular fields of view, so that without using circles the observer would waste an enormous amount of valuable observing time simply attempting to find the object to be studied.

Constellation boundaries

In the older star atlases, produced by the first celestial cartographers, there is often a great deal of confusion at the boundaries of constellations as to which one a particular star belongs to. In fact the early sky maps had no boundaries separating the different constellations. These were first introduced in 1801, by Bode, who drew arbitrary lines without thought of what effect long-term precession might have in displacing them. After Bode, other astronomers decided on their own modifications, so that the situation eventually became as confusing as before. In 1930, the International Astronomical Union decided to adopt a proposal by E. Delporte, a French astronomer, for a standardization of the boundaries, so that they ran 'squarely' exactly along the direction of the celestial co-ordinates RA and Dec. These boundary lines, like the stars themselves, are subject to precessional movement, so that when a new star atlas is constructed, it is always quoted as belonging to a particular epoch, e.g. 1920. All the charts in this book are based on epoch 1950, and are sufficiently accurately delineated so that for the purpose of this book an observer could use them long after the year 2000, without any alterations.

Finding one's bearings

On his first night out, the observer will quickly notice that the visible stars are not distributed uniformly over the dome of the heavens. The realization of this is actually the first step towards actual recognition of individual groups. Quite a short period of observation will show the observer that the stars, like the Sun and the Moon, rise in the east, climb up the sky until due south (if he is located in the northern hemisphere) and sink again towards the western horizon.

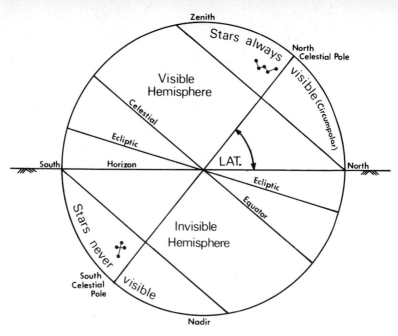

11 The celestial sphere in northern temperate latitudes.

More extended observations over two consecutive nights will show that the stars appear to make one complete circuit of the sky in about twenty-four hours. These observations will also show that the star sphere *appears* to be rotating round a 'pivot' (owing to the daily rotation of the Earth). Actually there are two 'pivots': one is in the northern and the other in the southern hemisphere. The altitude that these 'pivots' make to the southern and northern horizons depends on the latitude from which the observer is looking; this angle is actually the real latitude and can be used for navigational purposes.

These 'pivots' are known as the north and south celestial poles. In the northern hemisphere the south celestial pole is invisible since it is located far below the observer's horizon (in the southern hemisphere it is the reverse situation). Since this book is aimed principally for star recognition by observers in the northern hemisphere, we shall start our constellation and individual star recognition by first locating the north celestial pole. Once this is found, and the position remembered, it becomes a key which will open the door to the rest of the heavens.

Firstly to make it easier: in the British Isles and North America, or other locales lying in the northern temperate zone, the north celestial pole is situated approximately halfway between the horizon and the point directly overhead (the zenith) when the observer faces *true* north. Very close by this celestial 'pivot' point is the star called Polaris (the Pole Star), which is actually located about two moon diameters away from the precise polar point.

Not too far distant will be found another key star configuration. This star group is known as the Plough and forms part of the constellation of Ursa Major (Latin for Great Bear). Since it is rotating about the north celestial pole, in common with other adjacent constellations, it may be found at any position of the 'clock face', depending on the month of the year and the time of day, if we imagine Polaris to be the pivot point of the hour hand.

We have already discussed the highly imaginative figures that the ancients gave to the constellation forms. The Great Bear is typical of the animals perpetuated in the sky, although there is some argument between authorities as to why such a figure should appear at all in mythology and also in which way it should actually be depicted. (Some argue that where the traditional tail is now placed should be the head!) The origin has been ascribed to the fact that it was the only well-known northern constellation familiar to the Greeks, and because they also knew that the polar bear came from the north, the two became associated by geographical connections.

To the later, more mundane, less imaginative Saxons and us moderns, the seven principal stars give the appearance of a wagon or a plough – or better still a saucepan with a bent handle (or a dipper). The two brightest stars Alpha (α) and Beta (β) point directly to the 'pivot', which is situated at a distance equal to about five times the distance separating the two stars. Once the Great Bear is recognized, and its hourly and daily movements familiarized, the observer has a means of finding true north, even if he decides not to bother learning another constellation!

It will soon be noticed that any star whose distance from the Pole Star is less than the distance of the Pole Star above the northern horizon, can never set for the observer – or, in other words, disappear from view below the horizon. All such stars are called circumpolar, and the stars which form the Great Bear are an example.

You will recall it was said earlier that the star sphere appears to make a complete circuit approximately once every twenty-four hours owing to the Earth's rotation. But if the star sphere rotated in exactly twenty-four hours, the same stars would rise at the same time night after night, and we should see the same constellations in the summer as we do in the winter. Even the most casual of sky observers will soon see that this is certainly not the case, and the winter's stars and constellations are not the same as those of summer (except of course the circumpolar ones). The reason is that the stars do not make one daily circuit of the star sphere in exactly twenty-four hours – but in a period some four minutes shorter. Thus clock time is slower than star time, and even a week's observation will show the observer that a star or constellation as seen at *exactly* the same clock time each night has gradually shifted position. The reason for the gradual daily shift is, of course, that the Earth is not only spinning on its axis (once every twenty-four hours) but is also revolving round the Sun in a period of one year which causes a steady change of the observer's viewpoint of the Sun and stars from minute to minute and from day to day. The four minutes' accumulated difference each day multiplied by the days in the year equals twenty-four hours and, therefore, in one year we come back to the starting point again.

It is important that the reasons for the seasonal change in position of the constellations is clearly understood, since it makes easier the actual identification of the different constellations in different seasons.

Star brightness

The first inspection of the sky by the observer shows him that the stars differ among themselves in apparent brightness. These differences depend on two main factors: different luminosities, and the fact that the stars are located at varying distances from the Earth.

It was Hipparchus, in 127 B C. who first divided the stars into six different brightness categories. The very brightest were said to be 1st magnitude and the next 2nd, and so down to the 6th – which is approximately the faintest that can be seen on a clear, moonless night with the naked eye. This simple system was quite adequate for astronomy before the invention of the telescope, but it was found to be too pragmatic when observational astronomy began making rapid advances in the nineteenth century, and in about 1850 it was given a precise definition. At this time it was agreed to base the system of magnitudes on a logarithmic scale, whereby a 1st-magnitude star was 2.512 times brighter than a 2nd-magnitude star. This meant in practice that a 6th-magnitude star was about one hundred times less bright than one of the 1st magnitude. Nowadays, we also have stars with so-called negative magnitude, implying that these are *brighter* than magnitude 0 stars. For example, in the case of Sirius (*a* Canis Majoris), its brightness is represented by – 1.6, which means that it is 1.6 magnitudes *brighter* than a star of magnitude 0.0. On this scale of brightness, the planet

Venus, at its most brilliant in the evening or morning skies, is about magnitude -3.0. The Moon is -12.0, and the Sun -27.0. However, even the ancient astronomers felt that whole magnitude numbers were insufficient to show precise differences between stars, and used fractions of a whole magnitude, e.g. one and one-third. Modern astronomers use a decimal system and represent stars to a tenth, a hundredth, or even a thousandth of a magnitude, using an instrument called a photometer which can detect, by electronic means, very minor differences in stellar brightness. With considerable practice, an experienced observer is able to detect differences of one-tenth of a magnitude by using the eye alone.

The seasonal charts depicted in this book omit many of the fainter naked-eye stars simply because these are not necessary in recognizing the principal star groups and seasonal constellation shifts. The more detailed charts, however, depict many more stars, including *all* the naked-eye ones, and some that can only be seen with binoculars or small telescopes. They also include many deep-sky objects of interest to observers.

How to find the constellations

We shall begin with the stars which form the northern circumpolar groups. It may be remembered that these are the stars which for the observer are always visible on each night throughout the year and which appear to be revolving round the north celestial pole in an anti-clockwise direction.

Which stars, and how many stars, are circumpolar for any particular observer depends on his location, or more precisely his latitude in the northern hemisphere. The charts of circumpolar stars provided in this book are the ones that may always be seen by an observer in the middle northern latitudes (approximately 50° latitude north), but remember that they do not always appear in the same position on the 'clock face'. For example, in the autumn, the Great Bear in the early evening is seen below the Pole Star. In spring at approximately the same hour, it is above the Pole Star (fig. 17). This also shows that the constellations are not always seen the same way up. The observer must constantly bear this in mind when he observes the constellations, at different hours of the night or different times of the year.

Note. Those observers who simply wish to identify and learn the brighter stars and constellations, and who for the present do not wish to observe the deep-sky objects, should now turn to Chapter 4 to begin actual star recognition.

CHAPTER 3
Observing aids

The majority of well-known observers started their sky-viewing careers in modest ways, and a lesson can be learnt from this. A modest beginning ensures that the observer develops his technique in a step-by-step fashion. Ideally a newcomer will learn the stars by naked eye – and if he can resist using or buying a telescope, he will thus serve his apprenticeship for perhaps a year. Then his first binoculars, or small telescope, will allow him to view the deep-sky objects that have long whetted his appetite.

It is of great importance that he appreciate the benefit that even modest optical equipment can bring, and fully explore its potential before rushing out to buy a larger instrument. Often a beginner is eager to start using a large telescope – purchased to the limit of his resources – which he will be quite unable to appreciate. He will conduct a short-lived orgy of looking at all the brighter celestial lollipops – that is if he has sufficient skill to locate them! The enthusiasm will predictably be short-lived, and the new toy will soon be relegated to the attic or the garden shed. Often such an observer will complain bitterly that he has no one to teach him. He may even be resentful of another local, experienced observer who refuses to give him lessons (though many will). He will be unaware that perhaps he is the twentieth person to come along with such a request. He will not understand that the experienced observer will have his own programme of work, for which, being an amateur, he will have precious little available free time; and that he has lost his enthusiasm for teaching rookies since his last pupil decided to take up philately!

The best method to learn the stars is by teaching yourself from a book. As Samuel Smiles found, self help is often the best help. One of the pleasantest and most memorable of all experiences is the actual process of learning the stars. I can vividly recall identifying my first star, which was Arcturus, in my schooldays during the luxury of the total black-out of the Second World War. I can recall following the new constellations from season to season and then, early one morning, watching Arcturus come round again just like an old friend returning. What an exciting experience it can be to possess for the first time a proper 2-in. telescope and then to wait eagerly for darkness to fall and see Jupiter with his four attendant moons strung out like pearls on a string; and what a thrill to glimpse the darker cloud belts just visible across the yellow oval disc. Although I soon graduated to much larger, more powerful instruments, my first observations remain the more vivid ones.

Modern observational astronomy began a little over three centuries ago with the invention of the telescope in about 1608. When Galileo heard about it, he quickly built one for himself and soon applied it to a comprehensive study of the heavens. Even with this very modest optical device, little better than half a modern opera glass, an entirely new world was opened to man. The wanderers, or planets, which to the ancients were merely points of light, were resolved into discs, and in the case of Jupiter, the four brighter moons were easily seen. The stars, although they still remained only scintillating points of light, were revealed to exist in innumerable numbers.

For simple star recognition there can be no better tool than the naked eye, but even a simple opera glass – similar to Galileo's first telescope – enables a casual watcher of the skies to see celestial objects beyond the power of unaided vision. Nevertheless, a newcomer to star recognition should first find his way about the sky without resort to any other means than his unassisted eyes. In this way he will develop a familiarity with the heavens which will provide a foundation for subsequent observation with binoculars and telescopes.

The principal advantage that optical assistance brings to observation is light grasp: the ability to detect faint images of celestial objects is determined by the surface area of the eye, or of the front object lens of binoculars or the telescope. The human eye, with a diameter of only one-fifth of an inch, compares very unfavourably with an 8 × 30 modern prismatic binocular, which has a light-collecting area over forty times greater.

Yet another advantage is what is known as resolving power. This is the ability to separate, or resolve, fine detail with objects which are close together and appear as a single one with the unassisted eye. This resolving power is expressed in seconds of arc, and is based on a formula first devised by an English amateur astronomer, the doctor-cum-clergyman Dawes, in 1850; nowadays this is often referred to as the 'Dawes limit'. Resolving power is highly important in the observations of double stars and planetary surface detail. In the case of double stars a 1-in.-diameter telescope will theoretically resolve (or separate) two stars which are 4.5″ (4½ seconds of arc) apart. Nevertheless, this ability is dependent on the quality of the optical surfaces and it also entails a minimum magnification, usually assumed to be about ×25 per inch of aperture (see p. 52).

Generally speaking, opera glasses and prismatic binoculars which are held by the hand alone, and otherwise unsupported, have a low magnification. This is because the smallest hand tremor is also magnified, and above a certain limit viewing becomes difficult. A magnification of ×8 is about the highest practical limit for portable binoculars. Other factors, however, do enter into binocular design. One is: the greater the magnification, the smaller the field of view; and for terrestrial viewing purposes the less brilliant the object, or view, which is being magnified. This is because the available light collected by the objective lens has to be spread over a larger area.

The older type of opera and field glasses (fig. 10) generally have low magnification, extending from ×2 to ×6, for they operate on the principle of the Galilean optical system which is now almost completely superseded by the prismatic optical system of modern binoculars. However, these older instruments are not to be despised, especially for astronomical purposes, for they give some glorious views of star fields and clusters – particularly those in the richer portions of the Milky Way.

Modern prismatic binoculars have a more complex optical system and can be designed to give a wide field of view in combination with higher magnification than the Galilean type. Typical of contemporary binoculars is one described as 7×35, which means magnification seven times, object lens (the front one) of each barrel 35 mm (1.4 in.) in diameter. This particular model (fig. 10f) gives a field of view of 11°30′ (often expressed on some binocular models as so many yards per thousand feet). Occasionally one finds binoculars with fields of view extending to 13°, but generally speaking such instruments are relatively expensive and may give blurred images at the outer edge of the field of view so that the wide-field advantage is lost.

All modern prismatics have coated lenses, and to gain the greatest advantage the internal prisms should also be coated. This 'coating' cuts down light which would otherwise be lost by reflection, instead of being transmitted (or refracted). It can lead in identical models, one coated and one uncoated, to differences of

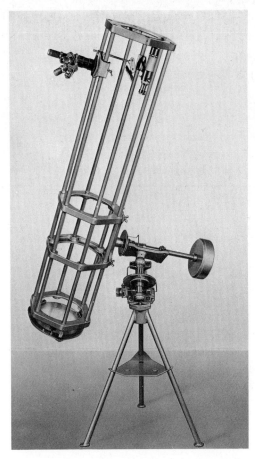

*12 8½-in. Newtonian reflecting telescope equipped with
circles for setting Right Ascension and Declination.*

one or more star magnitudes – so it can be seen that it is highly advantageous to have fully coated optical systems for the observation of faint objects near the borderline of visibility.

Many low-priced prismatic binoculars on the market will exhibit 'rainbow' colours when a bright object is viewed. This is an optical 'disease' known as chromatic aberration and is caused by unmatched optical components. Although the effect is a nuisance, for simple straightforward observations these binoculars are still very useful instruments – and are certainly better than none at all if your resources are limited. All early astronomical telescopes suffered from this chromatic defect, but it did not deter their users from making significant discoveries.

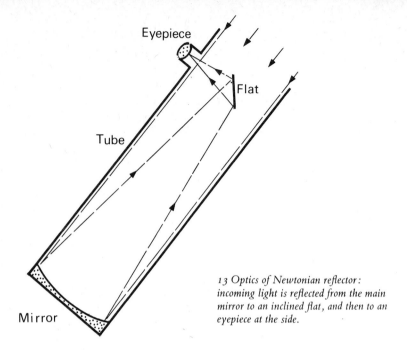

13 *Optics of Newtonian reflector: incoming light is reflected from the main mirror to an inclined flat, and then to an eyepiece at the side.*

By contrast, reflecting telescopes do not show these bright colours. This is because in the case of the *reflection* of light there is no tendency for the light beam to be split into its component wavelengths (or simply colours), as with *refraction*, when the light passes *through* the lens and is bent to a focus. However, some reflecting telescopes may still show signs of chromatic aberration owing to defects in their eyepieces, which rely on lenses.

Usually astronomical reflecting telescopes are constructed on the Newtonian optical system (fig. 13). The incident light rays are *reflected* and focused from a parabolic mirror to a secondary (flat) mirror which is angled at 45° to the main tube in order to project the image sideways to an eyepiece. It must always be remembered that both astronomical refractors and reflectors give inverted images, in other words the object is viewed upside-down. This does not matter in astronomy for it enables more light to be transmitted to the observer's eye – since fewer lenses are required in the eyepiece (and the glass lenses absorb light). Astronomical eyepieces often consist of either one or two lenses, whereas terrestrial ones (to make the image upright) require four.

Binoculars have an advantage not possessed by telescopes in that viewing with both eyes is more restful (except for those rare birds who cannot converge two light images in their brain). This means that binoculars can be used for longer periods of observation without fatigue – an important factor when straining the eyes for faint images of deep-sky objects such as nebulae and comets. Fig. 10 shows various pairs of prismatic binoculars which I use for my observing. The largest ones are 25 × 105, which, we have seen, means a magnification of × 25, with an object lens of 105 mm (4 inches). Many comet hunters use powerful 'glasses' such as these, and G. E. D. Alcock, a British amateur schoolmaster-astronomer, has discovered four new comets by using such an aid. Of course, they were not designed initially for astronomical work, in fact they were produced by the Germans as military reconnaissance binoculars, and after the Second World War they were sold on the surplus markets to be eagerly snapped up by those who realized their astronomical observing potential. Such instruments, if produced commercially for peaceful uses, would be prohibitively expensive.

Another instrument which is ideal for adaptation to astronomical viewing (fig. 10*d*) originally formed the observing telescope on military tracking predictors. It has a magnification of × 7 and a field lens of 2 inches – in effect a small compact telescope, which has now found its way to the far corners of the earth via the war-surplus markets.

When considering a new binocular purchase for deep-sky observing, the 8 × 30 model should be regarded as the median type. There are many varieties on the market, but by preference a pair with a wide-angle view should be chosen: say 450 feet at 1,000 yards (giving at least 7.5° true field – or one and a half times the distance between the Pointer stars in the Great Bear). If the money can be stretched a little further, it is worth investing in a pair of extra wide-angle 7 × 35's; say 500–550 feet at 1,000 yards, or a true field of 11° plus. Both these varieties of binoculars are also useful for ordinary terrestrial purposes.

The heavy, hand binoculars of the 7 × 50 'night glass' type, although theoretically they collect more light (i.e. by having a larger object lens), can only be fully effective in truly coal-black skies. In towns or semi-rural conditions they produce too bright a sky background so that no advantage is gained over the smaller, handier 8 × 30's or 7 × 35's – which are also much lighter in weight and therefore less fatiguing to hold.

Mounted binoculars of the 10 × 80, or 25 × 105 variety, as illustrated in fig. 10, are more difficult to come by these days, but may still occasionally be picked up by advertising or watching the columns of certain periodicals which specialize in optical goods of this kind. However, they will be expensive: the 10 × 80 model will cost at least as much as a good-quality 6-in. reflector, while the 25 × 105 model probably will be as expensive as an $8\frac{1}{2}$-in. reflector, or in models of first-order quality, a 12-in. reflector. If an investment of this kind is contemplated, it must first be considered whether the large binoculars are better suited for one's observing programme than the telescope, which will reveal a great deal more yet is not as convenient to use. The best situation is, of course, to own a whole series of instruments – like the golfer with his bag of clubs: one then has the right instrument for the job. For instance, it is no use looking at a variable star which varies from mag 5 to mag 7 with a 12-in. telescope, whereas a pair of binoculars is ideally suited. Likewise, a long-period variable with a minimum brightness of mag 13, will be just visible with a 12-in., but hopelessly beyond the range of 8 × 30 binoculars.

The naked-eye or binocular observer will find a garden chair especially suitable for gazing at the sky overhead. A garden chair with arms provides an ideal elbow rest to steady hand-held binoculars, and is essential when operating at the limit of their optical range in detecting faint objects. An alternative method of steadying binoculars is to mount them on a small table tripod by means of a special adapter which can be purchased from optical stores. This tripod method is useful when observing variable stars, for once a field is located, the binoculars can be left in position and the hands remain free to hold a star chart or record an observation.

Astronomical 'seeing'

Quite early on in your stargazing career you will be aware that meteorological conditions have a great bearing on the visibility of astronomical objects. Astronomical 'seeing' is a term used to describe the sky conditions in relation to the *steadiness* of the image; it does *not* describe the sky transparency, although the two are generally very closely related. Everyone is aware of the twinkling of the stars on cold, frosty nights. This effect is due to atmospheric turbulence, which causes the path of the starlight entering the Earth's atmosphere to be displaced at rapid intervals. Now if these are readily apparent to the optically unassisted human eye, it can be imagined what the result can be when any kind of optical system is used which involves magnification. It follows that the amount of disturbance bears some relation to the amount of magnification. This can easily be verified if an observer tries to use too high a power to view a celestial object: when the turbulence is high – or, as we say, when the 'seeing' is bad – the object will often, in severe cases, appear to 'boil' in front of the observer's eye. Magnification is often limited by the aperture of the telescope used and this is usually expressed by a figure giving magnification per inch of aperture of the telescope; however, it varies with different celestial objects, and it is also dependent on the quality of the optics within the system.

It so happens that the worst 'boiling' takes place on those crystal-clear nights when the stargazer feels that if he reached out, he could almost touch the stars. On nights such as these, planetary and double-star observers usually find observing conditions impossible; but to observers of nebulae, comets or faint star fields they are sheer joy – for these observers, *sky transparency* is more important than *good seeing*. On still, misty or foggy nights, when only the brighter naked-eye stars are visible, the reverse will be true – for the atmosphere is quiet and the comet hunter may go to bed and rest in peace!

Of course, astronomical 'seeing' is not so important to the naked-eye observer in that some kind of work is always possible, but in order to see the fainter stars he will need breezy, clear nights free of mist and fog.

Although it can be said that observations of planets and double stars are best performed on still, misty evenings, it must, nevertheless, be borne in mind that 'seeing' never reaches perfect conditions. In other words there will always be some atmospheric turbulence present, but the difference between 'good seeing' and 'bad seeing' is that during 'good seeing' the image may be perfectly still for a second or more between 'boils'. These are the periods to watch for, but nights of really top-class 'seeing' conditions, when large-aperture telescopes can be used to their best for resolving planetary detail or splitting double stars, are very few: in the British Isles no more than between ten and twenty nights a year could be described as ideal. 'Seeing' is often described by reference to a numerical scale consisting of five or ten divisions. The worst would be described as 1 and the best as 5 or 10.

In respect to 'seeing', geographical or topographical conditions often influence it. For example, in a valley at night the air can be ruinous to definition because cold air tends to flow downhill (i.e. frost hollows are common). The crest of a hill can also be impossible for double-star observers for the rise will be subject to constant air turbulence. Experience has shown that the best all-round observing can be gained from country covered with vegetation and trees, plus a sandy soil (the latter discourages the formation of dew on exposed instruments).

Lastly the would-be stargazer should bear in mind that observations of a celestial object directly over a chimney, or hot flue outlet, can produce a devastating effect on even naked-eye 'seeing'. Try it and judge for yourself!

Observing techniques

To make the most of one's natural vision is something that every stargazer should constantly be aiming for. The wearing of glasses does not necessarily mean that one's astronomical observing abilities are going to be any the less, and in point of fact a good number of people who have eye defects in normal everyday life turn out to have extraordinarily good vision for astronomical purposes. Many eye defects can be partially neutralized by focusing adjustments on telescopes and binoculars – particularly the defects of long- and short-sightedness.

However, even in stargazing, practice makes perfect. The eye needs to be trained and conditioned to what it is looking at. It is surprising how many beginners go outdoors to observe and come back in, disappointed by their views of the sky. They often consider that they have been let down and that descriptions by authors in published books are, to say the least, exaggerated. The reasons for this are many. One reason is that a great number of beginners expect to go outdoors and see the Andromeda nebula through a telescope exactly as it is depicted in the long-exposure photographs taken by some of the world's finest and largest telescopes. In many instances the authors of published works are to be blamed for not pointing out that these photographs are the result of extremely long exposures, measured in hours – so that the normal, faint images of objects are actually built up and become reinforced, over-exposed pictures that create the impression of a solid area of light. What an observer actually sees when he looks through his telescope is usually a faint, misty patch of light at the limit of visibility, and quite frequently he complains that he cannot see anything at all.

Part of this latter trouble is that the beginner is not aware of, or does not fully understand the importance of, 'dark adaptation'. He will rush outdoors from an environment that has been flooded with bright electric lighting and plunge into the inky blackness. Now the pupil of the human eye needs time to dilate, and this time varies considerably in different people. Some appear to adapt within a few minutes, while others may take fifteen minutes to half an hour. Actual dark adaptation begins fairly rapidly, but

44

continues to improve slowly over a long period outdoors. Those who sweep for comets are well aware of this slow process and quite often find they are able to see large faint patches much more easily at the end of a two-hour period of sweeping than they did fifteen minutes after starting, when the 'normal' adaptation had been achieved. Nebulae which are missed completely on the first sweeps are plain as pikestaffs an hour or so later. However, the casual observer need not worry too much about spending long periods under the darkened sky in order to see the stars, but it is recommended that he or she spend at least fully five minutes in the darkened outdoor environment before even attempting simple star-recognition work. For those interested in observing deep-sky objects with small telescopes and binoculars, full dark adaptation is absolutely essential, and it must also be remembered that all extraneous light must be kept to a minimum. When star charts have to be consulted to assist recognition, a red light is best since it does not appear to materially affect night vision. This light can take the form of an ordinary flash lamp or torch with the lens covered with red-tinted paper or cloth.

In my opinion, 'natural' views of the faint nebulae are far more aesthetically satisfying than over-exposed, unrealistic photographs. In particular, no photograph can depict the beautiful diaphanous, greenish, transparent light of the Orion nebula. Nothing can beat the experience of observation through a small telescope on a cold, black winter's night when the stars are shimmering through the atmosphere, producing an almost hypnotic effect on the eyes. No photograph can capture the myriad, animated, scintillating points of light that emerge from a globular cluster, such as the one in Hercules; and no photograph can capture the rich, ruby-red tint of stars such as the Garnet Star in Cepheus. If the deep-sky observer, equipped with small instruments, is patient and obeys the simple rules of dark adaptation, he will certainly not be disappointed. When his eyes become trained, he will find in the sky so many objects worthy of his attention that a lifetime of observing barely seems long enough.

Apart from the dark adaptation, there is another trick which the human eye can perform. The centre part of the pupil is surprisingly less sensitive to light than its outer edges, so that if one glances sideways ('averted vision') a faint patch at the extreme limit of vision can often be seen better defined. This phenomenon shows up readily when slowly sweeping for faint nebulae: when the field appears to be moving slowly, the eye will register a faint patch more positively than when it appears to be stationary.

Deep-sky observers differ in the kind of visual acuity they develop for astronomical observation. One observer might well become highly adapted at seeing faint *point* sources, another faint *diffuse* patches. Then again, another observer may well be better adapted at resolving fine planetary surface details. It is seldom that all three acuities become fully developed in the same pair of eyes – but generally some native talent (to a greater or lesser degree) of one of the three kinds appears to be present in every pair of eyes.

Clothing

14 Observer in garden chair, suitably clothed for deep-sky viewing in cold weather.

It is important to dress adequately for outdoor observing at night. This is perhaps stating the obvious, yet a beginner rarely gives it a second thought until he becomes frozen to the bone and hurries back indoors to his creature comforts and TV set – and second thoughts about his future star-recognition forays.

What should one wear? The possibilities are many, but one should remember that many layers of light clothing are preferable to one layer of heavy clothing. In this way optimum temperature control can be achieved simply by adding more layers or removing some. Loose clothing is also more thermally efficient than tight clothing. In my experience, duffle jackets – the kind of garment popularized by seamen in the Second World War – are not very suitable for prolonged exposure outdoors. In a sitting position they offer little protection to the knees and thighs, and their hoods tend to interfere with visibility. Far preferable, and highly recommended, are ski jacket and ski pants. These garments are light in weight yet windproof, and are not draughty in the lower quarters. They also possess useful pockets in which can be carried eyepieces, a torch, star charts – and this book! The hood of a ski jacket is fashioned in such a way that it provides full weather protection to the head, if required, and yet allows complete freedom of visibility, which is highly important for all-round observation of the sky.

The feet and hands are two parts of the body vulnerable to cold, particularly when there is little physical activity. Surplus disposal flying boots are excellent in combating cold. They are relatively inexpensive and the part-canvas ones are thermally the best – especially if they are purchased two sizes too large so that extra thick woollen socks can be worn.

For the hands, two pairs of gloves for really cold conditions: one pair of *thin* woollen, separately fingered, so that the hands have mobility, and a pair of sheepskin mitts attached to the body with a string harness, such as the Arctic and Antarctic explorers wear. The harness idea allows easy recovery after removal in the dark without having to resort to a light, which temporarily spoils one's night vision.

If the observer contemplates long periods of exposure outdoors, such as all-night meteor watches or marathon comet sweeps, then he has to resort to mountaineering clothing, electrically heated suits or flying jackets. Mountaineering clothing is more easily obtainable and nowadays relatively inexpensive. The jacket and trousers should be quilted, filled with eider-duck feathers. Such equipment will keep out many degrees of frost even when the observer is lying in a deck chair for hours on end.

Another dodge to keep the feet warm is to stand or rest them on a thermally insulated board, or just a square of timber. Never stand directly on a concrete or stone surface for long periods, since this quickly conducts heat away from the body. Also keep warm drinks to a minimum: although a cup of coffee or tea gives psychological uplift in the small hours, the heating benefits are, at best, only transitory, and frequent visits to the 'loo' are socially inconvenient to the rest of the sleeping household, especially in the small hours!

Observing variable stars

For observing variable stars, details of which appear later in the deep-sky lists of the constellations in Chapters 5–10, certain

47

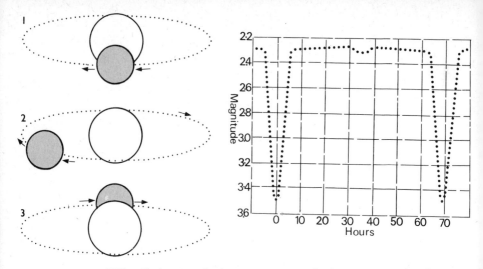

15, 16 *Why Algol varies in brightness: 1, minimum: brighter component eclipsed (steep dip in light curve); 2, maximum; 3, slight dip in maximum as fainter component is eclipsed.*

methods have been evolved over the years. It would be best to begin with one visible to the naked eye, such as β Persei, which is just a circumpolar star for observers above latitude 50° N. It is one of the oldest variable stars known to man, and there is good reason to suppose that it was first discovered by the Arabs, who called it Algol – the Demon Star (see p. 129). Algol is a variable star of the variety known as an eclipsing binary: the light variations are brought about by a 'dark' companion star periodically cutting off, or eclipsing, the brighter one as they both revolve round a common centre of gravity. This happens every sixty-nine hours, but the actual period of eclipse occurs over a much shorter period.

Ordinarily β Persei will be slightly fainter than α Persei, while the stars γ, δ, ε, and ζ Persei will all be fainter than Algol. Two other stars near by, α and β Arietis, will ordinarily be respectively brighter and fainter than Algol. Also near by are α and β Trianguli, which can be used as comparison stars when the brightness of Algol has begun to fade.

For the beginner who wishes to witness the light variations there are two methods open: he can either consult an ephemeris to find the exact time the events will take place, or he can, by regular observations, 'discover' one for himself. The latter method is recommended as the more interesting approach, and for our purpose we shall suppose that this is the method adopted.

When observations show that fading has begun by comparison with the nearby stars, estimates of brightness should periodically be recorded along with the time. Always observe it by comparing it with two stars: one brighter and one fainter. Algol's brightness can be gauged each time by looking up the magnitudes of each of the comparison stars and thinking in terms of differences in fractions by estimating Algol's relationship separately to each one. For example: 'Time 1975, August 1d 10h 15m, a $\frac{2}{5}$ V $\frac{3}{5}$ b' means that on 1st August at 10.15 Universal Time, Algol, denoted by 'V', was two-fifths of the interval *fainter* than comparison star 'a' and three-fifths of the interval *brighter* than comparison star 'b'. Simple arithmetic will then give Algol's actual magnitude, expressed to the nearest tenth of a mag. Once the variations have been noted, repeat the observations at half-hourly intervals until a sufficient number have been made to show how the brightness fluctuates with time (see fig. 16). Obviously there may not be time (or sufficient period of darkness) to catch the whole light cycle, for the decline and recovery takes Algol nine hours. The light diminishes for four and a half hours, remains constant for a few minutes, then gradually increases again for another period of four and a half hours. To detect even a part of the light cycle gives the observer deep satisfaction, and quite a thrill of achievement the first time he succeeds in catching it. Even if you have only very limited time for your nightly perusal of the heavens, methodical night-to-night inspection of Algol will one day catch the performance 'red-handed' during mid-eclipse.

Similar methods are adopted for observations of binocular or telescopic variables. However, many observers adopt methods other than the fractional estimate one. Some always work in units of one-tenth magnitude and acquire the ability to memorize differences of as little as 0.1 magnitude between the comparison stars and the variable. If one becomes hooked on variables, there are societies all over the world who specialize in this kind of work and are able to supply highly comprehensive field charts to their observing members.

Occasionally one finds observers who prefer, as I do, to estimate brightness of stars by observing their out-of-focus (extra-focal) images, which then appear as discs of light rather than point sources. Opinion differs as to the accuracy of this method, but many believe it to be very accurate indeed – particularly for observations of binocular variables, and it is also useful for estimating the brightness of comets, which are always very different in their appearances.

When choosing comparison stars, care should be taken to choose stars of the same colour as the variable, whenever possible.

Colour differences can lead to large errors, for the human eye is particularly sensitive to blue stars but not red ones – although some observers always see red stars as being brighter than others. The personal factor enters into observational astronomy a great deal and must be reckoned with if different observers' observational work is to be combined and compared. It is of interest that extrafocal estimates are more consistent when it is not possible to choose comparison stars of the same colour range, and they are often more consistent in estimates made by a range of observers than are the point-source estimates. It is also easier to carry the 'memory' of an extrafocal image out of the variable's field of view if another comparison star is not available nearby, as often happens when observing a nova, or new star.

Although we have briefly covered the kind of instruments and discussed the techniques that will take the beginner beyond the frontiers of naked-eye vision, it must never be forgotten that important and serious observational work can be done *without* optical assistance. Throughout history, many of the brighter novae have first been noticed with the naked eye by observers knowing the constellations like the back of their hands. There are many variable stars which can be studied throughout their light variations with the naked eye alone – a list is provided on p. 215. No telescope need ever be used to observe the aurora, meteors or fireballs. No optical equipment could have recorded the last great Leonid meteor shower of 1966 in such magnificent splendour as that seen by naked-eye observers in the USA and eastern Siberia.

There are also bright comets which suddenly appear in the evening and dawn skies, which have been seen first by people who did not even know what they were looking at. The heavens are never static; no one knows when the next new object will appear in the sky; it may even be tonight, and by fortuitous circumstances your part of the world may be in the ideal position to see it first.

If regular observing is carried out, it is well worth while to keep an observing book to record all that is seen. Methodical entries over a period of time can give a great deal of pleasure when read in retrospect, and, when looking for certain objects, even negative results can sometimes be useful by indicating the invisibility of an object at different periods.

If that rare event happens, and a strange object is seen in the sky, first seek out another local amateur astronomer before announcing your 'new' discovery to the world. After all, it may be a perfectly well-known variable star that has previously escaped your notice, and even professional astronomers have been known to make mistakes, like the very experienced observer who was led by the reflection from a street lamp on a TV mast to think he had discovered a bright new comet!

Do's and don'ts

1 *Don't* use an old rag to clean lenses. Always use a chamois leather, silk handkerchief or specially manufactured cloth, but beware of patent spectacle cleaners which remove the high transmission coating from modern optical instruments.

2 *Don't* ever look at the Sun directly with the naked eye, binoculars or telescope, as this can lead to permanent eye damage. It can be observed by *projecting* the image on to a white card placed behind a telescope.

3 *Do* remember to allow sufficient time for the eye to adapt for night vision before trying to observe faint objects.

4 *Don't* bore the rest of the family by your initial over-enthusiasm at actually recognizing Orion: wean them to it slowly. And, for husbands, *do* be sure that your wife is suitably clothed before enticing her to the great outdoors. One of the worst enemies of astronomy is – cold feet!

5 *Don't* boast of your abilities to see faint objects to other less well-endowed stargazers. They will hate you for it, and anyway they will not believe you; wait until you have discovered a comet or nova – then you won't need to boast!

6 *Do* expect to have lots of fun with stargazing. Seek out your local astronomical group – the camaraderie is wonderful.

Note on abbreviations and conventions

a.u.

Astronomical unit(s). This unit, used for shorter distances (on the astronomical scale), is the Earth's mean distance from the Sun, or approximately 93 million miles.

binary

See double stars.

colours of stars

These are given (in decreasing order of temperature) as: greenish, blue, blue-white, white, yellow-white, yellow, yellow-orange, orange-red, red.

dia

The apparent angular diameter of an object as seen by the observer, measured in seconds ("), minutes (') or degrees (°).

dist

Latest known distance, or angular separation, between two stars, expressed in minutes (') or seconds (") of arc.

double stars

In descriptions of binary and double stars the position angle of the fainter star to the brighter is not given as this information may be confusing and is not essential to make an identification.

mag

Magnitude (see p. 34). The ability to see faint stars, or the limiting magnitude, depends principally on the aperture of the binoculars or telescope. The larger the diameter of the mirror or object glass, the fainter the stars that can be seen. Also, the ability to resolve, or divide, double stars depends on the aperture, and the table below indicates approximately the performance the observer may expect with different-sized telescopes. But remember, inferior instruments or sky conditions may lead to a much lower performance. Likewise, superior instruments and ideal sky conditions may allow a slightly better performance. Note that with low-power binoculars in the range ×6 to ×12, the magnification obtained is generally insufficient to divide double stars less than 1.5'.

object lens	naked eye	1-in.	2-in.	3-in.	4-in.	6-in.	8-in.	12-in.
closest stars divided	3'	4.56"	2.28"	1.52"	1.14"	0.76"	0.57"	0.38"
average faintest star	6	9.0	10.5	11.4	12.0	12.9	13.5	14.4

The limiting magnitude of nebulae and clusters, apart from the considerations above, is also very dependent on their apparent angular size, on sky transparency, and on the amount of scattered light. Generally speaking, their limiting magnitude is two magnitudes *brighter* than for stars, e.g. a 1-in. telescope can show mag 9 stars, but mag 7 nebulae. Yet when the sky is particularly transparent, after rain for example, their threshold magnitudes often approach those of the stars. Another important factor is that very low magnification often induces a brighter sky background, so that, for example, binoculars do not fully realize their theoretical aperture capabilities as indicated in the table.

numbering

For full explanation, see p. 28. Briefly, nebulae and clusters are given their Messier catalogue number (e.g. M31) or their New General Catalogue number (e.g. NGC 2031). Individual stars can be identified in any of the following ways: with lower-case Greek letters, by Bayer's method; by number only, which is the Flamsteed catalogue number; or – less frequently seen nowadays – by the numbering adopted in the star catalogues of John Herschel (Hh), W. S. Jacob (Jc) or F. G. W. Struve (Σ). All these methods entail using also the name of the constellation (in the genitive) or its official abbreviation, thus: a Ursae Majoris or a UMa. For variable stars see note, p. 216.

period

In variable stars, the cycle of light variation, and in the case of binary stars the period of orbital revolution.

U.T.

Universal Time. For convenience, astronomers use Greenwich Time almost exclusively in their tables and Ephemerides. It is called Universal Time to show that it is independent of the observer's longitude or time zone.

*

In star maps, this marks the position of a meteor shower radiant.

Note. The chart overleaf is designed for use at any hour, day or month of the year by observers in northern temperate latitudes, looking north. Hold the book so that the name of the required month is *uppermost*. The constellations are represented for approximately 11 p.m. at the *beginning* of any month. If you wish to observe before or after this time, or at a date later in the month, the constellations will be proportionally shifted backwards or forwards – bearing in mind that the northern circumpolar stars appear to rotate *anticlockwise* and each monthly division also represents 2 hours' clock time. Thus for every difference of 2 hours rotate the book one monthly division, *clockwise* if earlier than, *anticlockwise* if later than, 11 p.m.

The seasonal charts on pp. 70, 90, 116 and 134 depict the equatorial and zodiacal constellations for an observer located in mid-northern temperate latitudes looking south. The names of the months along the top of the chart refer to the constellations which can be seen beneath these about the *middle* of the month, due south of the observer, between about 10 p.m. and midnight. If you observe before or after this time or date, the constellations will be proportionally east or west – bearing in mind that the stars appear to move from east to west and each monthly division also represents 2 hours' clock time.

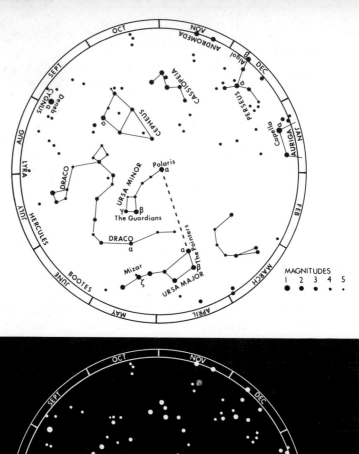

17 *The northern circumpolar stars (see note on p. 53). To locate the less conspicuous constellations and for individual star recognition refer to charts, pp. 194–214.*

CHAPTER 4

The northern circumpolar stars

CAMELOPARDALIS, *the Giraffe* (Cam)

This is a great, straggling constellation, and a relatively modern one, formed by Hevelius or Bartschius in 1614. It was not recognized by many authorities at the time, and does not appear in many star maps of even the late seventeenth century.

It stretches from a point fairly near the pole and its major part lies between Ursa Major and Cassiopeia. It contains no star brighter than the 4th magnitude and the apparent barrenness of the sky in the region serves as a good guide to its location.

Mythology

Although a new constellation to the western world, it was well known in ancient China as a separate group. Seven asterisms (groups of stars) lay within its boundaries, and these were: the State Umbrella, an obscure anatomical term, the Higher Minister, the Higher Guard, the Minor Guard, the Four Official Supporters of the Throne, and Unostentatious Virtue.

Principal stars

α Cam Mag 4.4, blue.

β   Mag 4.2, yellow. A 2-in. telescope will show a mag 9 companion, dist 80″.

γ   Mag 4.7, white.

121 (Piazzi's catalogue) Mag 4.7, orange-red, mag 4.4, white; a very close double and spectroscopic binary with 3.88-day period.

Deep-sky objects

11 & 12 Cam A wide binocular double; mags 5.3 and 6.0, blue and yellow, dist 180″.

Σ1694 Double; mags 5.8 and 5.31, dist 21″. The primary is also a spectroscopic binary, period 3.3 days.

Σ 485 Double; mags 6.1 and 6.1, dist 18″. Easy with 2-in. telescope.

T   Long-period variable; mag range 6.4–14.4, period 373 days, deep red.

NGC 1502 Open cluster; mag 5.3, dia 7′; about 15 stars, and easily seen with opera glasses or binoculars.

CASSIOPEIA, *the Lady on the Chair (or Throne)* (Cas)

After Ursa Major, probably the most easily recognizable constellation in the northern heavens. Its principal stars form a configuration in the shape of a badly formed 'W' or 'M' – depending on which side of the pole it is observed. It is also quickly located since it is always on the opposite side of Polaris to Ursa Major.

Mythology

This group belongs to the 'Royal Family' of constellations. Legend tells us that Cassiopeia was the wife of King Cepheus and the mother of Andromeda. She is said to have been extremely beautiful, and in a moment of vanity boasted that she was fairer than the Sea Nymphs. When the Nymphs complained to Neptune, he dispatched, in his anger, a frightful sea monster to ravage her country, and finally she was compelled to offer her daughter Andromeda as sacrifice. Fortunately, in the nick of time, Perseus came to the rescue (see Perseus, p. 128, and Andromeda, p. 118). In Julius Schiller's constellation reforms, 'the Lady on the Chair' became either Mary Magdalene, Deborah or Bathsheba, the wife of David.

Principal stars

α Cas *Schedar* or *Shadar*, meaning 'the Breast'; delineates the front leg of the traditional chair. A variable star; mag range 2.5–3.1, orange-yellow. The brightness fluctuations are of an irregular pattern. It is a highly suitable object for naked-eye observation. Estimates can be made by comparing it with other circumpolar stars in the same brightness range (and preferably the same colour, see pp. 49, 50). With 12×60 binoculars, or a 2-in. telescope, a mag 9 blue companion is visible, dist 62".

β *Caph*, 'the Tinted Hand', marks the back of the chair; mag 2.4, yellow-white.

γ An irregular variable; mag range 1.6–3.0, blue-white. Another excellent example of a star that can be studied entirely by naked-eye observation. Also a double, with a mag 11.0 companion, dist 2.1", but this requires 4-in. refractor or 6-in. reflector.

δ *Ruchbah*, 'the Knee'; mag 2.8, white.

η Binary system; mags 3.6 and 7.5, yellow-white and orange-red, dist 11". An interesting dwarf double system with a revolution period of over 500 years. A fine object in 2-in. telescopes.

ε Mag 3.4, blue-white.

ζ Mag 3.7, blue-white.

θ Mag 4.5, white.

Deep-sky objects

R Cas Long-period variable; mag range 4.8–13.6, period 430 days; a beautiful deep red. Can be followed with naked eye at maximum brightness.

SU   Cepheid-type variable; mag range 5.9–6.3, period 1.9493 days, yellow-white. Good object for study with opera glasses or binoculars.

NGC 663 Open star cluster; mag 7.1, diameter 11′; visible with 8 × 30 binoculars.

M 52 (NGC 7654) Open star cluster; mag 7.3, diameter 12′; visible with 8 × 30 binoculars.

M 103 (NGC 581) Open star cluster; mag 7.4, diameter 5′; visible with 8 × 30 binoculars.

One of the most famous stars on record, and now no longer visible, is 'Tycho's star'. He first fixed its position accurately a few days after it suddenly burst into view in early November 1572. It became so bright that it exceeded even the planets Jupiter and Venus, and for a time actually became visible in broad daylight. In December 1572 it began to fade quickly, and entirely disappeared from naked-eye view (this was before the invention of the telescope) in March 1574. Although Tycho positioned the star reasonably accurately, no optical trace of it has been found in modern times, so perhaps it has faded to beyond mag 24.0 – out of range for even the 200-in. Palomar telescope and the new 234-in. Soviet telescope. This star was certainly no ordinary nova, but of a variety known as a supernova, only three of which have been observed within our own galaxy by modern man. The physical processes that take place in the interior of such stars are little understood, but they may be closely related to neutron stars or pulsars. It is worth while for every sky observer to watch carefully the position where Tycho's star appeared. Many novae recur from time to time and this may happen at any moment, without any prior warning.

CEPHEUS, *the Warrior King* (Cep)

Although relatively inconspicuous in a casual glance at this part of the sky, and difficult to spot at full moon, this area, nevertheless, is strewn with glorious star fields which will be revealed with even the simplest optical assistance. It is located in a triangular area formed by the Pole Star, Cassiopeia and Cygnus. Since it is a circumpolar constellation, it must be borne in mind when attempting recognition, that at different times one sees a complete inversion of the star grouping.

Mythology

The mythological origin of this figure is controversial. One legend relates that Cepheus was an Argonaut who accompanied Jason to

Colchis, to obtain the Golden Fleece. However, a better-known one supposes that the figure immortalizes the name of an ancient king who reigned either in India or Ethiopia. Some trace back its beginning to the period 21,000–19,000 B C, when the stars *a* Cephei and *γ* Cephei were each respectively the Pole Stars and the group as a whole represented the ancient Ape God Kapi. To the Arabs it had a different meaning altogether, and represented a pastoral interpretation by depicting a shepherd attended by his dog keeping watch over his grazing fold.

Principal stars

a Cep *Alderamin*, 'Right Arm' – marking what is considered the right shoulder of the mythical Cepheus; mag 2.6, white. Owing to the Earth's precessional wobble, it was the Pole Star in 21,000 B C, and it will be Polaris again in A D 7500. If a line is projected from Alderamin to Deneb (*a* Cygni), the north pole of the planet Mars points to the half-way mark.

β *Alfirk*, 'the Flock', marks the waist of Cepheus; mag 3.3, blue-white. It is an optical double star, mags 3.3 and 8.0, dist 13.7″ – easily seen with 2-in. telescope. The primary is also variable in brightness (of the classical Cepheid variety, see below), mag range 3.32–3.73, period 0.1905 day, but without the use of special equipment the light variations are difficult to follow. It is also a spectroscopic binary.

γ *Errai*, 'the Shepherd', locates the left knee; mag 3.4, orange-yellow. It will be the Pole Star in approximately 2,600 years' time.

δ Variable star; mag range 3.9–5.0, yellow, period 5.3663 days. Also a double, companion star, mag 7.5, blue, dist 41.0″; very

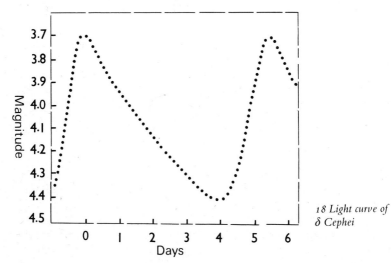

18 Light curve of δ Cephei

easily seen with 2-in. telescope and provides a splendid contrast of colours.

This star is now one of the most famous in the sky. It is the prototype star after which all other Cepheid-type variables are named, since this was the first example to be recognized. The Cepheids (pronounced 'sefid' or 'sefeed') have been of considerable interest since δ Cep was first spotted in 1784 by the English amateur, John Goodricke, who, although a deaf-mute, was one of the earliest and most successful naked-eye discoverers of variable stars. Astronomy suffered a great loss when he died at the early age of 22 years.

The light fluctuations of the Cepheids proceed with clockwork regularity in periods measured in days. Unlike the eclipsing binary variables such as Algol, the Cepheid variations are due to periodic pulsations in the star itself. When a number of Cepheids had been discovered, a peculiar relationship was noticed between the length of the period of light variations and the luminosity (or intrinsic brightness): the longer the period, the more luminous the star. This period/luminosity relationship, as it is now called, has furnished astronomers with a method of determining stellar distances both in our own Milky Way and in nearby galaxies. It is only necessary to measure the period of a Cepheid in order to deduce its intrinsic brightness, and then when this brightness is compared with its *observed* brightness, the distance can be deduced. Today several thousand Cepheid-type variables are known.

ε	Mag 4.2, white.
ζ	Mag 3.6, orange-yellow; spectroscopic binary.
η	Mag 3.6, yellow.
θ	Mag 4.3, white; spectroscopic binary.
ι	Mag 3.7, orange-yellow.

Deep-sky objects

U Cep Variable star of eclipsing binary variety; mag range 6.7–9.8, blue-white to yellow, period 2.4929 days.

μ Variable star of a distinct red colour, nicknamed the 'Garnet Star', by William Herschel. In 1848 it was found to vary in brightness between mags 3.6 and 5.1, in a cycle ranging between 5 and 6 years. It can easily be followed with the naked eye, but with binoculars its red hue is very striking – especially if it is directly compared with the brilliant whiteness of α Cephei, in the same field of view.

Kruger 60 Double star, located near δ Cep. Although only a faint binary pair – mags 9.0 and 9.2, dist 27″, both orange-red – they are of considerable interest, for both stars are members of a class known as Red Dwarfs. They are the closest known binary pair to the solar system, lying about 14 light-years away. The brighter member is only one-fifth the Sun's mass and the fainter only one-sixth. They are the least luminous stars known at the present time.

Note. The Milky Way passes through Cepheus and on clear, moonless nights, the rich star fields present a glorious sight in wide-angle binoculars. If the night is particularly transparent, the observer will also be able to see the dark obscuring dust-cloud nebulae – known as 'coal-sacks' because of their unique dark appearances contrasting with the milky backcloth of the stars surrounding them.

DRACO, *the Dragon* (Dra)

This is one of the more sprawling configurations in the northern skies and, for most of its length, wanders between the two Bears. Although most of its stars are relatively faint to the naked eye, the serpent form is quite distinctive. The head is formed by β, γ, ξ, ν and μ, and the body by δ, ε, χ, ζ, η, θ, ι, a, κ and λ.

Mythology

This dragon, or snake, to many storytellers represents the monster which protected the golden apples in the garden of the Hesperides, and which was later slain by Hercules. When Juno married Jupiter and presented the apples to him, she retired Draco into the heavens as a reward for his vigilance. In ancient China the constellation had great significance and became their national emblem.

Principal stars

a Dra *Thuban*; mag 3.6, white. This was the Pole Star about 4,700 years ago, and since it was the middle star in the constellation at this time, the whole configuration appeared to circle around it like the hands of a clock. In China it was nicknamed 'the Right-Hand Pivot'. It is also a spectroscopic binary with a period of 50 days.

β *Rastaban*, 'Dragon Head'; mag 3.0, yellow. It has a faint companion, mag 14, dist 4", which may be a member of a long-period binary system.

γ *Eltamin*; mag 2.4, orange-yellow. This was a highly important star to the Egyptians, who called it Isis. At the period around 3500 BC, it rose directly in line with the centre passage of the temple of Hathor at Dendera, and of Mut in Thebes. In 2300 BC, it was used as a fixing point in the Rameses and Khons temples; at Rameses, the passageway along which the star could be seen was 1,500 feet long. In modern times it is also significant, for it lies almost exactly at the zenith of the old Greenwich Observatory, and extensive observations of it by James Bradley, the third Astronomer Royal, led him to the discovery of the aberration of light in 1725.

δ	Mag 3.2, yellow.
ε	Mag 4.0, yellow. Also a binary system, mags 4.0 and 7.1, dist 3.3″. Visible with 2-in. telescope and a moderately high power.
ζ	Mag 3.2, blue-white. Near this star lies the radiant point of the Draconid meteors (see below).
η	Mag 2.9, yellow. Also a binary system, mags 2.9 and 8.8, dist 6.1″. Visible with 2-in. telescope.
θ	Mag 4.1, yellow-white. Spectroscopic binary system.
ι	Mag 3.5, orange-yellow.
κ	Mag 3.9, blue-white.
λ	Mag 4.1, orange-red; colour very distinctive even with opera glasses.
ν^1	Mag 5.0, white; forms a wide double with ν^2, mag 5.0, white; distinctly split with 8×30 binoculars.
ξ	Mag 3.9, orange-yellow.

Deep-sky objects

TW	Dra Eclipsing variable of the Algol type; mag range 7.7–10.0, period 2.8068 days. At maximum can be seen with 8×30 binoculars and at minimum a 2-in. telescope will show it.
R	Long-period variable of the Mira type; mag range 6.3–13.9, orange-red, period 245 days. Easy object for binoculars at maximum but at minimum requires 8-in. telescope.
ζ	*Draconids*. Meteor shower which reaches maximum activity on 10 October. Its activity was spectacular in 1926, 1933 and 1946, and it has some connection with the Giacobini-Zinner periodic comet.
ι	*Draconids*. Meteor shower which reaches maximum about 30 June and is connected with the Pons-Winnecke comet. Normal range 27–30 June, and produces 7–10 *very* slow-moving meteors per hour.
	Quadrantids. Meteor shower which reaches maximum 2–3 January, normal range 28 December–4 January. Produces meteors with long paths at the rate of approximately 30 per hour. It is of interest that this is the only meteor shower to be given a different name from the constellation in which the apparent radiant point is situated. The reason is that it lies in a part of the sky previously occupied by the constellation Quadrans Muralis, the Mural Quadrant, invented by Lalande. This constellation is no longer recognized and has been re-incorporated into Draco and Boötes.

Ursa major, *the Great Bear* (UMa)

This is probably the best-known of all constellations in the northern hemisphere and in addition to the name of the Bear, it is also known as the Plough, the Dipper, the Chariot or Wagon, Charles's Wain, or the Bier.

Why the ancients imagined the figure in the form of a bear is shrouded in mystery. It is believed that the name is certainly Aryan, but no stretch of the imagination – at least to us moderns – can allow the grouping to adopt the pose which the traditional bear adopts; especially the tail, which is certainly the longest bear tail known to zoological science. Its great importance as a constellation in ancient times is doubtless due to the fact that seven bright stars form a distinctive, recognizable shape. The number seven, to the ancient world, was possessed with mystical properties, which have survived in folk-lore to the present day.

The Phoenicians were probably the first people to make use of the group for navigational purposes. Being prominent, it serves as a direction indicator to the much less conspicuous Little Bear and Pole Star. These early voyagers soon learnt the use of the two brightest members as celestial pointers to locate Polaris and so enable the navigators to sail in specific directions and make landfalls in approximately the area required.

Mythology

In Greek mythology the Great Bear is closely associated with the Little Bear. In one story they represented the nymph Callisto, with whom Jupiter was in love, and her son Arcas. The goddess Juno, wife of Jupiter, became jealous of Callisto's beauty, in particular the constant attention paid to her by Jupiter, and transformed mother and son into bears. In one version of the legend, Jupiter transformed them both into constellations, to guard them from death at the hands of hunters, and they circled the pole for ever more, where he could watch over them. There are numerous versions of this story, but all hinge on the theme of jealousy and revenge, and on Jupiter for his misplaced love.

To the North American Indians, the figure also represented a bear form, which is a coincidence almost beyond belief. Whether the legendary form was transported from Asia during the Indian migrations across the Bering Straits or whether it is simply coincidence, cannot be ascertained. The Red Indian mythological story relates that the three traditional tail stars depicted hunters after a bear, but the bear was never caught and always evaded capture by circling the northern heavens year after year.

Principal stars

α UMa *Dubhe*, Arabic name meaning 'the Back of the Greater Bear'; mag 2.0, yellowish-orange. The brightest member in the seven-star group. With β it forms 'the Pointers'. A line projected from β to α and extended for another five times its length finds approximately the position of Polaris. Alpha is also a binary system, the 4.8 mag companion at a dist 0.6″, but this is beyond reach of ordinary telescopes.

β   *Merak*, from the Arabic *Al Marakk*, 'the Loins of the Greater Bear'; mag 2.4, white.

γ   *Phad* or *Phekda*, 'the Thigh of the Greater Bear'; mag 2.5, white.

δ   *Megrez*, 'the Root of the Tail'. The faintest member of the seven-star group; mag 3.4, white.

ε   *Alioth*, 'the Fat Tail of the Eastern Sheep'; mag 1.7, white. Also a spectroscopic binary system with a longish period of 4.2 years.

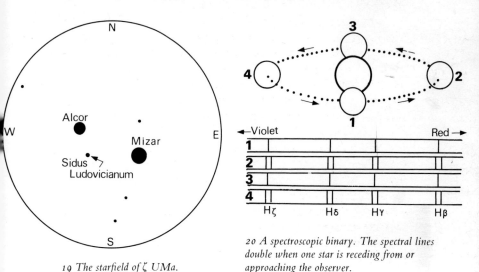

19 *The starfield of ζ UMa.*

20 *A spectroscopic binary. The spectral lines double when one star is receding from or approaching the observer.*

ζ   *Mizar*, 'the Girdle'; mag 2.2, white. It forms a naked-eye double, and the companion star, *Alcor*, mag 4.0, white, dist 11′, was supposed by the Arabs to form a test for naked-eye acuity; the pair are also known as 'the Horse and his Rider'. It is easily seen in opera glasses or prismatics, and the latter instrument will show another, fainter star (see fig. 19), known by the odd name of Sidus Ludovicianum. This was named by an eccentric German amateur astronomer in 1723, who thought he had discovered a new planet and named it after a contemporary German prince, Ludwig V. Mizar is also a double; mags 2.4, 4.0, dist 14.5″, and is an ideal subject for 2-in. telescopes. This double star system was the first pair ever to be photographed successfully, and by strange coincidence it was also the first spectroscopic binary system to be discovered; this was the work of Professor Pickering of Harvard College Observatory in 1889, using a powerful new tool called the spectroscope. He noted that the spectrum lines periodically became double and later changed to single again, and he deduced that there were two bodies present in the system, too close to be seen with the most powerful telescopes, but they could not escape the light analysis of their separate chemical make-up. Both these bodies revolve round a common centre of gravity, taking 20.5 days.

η *Benetnasch* (alternatively *Alcaid*, *Alkaid*), 'Governor of the Daughters of the Bier' (the chief mourners). The Chinese named it 'Revolving Light'; mag 1.9, blue-white.

θ Known at one time as 'the Throne of the Mourners', but nowadays unnamed; mag 3.3, yellow-white. It is also a binary system; the companion star, mag 13.7, dist 5″.

ι Another binary system; mag 3.1, white; companion star, mag 10.8, orange-red, dist 5″.

λ Marks the Bear's left hind foot; mag 3.5, white.

μ Also marks the left hind foot with λ, the two being known as Tania australis and Tania borealis; mag 3.2, orange-red.

Deep-sky objects

ξ UMa Binary system: combined mags 3.9, separate 4.4, 4.8; both yellow, dist 2.5″, period 60 years. A fine object for 2-in. telescopes. The first binary pair to have an orbit computed (1828). Both stars are also spectroscopic binaries, periods 670 days and 4 days.

T Long-period variable; mag range 6.4–13.5, period 256 days, orange-red. At maximum brightness can be picked up with 8×30 binoculars but at minimum requires at least 8-in. telescope.

R Long-period variable; mag range 6.2–13.6, period 301 days, orange-red. Also a binocular star at maximum.

M 81 (NGC 3031)

M 82 (NGC 3034) Two galaxies which lie within $\frac{1}{2}$° of each other. Can be glimpsed in same field of view with 8×30 binoculars when the night is moonless and the sky transparent; mags 7.9 and 8.8, dia's $16' \times 10'$ and $7.0' \times 1.5'$. Both galaxies lie about 10 million light-years from the Sun, and about 150,000 light-years apart. In 1961, M 82 was discovered to have an unusual radio-wave emission, and the two galaxies are now known to be physically connected. Long-exposure photographs show extensive faint loops between them in a highly magnetic field.

Ursa Major is particularly rich in extragalactic nebulae, or 'Island universes', but unfortunately most of them are too faint to be observed with small binoculars. Their visibility with small telescopes, 3 to 6 in., depends very much on sky conditions and how far out of town the observer is located. On a moonless night, when the air is sparkling clear after rain or snow, many nebulae can be fished up with 10×80 binoculars or a 3-in. refractor. Remember to make use of the averted vision method (see p. 45), and you may see many faint misty blobs as you *slowly* sweep through the constellation.

Ursa minor, *the Lesser Bear* (UMi)

In modern times this is one of the most important of all constellations since it contains the present Pole Star (Polaris), which is situated so close to the true north pole as to make the location of north a simple matter. It was well known to the Phoenician navigators, who called it Doube, and later the Arabs nicknamed it 'the Guiding One'. The constellation, in spite of the relative naked-eye faintness of the principal stars, is easily recognizable, and like the Great Bear the primary configuration pattern is formed by seven stars. Two of the brighter stars, β and γ, are sometimes referred to as 'the Guardians of the Pole', or simply 'the Guards'.

Mythology

According to Greek tradition the group is named in memory of Arcas, son of Callisto (see Ursa Major). It is strange, however, that, as a constellation, it was not known to the Greeks until about 600 BC. Yet long before this it was known to the Mongol races, to whom one of its names was 'Lode Star', meaning that it was the constellation to which the lodestone pointed. It was also certainly known by the successive civilizations of the Euphrates Valley.

In Red Indian legend, the Lesser Bear was well known: it is said to have originated when a group of braves became lost in the forest, and in answer to a prayer for guidance, a vision appeared in the form of a young girl who pointed out Polaris, by which they eventually found their way home. As a reward the hunters placed her in the sky where she could always be seen as a guide to the pole and true north.

The Chinese named Polaris after the goddess Tou Mu, who had supernatural powers and saved sailors from shipwreck. On her death she was transported to the sky with her husband and her son – where she now dwells at the pole.

The Arabs thought of the constellation as the Lesser Bier. They imagined Polaris to be the greatest villain of the skies who had slain the warrior that lay in the coffin of the Greater Bier (Ursa Major). For his sins, and as his punishment, he alone must remain constantly fixed at the apex of the unfriendly, bleak, northern heavens – to be scorned by his fellow stars that ever circle round him and keep their distance.

Principal stars

α UMi *Alruccabah*, Polaris, Stella Polaris, the Pole Star. A double; mags 2.1 and 9.5, yellow, dist 18″. This is by no means an easy double to see with small telescopes although it can occasionally be glimpsed with 2-in. × 75 instruments. The primary star is a Cepheid variable, mag range 2.1–2.3, period 3.97 days; it is also a spectroscopic binary, period 29.6 years.

β   *Kochab*; mag 2.2, orange-yellow.

γ   A wide binocular double formed with 11 UMi, mags 3.1 and 5.1, white and orange-yellow. This star, with β, forms 'the Guardians of the Pole'; it is of particular value to navigators and was used as a clock in primitive cultures.

δ   *Yildun*; mag 5.9, white.

ζ   Mag 4.3, white.

ε   Mag 4.4, yellow; a spectroscopic binary which experiences minor light variations, difficult for the inexperienced observer to detect; period 39.5 days.

η   Mag 5.0, white.

Deep-sky objects

π^1 UMi A wide double; mags 6.1 and 7.0, dist 31″. An easy and beautiful object with 2-in. telescopes; not usually visible with 8 × 30 binoculars, but just so with 12 × 60's.

CHAPTER 5
The Milky Way

When observing the constellations outdoors at night, you will notice, particularly if the sky is transparent, that a band of faint milky light extends right across the heavens. Its position in the sky will depend on the time of night and the season of the year. In winter, during the early evening, it will be directly overhead, while in the late summer evenings it will be lying low down near the northern horizon.

This band of light extends over more than one-tenth of the visible heavens and in fact represents the galaxy of stars to which the Sun and its attendant planets belong. Most of the stars are located within a horizontal plane, but they are so far distant that we cannot see them as individual points of light with the naked eye. The milky appearance is simply the effect of myriads of faint stars merged together to form a nebulous mist.

However, even with opera glasses and binoculars the milky light can be resolved into innumerable stars, and long-exposure photographs (see fig. 21) reveal a magnificent structure of star clouds, containing so many individual members that the human eye cannot possibly count them by normal methods. The Milky Way is inclined to the celestial equator by about $63°$, and intersects it in the constellations of Monoceros and Aquila. Its width is irregular, in parts only $3°-4°$ wide, in others $12°-16°$.

Beginning in Scorpius and travelling northwards, it traverses Sagittarius, Scutum, Aquila, Sagitta, Vulpecula, Cygnus, Lacerta, and projects an 'arm' into Cepheus. It passes through Perseus, Auriga, between Gemini and Orion, then Monoceros and Canis Major. In the southern skies it extends across Puppis, Pyxis, Vela, Carina, Crux, Musca, Centaurus, Lupus, Circinus, Norma, Ara and back into Scorpius.

In the night skies surrounding modern urban developments the Milky Way can rarely be seen at its best. Only in the pitch-black, transparent skies of the tropics do we see it as the ancients once did before air pollution obscured our modern skies. Aratos

21 'Fish-eye' photograph of the Milky Way. The dark bars are the supports of the film holder.

in his classic poem said: 'that shining wheel, men call it Milk'. To the ancient this band of milky light was a great puzzle. The Greeks called it the *Galaxy* (from *gala*, milk). To Aristotle, noted for his vivid unscientific imagery, it was, 'a vast mass of arid vapours which takes fire from glowing trees, above the region of ether and far below that of the planets'. Yet to the more scientific Democritus in 460 BC, 'it is the lustre of several small stars which are very near together' – an excellent guess indeed at its true nature.

In early Akkadian times it was connected with the mythological idea of a Great Sky Serpent, or a Snake River of sparkling dust. The later Arabs also knew it as 'the River', and in China it was 'the Celestial River' or 'Silver River'. It was known as 'the

Path of the Ghosts' in Norse mythology, the route which the fallen warriors took on their journey to Valhalla. In one story of classical Greek folk-lore the Milky Way was marked out by the corn ears dropped by Isis in his flight from Typhon. To the North American Indians, it was 'the Path of Souls', and French peasants nicknamed it 'the Road of St Jacques de Compostelle'.

It was not until Galileo turned to it with his newly constructed telescope that its true nature was confirmed, and he later wrote in his classical work *Sidereus Nuntius*: '. . . it was nothing else but a mass of innumerable stars planted together in clusters.' Nowadays, we know a great deal more about its physical make-up. We know that the irregular structural features we observe are only due in part to the non-uniform distribution of stars contained within it, but that also a significant element is the presence of an absorbing medium in the form of dark nebulae, or 'coal-sacks', probably consisting of a mixture of various dusts and ices. We know that the Milky Way rotates, and that the Sun takes 200 million years to complete one revolution. We know of places where the stars are created, and we know, for the most part, which celestial objects belong to it, and which are located beyond, in deeper space, at distances truly unimaginable to the mind of man.

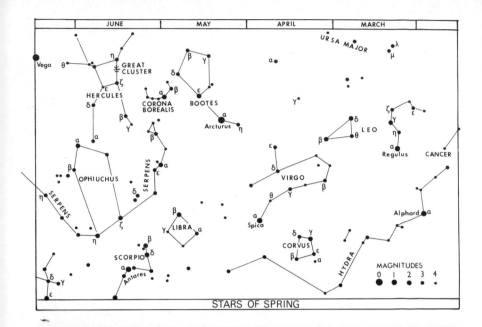

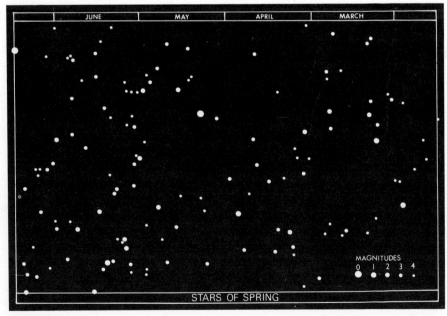

22 *Stars of spring (see note on p. 53). To locate the less conspicuous constellations and for individual star recognition refer to charts pp. 194–214.*

CHAPTER 6

Stars of spring
March, April, May

Refer to fig. 22 at required month and time.

With the arrival of spring, the winter constellation of Gemini is low down in the western sky and is due to set. Facing south, and allowing the eye to travel back eastwards (to the left), the five-star sickle shape of Leo (The Lion) can be picked out. Its bright star Regulus, or *a* Leonis, is a 1st-magnitude one and forms the lower apex of a large triangle with the Twins and Procyon. Regulus was once known as Cor Leonis, or the Lion's Heart, and the ancient astronomers thought it a truly royal star.

Casting your eye eastwards (left) from Leo, but lower down in the sky, you will see another 1st-magnitude star called Spica (*a* Virginis). This star is a giant and is 1,500 times brighter than the Sun.

Above Spica is a very noticeable spring star called Arcturus, the *a* star in the constellation of Boötes – pronounced Bo-o-tez – (the Herdsman). It rises early in the spring evenings and is visible all night long in the southern sky. To the east of Boötes is Corona Borealis, the Northern Crown as it is popularly known, one of the smallest constellations in the skies. Its brightish stars form a semicircle which depicts the legendary star crown of Ariadne, daughter of Minos, King of Crete.

Turning north to face the circumpolar groups, Ursa Major is now high overhead, completely reversed, and perhaps not easy to trace out owing to its extreme altitude. However, between the celestial pole and the northern horizon, Cassiopeia is clearly visible in her distinctive form of a distorted letter 'W'.

Boötes, *the Herdsman* (Boo)

An easily recognizable constellation, visible for much of the year for northern observers and dominated by the yellow-orange 1st-magnitude star Arcturus forming a distinctive equilateral triangle with Spica (*a* Virginis) and Denebola (*β* Leonis) which lies approximately due south on spring evenings.

Mythology

The mythical figure of Boötes is generally depicted as a rustic character holding in one hand a club or spear, but in some representations a staff or a sickle. He is sometimes shown holding in leash two hunting dogs (Canes Venatici) which appear to be chasing the Great Bear round the pole. There are varying and conflicting stories about his origin: he has been identified with Arcas, the son of Callisto, but, generally, opinion attaches this story to Ursa Minor. He has also been confused with stories concerning Auriga. More positive associations are with Mons Menalus which lies supposedly beneath his feet and which is a mountain in Arcadia, sacred to Pan and frequented by shepherds.

Principal stars

α Boo *Arcturus* – a name derived from its confusion with the Arcas story of the Bears (p. 62); mag 0.2, yellow-orange. The fifth brightest star in the heavens and the first to be observed with a telescope in daylight; this was done in 1635, by Morin, one of the last astrologers of France, who cast horoscopes for Louis XIV.

  In 1933, the light beam of Arcturus was used to trigger off the lights of the Chicago World's Fair. It is a large star with a diameter about 27 times that of the Sun.

β   *Nakkar* – an Arabic name for the whole group. It marks the hand of the mythical figure; mag 3.6, yellow.

γ   *Seginus*; mag 3.0, white, slightly variable in brightness over 0.05 magnitude.

δ   Mag 3.5, yellow.

ε   *Pulcherrima* – a modern title; mag 2.6, yellow-orange; also a binary system, mags 2.7, 5.1, dist 2.9″, comparison star, white. A fine object for 2-in. telescopes and high powers.

ζ   Mag 3.9, white; a close binary system, mags 4.4, 4.8, dist 1.1″; period 125 years.

η   *Muphrid* 'the Solitary Star'; mag 2.8, yellow; also a spectroscopic binary, period 484 days.

λ   Mag 4.3, white.

σ   Mag 4.5, yellow-white.

ρ   Mag 3.8, yellow-orange; in combination with σ Boötis the two stars were called Kang Ho, after a river in China.

Deep-sky objects

κ Boo Mag 4.6, white, double, mags 6.6, 4.6, dist 13″. Easy object for 2-in. telescopes.

ζ   Binary system; mags 4.8, 6.8, dist 7″, yellow and yellow-orange. A fine pair for 2-in. telescopes.

ι   Mag 4.8, white; double, mags 4.5, 7.5, dist 38″. Easy telescopic pair.

ν   Mag 4.3, white; triple system which includes an easy double, mags 4.5, 6.7, white and yellow, dist 108"; the fainter component resolves into a further pair, mags 7.2, 7.8, dist 2".

R   Long-period variable; mag range 5.9–13.1, period 223.36 days, orange-red.

RX Semi-regular variable; mag range 6.9–9.1, period 78 (?) days, orange-red. Can be followed through entire range with 2-in. telescope.

V   Long-period variable; mag range 6.4–11.5, period 258.81 days, orange-red. Easy to locate near γ Boötis.

W   Irregular variable (?); mag range 5.0–5.4, orange-red. A star worth investigating by binocular observers. Very close by ε Boötis.

COMA BERENICES, *Berenice's Hair* (Com)

A small constellation which with the naked eye appears as a woolly aggregation of approximately 30 stars of magnitude 4 to 6. Best located by projecting a line from η Ursae Majoris (Alkaid) through α Canum Venaticorum (Cor Caroli); halfway towards β Leonis (Denebola) lies the main body of the group.

On a sparkling clear night the constellation has been described by one nineteenth-century naked-eye astronomer as 'gossamer spangled with dewdrops'. With medium telescopic power the area is found to be strewn with distant galaxies, some of which are visible with quite small instruments.

Mythology

The name 'Berenice's Hair' is derived from an old, highly romantic Middle Eastern legend. Berenice, the daughter of Philadelphus, fell in love with and married her own brother, Euergetes, one of the kings of Egypt. Euergetes was required to take part in a dangerous expedition, and she vowed that if he returned safely to her, she would dedicate her beautiful hair to Venus.

Subsequently he returned safely and Berenice, true to her promise, cut off her long tresses, and hung them in the temple of Venus. However, they mysteriously disappeared and, when the wise men were consulted about it, one of them, an astronomer named Conon, declared that Jupiter was so enraptured by them that he had set them for ever in the heavens. Being sent for by Euergetes, Conon pointed out the new constellation, saying, 'There, behold the locks of the Queen.'

Principal stars

α Com Mag 4.5, yellow-white; also a very close binary system, mags 5.2, 5.2, dist 0.7", period 26 years; beyond the reach of ordinary telescopes, at their widest separation again in 1981.

β   Mag 4.8, yellow.
γ   Mag 4.6, orange-yellow.

Deep-sky objects

24 Com Double; mags 5.2, 6.7, dist 20″. Companion star is a spectroscopic binary, period 7.4 days.

12   Wide double, easy with small telescopes; mags 4.7, 8.5, dist 66″.
With a 6-in. telescope a third star is visible, mag 11.5, dist 35″.

17   Mag 5.1, white; also a wide double, visible with 8 × 30's, mags
5.4, 6.7, dist 145″.

32   Wide, easy binocular double; mags 5.3, 6.1, dist 195″.

M 53 (NGC 5024) Globular cluster; mag 7.6, dia 3.5′; just visible on
really transparent nights with 10 × 50's as a nebulous star.

M 64 (NGC 4826) Spiral galaxy; mag 8.8, dia 8′ × 4′, rather a faint
object in 2½- or 3-in. telescopes, but very apparent with 10 × 80's.

M 85 (NGC 4382) Spiral galaxy; mag 9.3, dia 4′ × 2.5′. An object for
3-in. telescopes; however, 10 × 80's will show it.

M 88 (NGC 4501) Spiral galaxy; mag 10.2, dia 6′ × 3′, rather faint in
small telescopes (3-in.), but fairly obvious in 25 × 105 binoculars.

M 99 (NGC 4254) Spiral galaxy; mag 10.1, dia 4.5′ × 4.5′, can be
glimpsed with 3-in. telescopes.

Note. Along the southern boundaries of the constellation, and
overlapping into neighbouring Virgo, the area is rich in spiral
galaxies. On a really transparent night, a 6-in. reflector will show
up to thirty, which will appear as faint, hardly perceptible,
nebulous wisps.

CANES VENATICI, the Hunting Dogs (CVn)

This was one of the new constellations introduced by Hevelius
in the seventeenth century to occupy the 'empty' space between
Boötes and the 'hind legs' of Ursa Major. Apart from its principal
star, Cor Caroli, there is little for the naked-eye observer, but the
whole region is rich in telescopic objects – particularly galaxies –
some of which can be seen with small instruments.

Mythology

The mythical dogs are represented as barking at the Great Bear.
They are traditionally in the charge of Boötes, who secures them
on leads, and for this reason he has been nicknamed the Bear
Driver as he chases it round the pole.

The northernmost dog is called *Asterion*, and the southernmost
Chara – the one who is 'dear to the heart of her master'. The Chinese
designated the three stars near the head of Asterion as the 'Three
Honoured Guards of the Heir Apparent'.

Principal stars

a CVn *Cor Caroli* – so named in honour of Charles II, in 1660, at the suggestion of the court physician, Sir Charles Scarborough, who stated that it shone with special brilliance on the evening of the King's return to London in May of that year.

A beautiful binary system, mags 2.9 and 5.4, both white, dist 20″. Easily seen with 2-in. telescopes.

β *Chara*, the Southern Hound; mag 4.5, yellow.

Deep-sky objects

15 & 17 CVn A wide optical double, ideally suited for binocular study; mags 6.2 and 6.0, dist 290″; blue and yellow-white.

2 Binary pair; mags 5.8 and 8.0, dist 11″; orange-red and yellowish-white. Fine object in small instruments.

R Long-period variable; mag range 6.1–12.8, period 328 days, orange-red.

Y Semi-regular variable; mag range 5.2–6.6, period 158 days, deep red. Named *La Superba* by the famous nineteenth-century Jesuit priest and astronomer, Father Secchi, because of its brilliant, intense red colour.

M 3 (NGC 5272) Globular cluster; mag 6.4, dia 10′. A most beautiful object in binoculars, appearing like a small comet.

M 51 (NGC 5194) Spiral galaxy; mag 8.1, dia 12′ × 6′. One of the first nebulae to be seen in its true spiral form, with the aid of the Earl of Rosse's 72-in. telescope in the 1860's. With modern instruments the spiral structure can be seen even with a 12-in. telescope. In binoculars it appears as a faint misty blob, but quite distinct in a 3-in. telescope.

M 63 (NGC 5055) Spiral galaxy; mag 9.5, dia 8′ × 3′. Quite distinct with 10 × 80 binoculars and just visible with 10 × 50's – if held steadily – in dark, transparent skies.

M 94 (NGC 4736) Spiral galaxy; mag 7.9, dia 5′ × 3′. Can be glimpsed with 10 × 50's.

CORONA BOREALIS, *the Northern Crown* (CrB)

The Northern Crown is among the smallest configurations in the northern skies. Yet, in spite of its size, it can easily be located by projecting a line north-east of Arcturus (a Boötis) towards Vega (a Lyrae). At one-third the distance between them the eye will arrest on a neat semicircle of six bright stars that form the traditional crown, or garland.

Mythology

There can be no doubt that the name Corona Borealis was suggested by the form taken by its brighter stars. In Greek legend, one story, recorded by Pherecydes about 500 BC, says that it was the crown of Ariadne, daughter of Minos, King of Crete, presented to her by Bacchus to console her for her desertion by the faithless Theseus. After her death, the crown was placed among the stars. Ovid, in his *Fasti*, mentions that Ariadne herself became the constellation. A crown, to the Greeks, meant a wreath or garland. To the Arabs the constellation was a broken plate, while to one tribe of Australian aboriginals it was a boomerang, and to another tribe an eagle's nest. The Shawnee Indians knew it as 'the Celestial Sister'. Such are the imaginings of different cultures.

Principal stars

α CrB *Alphecca*; mag 2.3, white. Its Arabic name means 'the Bright One of the Dish'. It has been nicknamed 'the Pearl of the Crown' or simply 'the Pearl'. A spectroscopic binary, stars separated by 5m. miles, period 17 days.

β   *Nusakan*; mag 3.7, white. Also a spectroscopic binary.

γ   Mag 3.9, white; a very close binary system, mags 4.2, 5.6, dist 0.7″, period 91 years; also a spectroscopic binary.

δ   Mag 4.7, yellow.

ε   Mag 4.2, yellow-orange.

θ   Mag. 4.2, blue-white.

Deep-sky objects

ζ CrB A visual double; mags 5.1, 6.0, dist 6″, blue-white. A beautiful object in small telescopes. ζ² is also a spectroscopic binary, period 12.58 days; each component is thirteen times as massive as the Sun and they are 14.5m. miles apart.

η   Very close binary system; mags 5.6, 6.1, dist 0.4″, yellow-white, period 41.56 days. Requires a 6-in. telescope to separate them.

σ   Binary system; mags 5.7, 6.7, dist 6.3″, yellow-white, yellow. Period may be greater than 1,000 years. Fine object for 2-in. telescopes.

U   Eclipsing variable; mag range 7.6–8.9, period 3.4522 days, white; can be followed through entire range with 10 × 50 binoculars.

S   Long-period variable; mag range 5·8–13·9, period 360 days, orange-red.

R   One of the most interesting variables in the entire sky and of unique variety; mag range 5.8–14.0, period irregular. Discovered in 1783, and owing to its irregular nature often remains at a constant brightness for years on end. This star is well worth watching with small instruments.

T   'The Blaze Star'. In 1855 it was observed and catalogued as a mag 9.5 star, but on 12 May 1866 it was spotted by the Irish amateur Birmingham, as a bright nova shining at mag 2.0. It was the first nova to be studied by spectroscopy. Like all novae it gradually faded in brightness and after some minor fluctuations it fell back to its previous magnitude. It remained quiescent for nearly eighty years until 8 February 1946, when it was spotted again, as a mag 3.0 star, almost simultaneously by a number of keen-eyed amateur astronomers who had risen early to make their routine observations. The star has now fallen back to its previous obscurity, but no doubt it will one day burst forth again. Consequently it should be carefully watched by all sky observers and its position is marked on the chart accordingly.

Note. Within the boundaries of the Northern Crown there are no nebulae (or clusters) visible with ordinary telescopes, although long-exposure photographs taken with large reflectors show the whole area strewn with systems. This lack of brighter nebulae makes Corona Borealis an easy and attractive constellation for the comet hunter. Any suspect object encountered visually with ordinary telescopes will almost certainly be a comet. It was in this constellation, on a summer night in late August 1959, that the English amateur G.E.D. Alcock discovered his first comet after years of fruitless searching. It was the first time that a comet had been discovered first and outright in Great Britain since 1894, when the celebrated Denning made the last of his finds. Between these years comets had been discovered in Great Britain, but they were only independent discoveries of comets which had already been found elsewhere. Alcock went on to make further history by finding a second comet the following week – thus paralleling the performance of the American amateur Metcalf who discovered two comets within two days in 1919.

CORVUS, *the Crow* (Crv)

Another of the very ancient constellations which, although rather small and with few bright stars, can easily be recognized. Its form is a highly distinctive, four-sided rhombus-like figure, not unlike the flowerpot of Hercules, but with north and south reversed. It is located by imagining a long line from Vega (a Lyrae) through Spica (a Virginis) and extending a further 15° southwards.

Mythology

Although it is the Crow which is now generally represented in the legendary stories, the Raven is often preferred. The Crow is supposedly the same bird into which Apollo transformed himself to escape from the giant Typhon on the same occasion when Pan assumed the figure of Capricornus. There is also a popular legend that appears in Ovid's *Fasti* which tells that the bird was sent by its master for a cup of water but lingered near a fig tree until the fruit ripened. It later returned with a water snake in its claws and a falsehood in its mouth, asserting that the snake was the cause of its delay. As punishment it was exiled to the heavens, with the cup (Crater) and a snake (Hydra), and sentenced by the keeper of the snake to everlasting thirst.

The principal Raven story asserts that it is the bird whose memory is perpetuated for the assistance it gave in the victory of Valerius over one of the Senones. Both Hebrews and Greeks knew it as a raven, and it constantly occurs as a symbol in many of the marbles on which the Mithraic emblems are engraved.

Principal stars

α Crv *Al Chiba*, 'the Raven or Crow'; mag 4.2, yellow-white. Somewhat faint to be the principal star and therefore, there may be good reason to suppose that it may have diminished in brightness since early times. However, it must be remembered that when Bayer, in 1603, designated the constellations with Greek letters, his method was very arbitrary.

β   Mag 2.8, yellow.

γ   *Gienah*, 'the Right Wing of the Raven'; mag 2.8, blue-white.

δ   *Algores*, or *Algorab*; mag 3.1, white; also a double, companion star, mag 8.4, dist 24″, yellow-orange. Shown by 2-in. telescopes.

ε   Mag 3.2, yellow-orange.

ζ   A binary system, faint companion, mags 5.3, 13.8, dist 8″. Beyond reach of small instruments. Also a wide optical double as a mag 6.2 star lies close by. In ancient China it was known as Clang Sha, 'a Long Sandbank'.

η   Mag 4.4, yellow-white; forms a wide naked-eye double with δ Corvi.

CRATER, *the Cup*, (Crt)

Situated close by Corvus in the back of Hydra; for northern observers it can be found lying due south of the distinctive triangle of Leo and also by the prominent rhombic shape of Corvus immediately to the east of it.

Mythology

One legend considers that the cup so represented belonged to Bacchus, while other stories refer to it as 'the Goblet of Apollo'; to the Romans it was known as 'the Cup of Apollo'. A Greek writer refers to it as 'the Cup of Oblivion' of the Platonists.

At various times it has also been more mundanely described as 'the Water Bucket', 'Urn' or 'Two-Handed Pot', and others again think it purely symbolic of the cultivation of the vine by Noah. In Julius Schiller's biblical reformations he incorporated it as part of 'the Ark of the Covenant'.

Principal stars

α Crt *Alkes* – 'at the base of the Cup'; mag 4.2, yellow-orange.
β   Mag 4.5, white.
γ   Mag 4.1, white; a double, companion star, mag 9.5, dist 5.2.
       A 2½-in. telescope is required to show it.
δ   Mag 3.8, yellow-orange.

Deep-sky objects

Jc 16 Double; mags 5.8, 8.9, dist 7.7″, white.

HYDRA, *the Water snake* (Hya)

An extremely long constellation, extending more than 100°
from west to east. The head of the mythical snake lies below Cancer
and then winds eastwards between Leo and Virgo, and finally ends
near Libra. The constellation is not well placed for observers in the
northern temperate zone and it requires a clear, moonless night
to trace out the sinuous form. Its only prominent star is Alphard,
mag 2.2.

Mythology

Its mythological history is obscure. One story asserts that it
represents the water serpent killed by Hercules. Another story, a
more traditional one, connects it with the legend of Corvus, the
Crow (p. 77). Interpretations in which it is named as the Lernaean
serpent say that this monster lived in a swamp near a rivulet and
was accustomed to ravage the country of Argos. The beast
possessed several heads, and the middle one was immortal. Hercules attacked it, but was startled to find that each time he cut off a
head, two new ones appeared. His companion Iolaus suggested
burning each stump as he severed the head, and this successfully
prevented new growth. When the immortal head was cut off
the monster died, and Hercules buried the head securely under a
rock. Afterwards, he used the serpent's blood to dip his arrows,
which, it is said, made even the lightest wound inflicted by them
fatal. According to another legend, the spiteful Juno, envious of
the success of Hercules, sent a crab to bite his feet while he was
preoccupied with his battle.

In ancient China the stars of Hydra were an ill omen to those
who fell under its sign for they would be deprived of the birth of a
son to enrich their family – probably the greatest personal tragedy
that could befall ancient Chinese families.

World mythology and folk-lore is rich in stories concerning
Hydra and its more northerly counterpart Draco; both have been

identified with every kind of serpent or dragon conjured up by the imagination of man.

Principal stars

αHya *Alphard*, 'the solitary one in the Serpent'; mag 2.2, yellow-orange. A prominent star, since it is by far the brightest in this part of the sky. Tycho Brahe nicknamed it Cor Hydrae, 'the Hydra's Heart', but an alternative name is 'Hydra's Neck'.

β   Mag 4.4 blue-white; also a binary system, mags 4.8, 5.6, dist 1.2″. Very far south for northern observers.

γ   Mag 3.3, yellow.

δ   Mag 4.2, white.

ε   Mag 3.5; very close binary system, mags 4.1, 4.4, dist 0.2″, both yellow-white. Also an invisible (spectroscopic binary) component star present with the primary, making it a triple-star system.

ζ   Mag 3.3, yellow.

η   Mag 4.3, blue-white.

θ   Mag 3.8, white; a spectroscopic binary and also an optical double, companion star, mag 10.8, dist 38″.

ι   Mag 4.1, yellow-orange.

λ   Mag 3.8, yellow; a spectroscopic binary.

μ   Mag 4.1, yellow-orange.

ν   Mag 3.3, yellow-orange.

ξ   Mag 3.7, yellow.

π   Mag 3.5, yellow-orange.

σ   Mag 4.5, yellow-orange.

Deep-sky objects

54 Hya Mag 5.0; double, mags 5.2, 7.1, dist 9″, both yellow-white.

17   (*Crateris*) Used to be within Crater before the constellation boundaries were reformed, and still retains this title in the Double Star Catalogues. Mag 5.1; double, mags 5.8, 5.9, dist 9″, both yellow-white.

R   Long-period variable; mag range 3.5–10.9, period 387 days; visible with naked eye at max.

U   Irregular variable; mag range 4.8–5.8, red. Ideal star for either naked-eye or binocular study.

V   Semi-regular variable; mag range 6.0–12.5, deep red, period 532 days. Another ideal binocular star, showing red colour very distinctly.

W   Long-period variable; mag range 6.7–8.0, period 385 days, orange-red. Observable through entire range with binoculars.

Y   Semi-regular variable; mag range 6.9–7.9, period 95 days (?), deep red. Binocular star.

M 48 (?) (NGC 2548) Large open star cluster; mag 5.3, dia 30′ (full moon size); about 80 stars, very easy object with binoculars. This cluster may be the 'lost' Messier object No. 48, which was originally catalogued some 3° to the north.

M 68 (NGC 4590) Globular cluster; mag 8.2, dia 3′. Object for 2-in. telescope or 10×80 binoculars. Very low in south for north temperate zone observers.

Leo, *the Lion* (Leo)

Easily recognizable because of the highly distinctive form of a sickle made by some of its principal stars. The fifth sign of the Zodiac. The traditional symbolic zodiacal figure ♌ most probably represents the head and mane of a male lion.

The group is rich in both bright stars and binocular-telescopic subjects. Within its boundaries can be counted at least 100 naked-eye stars, and in north temperate latitudes it dominates the southern midnight sky during the spring months. From a position inside its famous sickle originated the greatest meteor shower ever witnessed by modern man.

Mythology

In Greek mythology the Lion represented the terrifying animal that inhabited the Nemaean forests. One legend supposes that the twelve zodiacal signs represent the labours of Hercules, and his first was the combat with this lion. However, the figure of the Lion was recorded by the Egyptians long before the invention of the fables of Hercules' exploits. To the Egyptians, it signified the period of intense heat of summer, when the Sun entered the sign. He was an emblem of violence and fury, for the ancient Egyptians suffered great inconveniences from lions which, during the great heat of summer, left their desert haunts for the cooler banks of the Nile.

The best-known story of the Lion and Hercules is the one which relates how Hercules, after being commanded by Juno to bring her the skin of the fiercest lion which roamed at large, finally caught up with it but could not kill it with either club or arrow. He finally resorted to strangling it and when he returned to her with the dead lion draped across his shoulders, the sight so terrified the relatives of Juno that they instructed him to tell the story of his brave deed well outside the limits of the town boundary. To the Hebrews it has always represented the Lion of Judah.

Principal stars

α Leo *Regulus*, 'Ruler of the Affairs of the Heavens' – so named by Copernicus. Mag 1.3, blue-white; also a wide double just in range with 2-in. telescopes, companion mag 8.5, dist 3′, yellow-orange.

Regulus was, to the ancients, leader of the four Royal Stars

(Regulus, Aldebaran, Antares, Fomalhaut), and because of their approximate equi-distance, they marked off the four quarters of the celestial sphere. It was also called 'the Lion's Heart' in classical times. As it lies on the ecliptic, it is often occulted by the Moon, and, more rarely and spectacularly, by one of the planets.

β   *Denebola*, 'the Lion's Tail'; mag 1.6, white. It once formed part of a Chinese group called Woo Ti Tso, 'the Seat of the Five Emperors'. Whereas Regulus was supposed to be of good influence, Denebola was considered to be a very unlucky star by astrologers of the Middle Ages.

γ   *Algieba*, which, although literally it means 'on the Lion's Forehead', is actually situated in the position of the tail. Mag 2.3. It is one of the finest binary systems in the sky, both members being giant stars, mags 2.6, 3.8, dist 4.3″, orange-yellow, period 618 years.

δ   *Zosma*, 'the Girdle'(?) or *Duhr*, 'the Lion's Back'; mag 2.6, white. It was on Flamsteed's observing list in the night he also observed Uranus, 13 December 1690, but unfortunately he did not recognize the latter as a planet, and it was discovered by William Herschel in 1781.

ε   *Algenubi*, 'the Southern Star in the Lion's Head'; mag 3.1, yellow.

ζ   *Adhafera*, 'the Crest of the Mane'; mag 3.6, yellow-white. Also an easy optical double, companion mag 6, white, dist 5′.

η   Mag 3.6, white.

θ   Mag 3.4, white; one of the named Chinese stars – 'the Second Minister of State'.

μ   *Rasalas*, 'the Eyebrows'; mag 4.1, yellow-orange.

Deep-sky objects

τ Leo Wide binocular double; mags 5.5, 7.0, dist 90″, yellowish-white and blue-white.

7   Wide double; mags 6, 8, dist 42″.

54   Binary system of long period; mags 4.5, 6.3, dist 6.5″, blue and white. Fine object with 2-in. telescope.

83   Double; mags 6.3, 7.2, dist 29″. Easy with 2-in. telescope.

88   Double; mags 6.1, 8.6, dist 15″, yellow and blue.

90   Double; mags 5.7, 7.1, dist 3.4″, white and blue. Object for 3-in. telescope.

93   Wide double; mags 4.7, 8.4, dist 74″, yellow and white.

R   Long-period variable; plainly visible with naked eye at maximum brightness; mag range 4.4–11.6, period 313 days, brilliant red. Can be followed to minimum brightness with a 3-in. telescope.

M 65 (NGC 3623) Spiral galaxy seen edgewise; mag 9.3, dia 8′ × 2′. Visible with 2½-in. telescope and 10 × 80 binoculars.

M 66 (NGC 3627) Spiral galaxy – another seen edgewise; mag 8.4, dia 8′ × 2.5′. Can just be glimpsed with 2-in. telescope in a transparent sky.

M 95 (NGC 3351) Spiral galaxy seen face on; mag 10.4, dia. 3′ × 3′. At limit of visibility with 3-in. telescope.

M 96 (NGC 3368) Spiral galaxy; mag 9.1, dia 7′ × 4′; visible with 3-in. aperture – easy with 10 × 80 binoculars.

Leonids. Meteor shower which produced the most brilliant and prolific displays seen by man in modern times. Originates from a radiant point within the 'Sickle', a little west of ζ Leonis. In 1966, at the height of the last big display, between 2,000 and 2,500 meteors were seen each minute and the sky was ablaze. Unfortunately, owing to the position of the Earth at that time it was missed by observers in Europe, but observers in the western United States and eastern Siberia enjoyed their greatest celestial spectacle of all time.

The shower reaches peak activity each year between 14 and 17 November, and produces meteors moving very swiftly with short paths. In an average annual display the observer, if the Moon is absent, will see approximately 70 meteors per hour.

Research has shown that the Leonids have been recorded as far back as A D 903, and that they have tended to recur in great showers, or storms, at intervals of 33 years. One of the earliest great displays was in 1799, and they occurred again in 1833, and 1866. The displays in 1899 and 1933 were disappointing, and it was thought that the influence of the planet Jupiter had perturbed the meteor orbits so that the Earth missed the thickest concentrations. The great shower of 1966 was then a great surprise to all.

Leo minor, *the Lesser Lion* (LMi)

Another of Hevelius' modern constellations, formed about 1690 between Leo and Ursa Major.

Mythology

In the oldest planispheres it is depicted as a serpent occupying the area within its modern boundaries. To Aratus, it was a region of unnamed or ungrouped stars under the hind paws of Ursa Major. The Chinese astronomers formed two asterisms here, and to the Arabs it was 'the Gazelle with her Young', which is recorded on the Borgian globe (dated 1225).

Principal stars

β LMi Mag 4.4; binary system, mags 4.6, 6.3, dist 0.6″, both yellow. A large telescope is required in order to split this star.

10 Mag 4.6, yellow.

21 Mag 4.5, white.

46 Mag 3.9, yellow-orange; Hevelius named it *Praecipua*, 'Chief'.

Deep-sky objects

R LMi Long-period variable; mag range 6.2–13.3, period 372 days, orange-red.

LIBRA, *the Balance, or Scales* (Lib)

The seventh sign of the Zodiac and the only inanimate object represented among the twelve. Originally it appears not to have been recognized as an independent constellation and was included as part of the *Chelae*, or Claws of the Scorpion.

Most of the group is located low in the sky in northern temperate latitudes, and its principal stars are best found by referring to Antares (α Scorpii) and then projecting a line towards Arcturus (α Boötis).

Mythology

It was not known in Chaldean times and only appeared in Greco-Roman folk-lore. An early Greek legend supposes that the Balance was placed among the stars to perpetuate the memory of Mechus, the inventor of weights and measures. A later story makes it refer to Roman history, and represent the figure of Julius Caesar holding a pair of scales in his hand as a token of his wisdom and justice. A third story regards the scales as those of Astraea, the goddess of justice, in which the fate of all mortal men must be weighed.

Principal stars

α Lib Mag 2.9, white; a wide double, companion mag 5.3, dist 230″, yellow-white. A fine binocular object.

β Mag 2.7, blue-white; often referred to as a green or emerald star by the older observers – an effect due to scintillation, owing to its extremely low position for observers in northern latitudes.

γ Mag 4.0, yellow.

σ Mag 3.4, orange-red giant.

Deep-sky objects

μ Lib Binary system; mags 5.8, 6.7, dist 1.8″, both white. Requires a 3-in. telescope to split them.

Hh 467 Double; mags 6.9, 7.7, dist 47″. Object for 2-in. telescope.

δ Algol-type variable; mag range 4.8–6.2, period 2.3273 days, yellow-white. Ideal star for binocular observations.

RS Long-period variable; mag range 6.5–13.0, period 218 days, orange-red. In same low-power field as Hh 467 (above).

SEXTANS, *the Sextant* (Sex)

To the naked-eye observer it is a desultory-looking group, and there are few objects to interest observers with only small-aperture telescopes. However, long-exposure photographs show the whole area to be strewn with extragalactic nebulae – vast myriads of island universes, in numbers practically uncountable.

The constellation is best located from the Leo 'sickle' and it lies due south of Regulus (α Leonis).

Mythology

The constellation was formed by Hevelius in 1680, to commemorate either the instrument called the nautical sextant invented by Hadley in 1730, or the instrument which he himself used at Danzig from 1658 to 1679. However, both these explanations have been disputed, for some say that it rather represents the instrument used by Tycho Brahe, an earlier pre-telescopic astronomer who observed from the Castle of Uraniborg in Denmark, and from which it is considered the alternative constellation name, Urania, is derived.

Principal stars

α Sex Mag 4.5, white.
β   Mag 4.9, blue-white.
γ   Mag 5.2, white; also a very close binary system, mags 5.8, 6.1, both white, dist 0.4″, period 80 years. Requires a very large telescope to divide them at the present time, but it will become easier towards the end of the century.
δ   Mag 5.2, white.
ε   Mag 5.4, yellow-white.

VIRGO, *the Virgin* (Vir)

The sixth sign of the Zodiac. An extremely long constellation, bounded on the east by Libra, on the west by Leo, to the north by Boötes and to the south by Corvus. In April its sprawling configuration straddles the meridian at midnight.

Virgo is dominated by the 1st-magnitude star called Spica which traditionally marks the ear of wheat in the Virgin's left hand. This star can be located from one of the ever-present circumpolar constellations by extending a curved line through α and γ Ursae Majoris. At approximately five times the distance between the latter stars, projected on, the eye will be arrested by the brilliant whiteness of Spica. It also forms a striking equilateral triangle with Arcturus (α Boötis) and Denebola (β Leonis).

Mythology

Various accounts have been put forward to explain the folk-lore origins of this group. Some say that the sign was Justitia, who, while on Earth, lived in the golden age and taught mankind their duty. However, when their crimes increased, she was obliged to leave the Earth and take her place in the heavens. Another story says that she was Ceres, and the ear of corn which this celestial maid holds in her hand evidently denotes the time of harvest among the people who invented the sign.

Yet the constellation of the Virgin is one of the most mysterious of the zodiacal groups, for although she is commonly thought to represent the figure of the Virgin, there appears to be little resemblance to a human form. Traditionally, her hand is supposed to lie towards Regulus, while the feet are made by two stars south of Arcturus. Four stars make the head, three the shoulder and another her outstretched right arm. Other members of the constellation form the draperies or clothing.

To the Greeks, the constellation name Virgo symbolized the integrity of an Earth as yet uncontaminated by decay. Some authorities contend that the title originated when the Sun was in Virgo at the spring equinox (at the time of the Egyptian harvest), but for this situation we must look back 15,000 years. The Egyptians also associated Virgo with Isis, and it is related that she formed the Milky Way by throwing millions of wheat heads into the heavens. Another variation of this story is that Isis let fall a sheaf of corn as she was fleeing to escape Typhon, but in his pursuit it became scattered over the sky, the sparkling, golden grains of corn becoming stars. According to Pliny, the appearance of a comet within the borders of Virgo implied grievous ills to all females.

Principal stars

α Vir *Spica*; mag 1.2, blue-white. Among the brightest stars in the heavens. A spectroscopic binary with a period of 4.01 days. In the nineteenth century, the American astronomer Gould claimed to have detected minor variations in its brightness, but others denied his claim. However, modern photo-electric measurements indeed show that there is a regular fluctuation of 0.1 magnitude every four days coinciding with the period of revolution of the binary pair.

Spica is well known to navigators, and is known as a lunar star since it is situated 2° south of the ecliptic (along the apparent path of the Moon). The Arabs called it 'the Solitary, Defenceless, Unguarded One', owing to its isolated position in the sky. To the Chinese astronomers it had great significance as a spring star. In ancient Greece several temples were deliberately orientated to it. On Flamsteed's star map it was designated 'the Virgin's Spike'.

β *Zavijava* or *Zarijan*; mag 3.8, yellow-white.

γ *Porrima* – so named by the Latins after an ancient goddess of prophecy, sister of Carmenta, who was worshipped by their women. Mag 2.7; one of the finest binary systems in the sky, mags 3.6, 3.6, both yellow-white, dist 5″, period 171 years; a fine object in a 2-in. telescope. The orbit of the companion star is highly eccentric and often the two stars are so close that only large telescopes can separate them. They were at their widest separation in 1922, and are now closing again.

δ   Mag 3.6, orange-red; a massive star, 700 times as luminous as the Sun.

ε   *Vindemiatrix* or *Almuredin*; mag 3.0, yellow.

ζ   Mag 3.4, white.

η   Mag 4.0, white; spectroscopic binary, period 72 days.

θ   Mag 4.4, white; a fine triple system of stars, mags 4.4, 9.0, 10.0, dist's 7″ and 70″. The double-star observers of the nineteenth century often described the mag 9 star as 'violet' in colour, but this is a subjective phenomenon and is due in part to spectral differences which produce what is termed 'dazzle tints', causing illusory colour effects. A 3-in. telescope will show both companion stars.

Deep-sky objects

R Vir Long-period variable; mag range 6.2–12.6, period 145 days, orange-red.

S   Long-period variable; mag range 6.0–13.0, period 377 days, orange-red. This was one of the variables discovered in 1852 by the English astronomer Hind, the famous comet and minor-planet discoverer, who made many of his finds from the Regent's Park Observatory, situated barely one mile from central London.

One of the best-known features in Virgo for deep-sky observers is what is known as the 'Field of Nebulae', where uncountable numbers of extragalactic nebulae can be photographed with large reflectors. The area is roughly outlined by the stars β, η, γ, δ, and ε, forming two sides of a square some 15° across. The region is not confined to Virgo and extends across the constellation boundaries into Coma Berenices. This region has often been labelled the 'Comet-Hunters' Nightmare'. However, only the brighter members are visible with small instruments. Within Virgo are listed ten Messier objects, ranging in visual magnitudes from 8.2 to 10; these include M 104, nicknamed the 'Sombrero Nebula', because of the unusual shape it portrays in long-exposure photographs. Magnitudes for nebulae can be very misleading, and their visibility depends much on the transparency of the sky. On a really clear night all these Messier objects can be readily seen with a 3-in. telescope, and some with instruments of smaller aperture. With a larger instrument the scope is greatly increased – for example, with my own 12-in. reflector 'comet-sweeper', more than 180 nebulae can, under ideal conditions, be observed within the boundaries of Virgo.

M 49 (NGC 4472) Elliptical galaxy; mag 8.6, dia 4.5′ × 4.0′.

M 58 (NGC 4579) Spiral galaxy; mag 9.2, dia 3.6' × 3.2'.
M 59 (NGC 4621) Elliptical galaxy; mag 9.6, dia 2.7' × 1.6'.
M 60 (NGC 4649) Elliptical galaxy; mag 8.9, dia 3.9' × 3.1'.
M 61 (NGC 4303) Spiral galaxy; mag 10.1, dia 6.0' × 6.0'.
M 84 (NGC 4374) Elliptical galaxy; mag 9.3, dia 2.9' × 2.6'.
M 86 (NGC 4406) Elliptical galaxy; mag 9.7, dia 3.8' × 2.9'.
M 87 (NGC 4486) Elliptical galaxy; mag 9.2, dia 3.3' × 3.3'.
M 89 (NGC 4552) Elliptical galaxy; mag 9.5, dia 2.2' × 2.2'.
M 90 (NGC 4569) Spiral galaxy; mag 10.0, dia 6.0' × 3.0'.
M 104 (NGC 4594) Spiral galaxy seen edge-on, Sombrero nebula; mag 8.7, dia 7.0' × 1.5'.

CHAPTER 7

Stars of summer
June, July, August

Refer to fig. 23 at required month and time.

During the period of summer stars, the observer in northern temperate latitudes will have only a short period of darkness in which to observe. However, one has the advantage of the warmer outdoor weather, and the softness of the still summer night skies provides an enchanting experience. Almost overhead will be a brilliant white star of the 1st magnitude called Vega. It is a of the constellation of Lyra, the Lyre or Harp. Although this is one of the smallest star groups, it is readily identified since Vega and the five other stars form a small equilateral triangle and parallelogram. Like Capella, Vega is just circumpolar and can often be seen flashing iridescently low down over the northern horizon in mid-winter. When photography was first applied to the heavens in 1850, Vega became the first star whose image was recorded on a primitive photographic plate.

To the east of Lyra is Cygnus (the Swan), which is generally referred to as the Northern Cross since five stars trace out the distinctive shape of a cross. The star a (or Deneb) is a giant star and emits 10,000 times more light than our own Sun.

Lying between Lyra and Boötes is the constellation of Hercules. Hercules is a large, sprawling constellation with no 1st-magnitude stars, but it can readily be identified by tracing out the 'flowerpot' shape that four of its stars make. On the right-hand side of the 'flowerpot' is located one of the most spectacular globular star clusters in the entire sky (M 13, see fig. 24). Long-exposure photography shows thousands of stars, but to the naked eye it can only be observed as a faint star on the darkest of nights at the extreme limit of naked-eye visibility by those with even the most acute night vision. To the west, Corona Borealis is now beginning to dip towards the horizon.

Below Cygnus, the Northern Cross, is a group known as Aquila (the Eagle) and its brightest member, Altair (a), is a prominent white 1st-magnitude star.

Late on a clear summer's evening is the best time to search

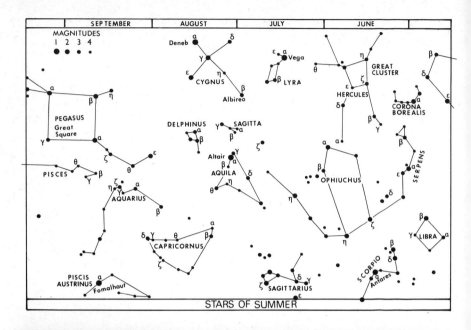

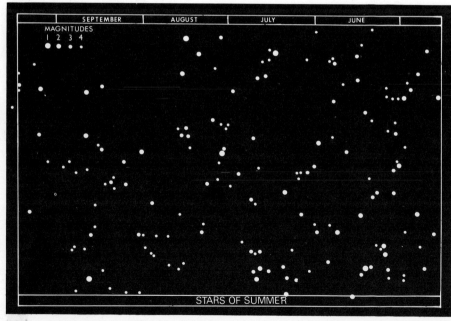

23 Stars of summer (see note on p. 53). To locate the less conspicuous constellations and for individual star recognition refer to charts, pp. 194–214.

24 Globular cluster M13 in Hercules.

for two other constellations which are barely visible in northern temperate latitudes. The first one, Scorpius (the Scorpion), is the easiest to find since its *a* star is a bright 1st-magnitude red giant called Antares which, owing to its extremely low position in the sky, will often appear to flash iridescently through the whole spectrum of colours. To the left (or east) of Antares can be traced out the fainter stars which form the constellation of Sagittarius (the Archer).

Looking northwards towards the circumpolar groups, the Great Bear (Ursa Major) is in the north-western sky with the tail uppermost, and the distorted 'W' shape of Cassiopeia is beginning to ascend in the north-eastern heavens. In the far north, low down, can be seen the iridescent light of Capella (*a* Aurigae), as it skims the permanent twilight zone of the far northern summer skies where the white nights prevail.

AQUILA, *the Eagle* (Aql)

A conspicuous constellation in the southern heavens during the summer and autumn months; lies south of Cygnus and Vulpecula, and north of Capricornus and Sagittarius. The configuration is dominated by the brilliant blue-white star Altair (α Aquilae) and β and γ, below and above, which gives the figure a distinctive pattern for easy recognition.

Mythology

Aratus in his poem simply describes it as a bird. In the Greek fables the constellation is said to represent the eagle which brought Hector to Jupiter while he lay concealed in a cave in Crete to avoid the fury of Saturn, his father. Aquila is supposed also to have assisted, by furnishing weapons, in the victory of the Gods over the Giants.

Another Greek story tells us that Aquila is a star group commemorating the bird which preyed upon the vitals of Prometheus. Yet another story says that the eagle was the bird of Zeus and is represented as carrying in his talons to heaven a beautiful youth called Ganymede whom Jupiter desired for his cup-bearer.

The group is certainly a very old one and was represented in many Roman coins; the figure also occurs on a stone depicting the heavens, found in the Euphrates Valley, dated about 1200 B C.

At one time a separate constellation called Antinous was recognized, but nowadays it is incorporated in 'the Eagle'. It was the creation of Tycho Brahe to perpetuate the memory of a youth much favoured by the Emperor Hadrian. When the youth died, a temple in his name was erected on the banks of the Nile as a monument.

Principal stars

α Aql *Altair*, 'Flying Vulture or Eagle' – same title as the constellation; mag 0.9, white.

β   *Alshain*, from the Persian title of part of the group; mag 3.3, yellow.

γ   *Tarazed*, also derived from the Persian; mag 2.8, orange-yellow. With α and β it forms a celestial measuring rod almost exactly 5° in length.

δ   Mag 3.0, blue-white.

ε   *Deneb*, 'the Eagle's Tail'; mag 4.2, yellow-orange.

ζ   Also known as *Deneb*; mag 3.0, blue-white. A binary system with an exceedingly faint companion which was discovered with the 26-in. refractor at Washington Observatory; mag 12.0, dist 7″; beyond reach of small telescopes.

η   Cepheid-type variable; mag range 3.9–5.1, period 7.1766 days, yellow. Discovered by Pigott, friend of the deaf-mute Goodricke, in 1784. A splendid star for study, either with naked eye, opera glasses or binoculars.

θ   Mag 3.4, blue-white; spectroscopic binary, period 17 days.

Near by is a yellow-orange star, 66 Aquilae, mag 5.6.

λ   Mag 3.6, blue-white.

12   Mag 4.2, yellow-orange.

Deep-sky objects

π Aql Binary; mags 6.0, 6.8, dist 1.4″, yellow and white. Requires 3½-in. telescope with high power to split them.

11   Optical double; mags 5.7, 9.2, dist 16″. Can be glimpsed with 2-in. telescopes.

57   Double; mags 5.2, 6.2, dist 35″, yellow and blue. A beautiful sight in 2-in. telescopes.

R   Long-period variable; mag range 6–12, period 310 days, orange-red.

U   Cepheid-type variable; mag range 6.2–6.9, period 7.0238 days, yellow. Ideal for binocular study.

V   Irregular variable; mag range 6.7–8.2, deep-tinted orange-red. Can be followed through entire light cycle with 8×30's.

Note. Since Aquila lies immersed within the Milky Way, it is worth while making a regular study of this constellation to watch for possible novae. At least four novae have been found within its boundaries since 1899, and chances for both naked-eye and binocular observers are good. With binoculars it is also possible to make routine sweep-searches during bright, moonlight periods when fainter deep-sky objects are rendered invisible.

CAPRICORNUS, *the Goat* (Cap)

The tenth zodiacal sign, although quite small in extent, is distinct as a group and can easily be found by projecting a line from Vega (*a* Lyrae) through Altair (*a* Aquilae) and then extending it approximately the same distance southwards.

Mythology

In some stories Capricornus represents the goat Amalthea which nourished Jupiter during his infancy – but this story is more likely in connection with Auriga. Another fable relates that Pan, with other deities, was feasting near the banks of the Nile, when without warning the giant Typhon appeared among them. They all became so afraid that they changed themselves into different forms and fled in various directions. However, Pan, who was guardian of the hunters and shepherds, plunged into the river and assumed the combined form of a fish and a goat, in which many of the early star maps actually depict him (fig. 25). On oriental zodiacs he is often shown as a fish swallowing an antelope. Like its neighbour, Sagittarius, Capricornus was always considered a fortunate sign by the old astrologers, and the Arabians nicknamed

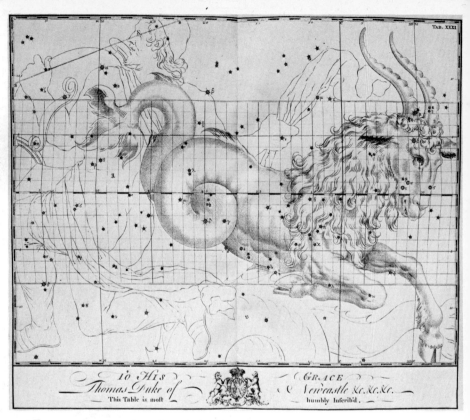

25 Capricornus, from the Atlas Celeste of John Bevis, 1786.

the α and β stars 'the Lucky Stars of the Slaughterers', and γ and δ 'the Fortunate Stars of Good Tidings'.

Principal stars

α^1, α^2 Cap *Giedi*, 'the Lucky One of the Slaughterers' – a name derived from early Arabic times when sacrifices were offered to the Sun as it rose in Capricorn. Consists of two stars both visible with the naked eye; mags α^1 4.5, α^2 3.8, both yellow, dist 6' 16"; α^1 also a telescopic double; mags 4.5, 9.0, dist 45", and α^2 is a telescopic triple system; mags 3.8, 11.5, 11.5, dist 8.3" and 1.2".

β *Dabih Major* and *Dabih Minor*; a highly complex system involving five connected stars; *A* and *B* form a wide double; mags 3.2, 6.2, dist 205". *A* is also a spectroscopic triple and the *B* star has a faint telescopic companion.

γ *Nashira*, 'the Fortunate One', also known as 'the Bringer of Good Tidings' when associated with δ; mag 3.8, yellow-white.

δ *Deneb Algedi*, 'the Tail of the Goat'; mag 3.0, white. Near this star the planet Neptune was found by Galle at the Berlin Observatory in 1846, after he had received the predicted position from the Frenchman Le Verrier.

94

ε	Mag 4.7, blue-white.
ζ	Mag 3.9, yellow.
η	Mag 4.9, white.
θ	Mag 4.2, white.
ι	Mag 4.3, yellow.

Deep-sky objects

o Cap Double, probably binary system; mags 6.1, 6.6, dist 22″, both white. Fine object for 2-in. telescopes.

σ A wide optical pair; mags 5.5, 9, dist 54″, orange-yellow and blue-white.

M 30 (NGC 7099) Globular cluster; mag 5.5, dia 6′. Visible as a nebulous star with 8 × 30's near 41 Capricorni.

CYGNUS, *the Swan, or Northern Cross* (Cyg)

The Northern Cross is one of the easiest groups to recognize, owing to its distinctive cross shape. It lies immediately to the east of Vega. Its principal star, Deneb (*a* Cygni), forms with Vega and Altair a well-known stellar triangle, which is visible for much of the year in northern latitudes.

Apart from its prominent configuration of naked-eye stars, it also contains an extensive list of interesting binocular and telescopic objects. It is immersed completely in the star clouds of the Milky Way so that, with even the simplest of optical aids, the background stars spawn in their thousands.

Mythology

The name has resulted from the resemblance seen by the ancients to the figure of a flying swan. To the later Greeks and Romans it was known simply as 'the Bird', while to the Arabs it was a 'Flying Eagle' or 'the Hen'. In Greek mythology, according to the poets (although there is some doubt as to the source), it was Orpheus, the celebrated musician of antiquity, who, having been murdered by the cruel priestesses of Bacchus, was after his death transformed into the swan and placed near his lyre. Since Orpheus was one of the Argonauts, this legend can be considered as the principal one; although Roman mythology regarded it as the mythical swan, identified with Cycnus, the son of Mars, or alternatively the friend and kinsman of Phaethon (p. 145), who was transformed into a swan at the River Padus and placed in the heavens.

In the later Christian reformation of the constellation figures, it became the 'Cross of Calvary', 'Christi Crux' and 'Crux cum S. Helena'.

Principal stars

α Cyg *Deneb*, 'the Hen's Tail'; mag 1.3, white. A giant star and one of the most luminous known: it gives out 8,000 times more light than the Sun.

β   *Albireo*, 'the Hen's Beak'; mag 3.0; a beautiful binary system, mags 3.2, 5.3, dist 34″, yellow (gold) and blue. A splendid object in 2-in. telescopes.

γ   *Sadr*, 'the Hen's Breast'; mag 2.3, yellow-white. In the area round this star is some of the most glorious 'star sweeping' to be found in the entire heavens. On black, transparent nights and comfortably reclined in a garden chair with binoculars, the observer can see more stars in this field than is humanly possible to count. In his own star gauge, it is recorded, Sir William Herschel estimated that there were over 300,000 stars within the space of 5° sq. hereabouts.

δ   Binary; mags 3.0, 6.5, dist 2.1″, white, period 500+ years.

ε   *Gienah*, 'the Wing'; mag 2.6, yellow-orange; there is also a mag 12 companion, dist 44″. Also a spectroscopic binary system.

ζ   Mag 3.4, yellow.

η   Mag 4.0, yellow-orange.

Deep-sky objects

o^2 Cyg Wide triple system; mag 4.0, 5.5, 7.5, dist 358″, 107″. An ideal subject for binocular study. The primary star is yellow-orange and also a spectroscopic binary that shows minor variations in brightness.

16   Double; mags 5.1, 5.3, dist 38″. Not physically connected.

ψ   Binary pair: mags 5.0, 7.5, dist 3″, white and blue.

61   Binary; mags 5.6, 6.3, dist 28″, yellow-orange, orange-red. Appears as a beautiful pair in 2-in. telescopes. This star is of great historical interest since it was the first one to have its parallax measured. The German astronomer Bessel, in 1838, using trigonometrical methods, found it to be 10 light-years from the Sun.

Note. Cygnus is very prolific in interesting variable stars, and the following list of various types is included to whet the observer's appetite for further study:

χ   Long-period variable; mag ranges 2.3–14.3, period 407 days, orange-red. A very interesting star since at its brightest, near maximum, it can be followed with the naked eye or binoculars. Easily located near η Cygni.

X   Cepheid-type variable; mag range 5.9–7.0, period 16.3866 days, yellow. Observable through entire light cycle with binoculars.

SU   Cepheid-type variable; mag range 6.2–7.0, period 3.8457 days, yellow; binocular variable.

W   Semi-regular variable; mag range 5.0–7.6, period 131 days, orange-red; binocular variable.

U   Long-period variable; mag range 6.1–12.3, period 462 days, deep orange-red.

M 39 (NGC 7092) Open cluster; mag 5.2, dia 30'. Visible with opera glasses.

NGC 7000 Gaseous nebula; dimensions 120' × 100'; known as 'the North America Nebula' because of its unique form which distinctly resembles a rough approximation of the coast round the Gulf of Mexico (see fig. 26). When the sky is very transparent, it can be picked out with binoculars.

26 The North America nebula in Cygnus.

'*Coal-sack*'. Between α and ε Cygni can be observed, with the naked eye, one of the dark 'coal-sack' nebulae. These consist of clouds of opaque, dusty material within the Milky Way which completely obscure the stars behind, so that from the Earth it appears as if we are observing a black hole completely devoid of stars.

DELPHINUS, *the Dolphin* (Del)

A small but highly distinctive constellation to the east of Aquila. Its four brightest stars are arranged in the shape of a diamond and

97

it has been aptly described: 'as neat as a miniature and compact as a jewel'.

Mythology

In Greece, Delphinus was the sacred fish. It was the dolphin which saved the life of Arion, the famous lyrical poet and musician of Lesbos. The story relates that Arion had amassed a vast fortune in Italy through his great personal skill and finally resolved to return to his native country with his wealth. While on the voyage home, the sailors of the ship learnt of his fortune and hatched a plot to kill him. When they prepared to carry out their plan, he begged them to permit him to play some of his own melodious tunes for the last time. They agreed, but Arion took them by surprise and flung himself into the sea in a desperate attempt to escape.

Meanwhile, a number of dolphins had been attracted to the ship by the sweetness of the music, and one of them swam up to Arion and allowed him to ride on his back. Subsequently Arion was delivered safely to land, and Neptune, as a reward, transformed the Dolphin into a constellation and signified it as a friend and protector of mankind.

Principal stars

α Del Mag 3.9, blue-white. Although various names have been associated with both α and β, none is recognized at the present time.

β Mag 3.7, yellow-white; a binary system, mags 4.1, 5.1, dist 0.2″, period 27 years. The pair will be at their widest in 1977, and closest in 1993, but it requires a large telescope to split them. There is also a third member present, mag 11.0, dist 6″, blue-white, which appears to be physically connected.

γ Mag 4.4; binary system, mags 4.5, 5.5, dist 10″, yellow-orange and yellow-white. A fine object for 2-in. telescopes.

δ Mag 4.5, white.

ε Mag 4.0, blue-white.

Deep-sky objects

U Del Irregular variable; mag range 5.6–7.5, orange-red. Can be followed through entire cycle with binoculars.

Nova Delphini 1967 Discovered by the British schoolmaster and amateur astronomer, G.E.D. Alcock, with 11 × 80 binoculars on 8 July 1967. It is one of the most peculiar novae yet observed. On discovery it was mag 5, but then over a period of six months it brightened to mag 3.5, with considerable erratic fluctuations in light output. In December 1967 it began to fade again, but much more slowly than any other true nova yet observed. It was a mag 12 object prior to its outburst, and in February 1970, it was still observable with binoculars and small telescopes (see HR Del, p. 212).

EQUULEUS, *the Foal* (Equ)

A very small constellation distinguished by a trapezium of four stars of magnitude 4, between Pegasus and Delphinus.

Mythology

The origin of this group is wrapped in mystery since it is not mentioned by Aratus or Hipparchus. Its first mention is by Geminus as 'the Fore-Section of a Horse', and, like its neighbouring constellation Pegasus, it represents only the fore-part of the animal.

The later popular Greek legend tells that the horse is Celeris, given by Mercury to Castor, who was celebrated for his skill in the management of the animal. The horse is depicted inverted for northern observers, as is Pegasus.

Principal stars

α Equ *Kitalpha*, 'the Little Horse'; mag 4.1, yellow-white. Also a spectroscopic binary, period 97.5 days.

β Mag 5.1, white; spectroscopic binary.

γ Mag 4.8, yellow-white; true binary of long period, faint companion star mag 11.0, dist 2.5″.

δ Mag 4.6; very close binary, mags 5.3, 5.4, dist 0.4″, both yellow-white, period 5.7 years.

Deep-sky objects

ε Equ Triple system; the *A* and *B* stars constitute a close binary pair, mag 5.7, 7.0, dist 0.2″, period 100 years; the *C* star, mag 7.1, dist 11″, is also probably physically connected, but its revolution must be very long. *C* star easily seen with 2-in. telescope.

HERCULES (Her)

One of the major constellations, which covers an extended area of the sky yet surprisingly contains no star brighter than the 3rd magnitude. It can readily be identified lying between Lyra and the Northern Crown by the distinctive 'flowerpot' configuration that four of its principal stars make.

Mythology

The earliest civilizations all appear to have depicted him as a kneeling giant, or youth. He was often termed 'the Kneeler' or 'the One who Bends Down'. No one knows who this kneeler was – or what he was actually doing. In more modern times he has always been identified with the 'twelve labours' of Hercules – if only because man does not respect anonymity.

In classical mythology he is the son of Jupiter by Alcmene, wife of Amphitryon. Hercules was reputed to possess great strength and courage. One of the feats of his labours was the destruction of the dragon which guarded the garden of the Hesperides.

The Phoenicians worshipped the group as a great sea god, Melkarth, and Julius Schiller, in his biblical reforms, represented him as the Three Magi.

Principal stars

α Her *Ras Algethi*, 'the Kneeler's Hand'; a binary system, but the primary star is also a giant, orange-red, irregular variable; mags (3.1–3.9), 5.4, dist 4.6″. The primary star is an extremely massive one with a dia of 200m. miles, and at least 700 times more luminous than the Sun. The fainter component is also a spectroscopic binary, period 51.6 days.

β *Korneforos*, 'Golden Red' (?); mag 2.8, yellow; a spectroscopic binary, period 410 days.

γ Double; mags 3.8, 8, dist 40″, white and blue. A fine object with 2-in. telescopes.

δ Optical double; mags 3.2, 8.3, dist 9.5″, white and yellow.

ε Mag 3.9, white; a spectroscopic binary, period 4 days.

ζ Mag 3.0, a true binary pair; mags 3.1, 5.6, dist 1.4″, period 34.4 years, yellow and blue. The pair were at their closest in 1967, and will be at their widest in 1991. A beautiful object in 3- to 4-in. telescopes.

η Mag 3.6, yellow.

θ Mag 4.0, orange-yellow. Part of an ancient Chinese group Tien Ke, 'Heaven's Record'.

ι Mag 3.8, blue.

π Mag 3.4, yellow.

Deep-sky objects

95 Her Mag 4.4; probably binary of long period; mags 5.1, 5.2, dist 6.3″, white and yellow. Object for 2-in. telescope.

μ Binary; mags 3.5, 9.5, dist 33″, yellow and red. Requires 3-in. telescope.

κ Mag 5.0; double; mags 5.3, 6.5, dist 30″. Another mag 6 star close by.

S Long-period variable; mag range 5.9–13.6, period 307 days, orange-red.

68 A β Lyrae-type variable, mag range 4.6–5.1, period 2.051 days. A good star for either naked-eye or binocular studies.

30 A semi-regular variable of red-giant variety; mag range 4.6–6.0, period 80 days (?). Another ideal star for regular binocular study.

M 13 (NGC 6205) Globular cluster, 'the Great Cluster of Hercules', consisting of many thousands of stars – perhaps upwards of 100,000; mag 5.7, dia 10′. Very easy to locate between η and ζ, and an opera glass will show it as a nebulous star. In small telescopes it is a very fine object. With a 6-in. telescope, the stars can be resolved into myriads of scintillating, separate points.

M 92 (NGC 6341) Globular cluster – another bright one; mag 6.1, dia 8'. Easy with binoculars.

Lyra, *the Harp or Lyre* (Lyr)

Although among the smallest of constellations, it is one of the easiest to recognize. It consists of a compact group of stars depicting the shape of the Lyre or Harp, dominated by the blazing, blue-white Vega. In the latitudes of Great Britain and North America, the constellation is almost a circumpolar one and therefore is visible for the greater part of the year. Its brightest member, Vega, is located at the apex of a bold triangle with Polaris and Arcturus (a Boötis) forming the base. In latitudes approximating to 50° N, it can often be observed directly overhead at the zenith point.

Mythology

The Lyre or Harp represents the fabled instrument invented by Hermes and given to his half-brother Apollo, who in turn transferred it to his son Orpheus, the musician of the Argonauts. A variation of this legend states that the lyre is the instrument by which Orpheus captivated the fair Eurydice.

In some early celestial maps the constellation is represented by a vulture in addition to the lyre, and was known as the 'Descending Vulture' – as against the 'Ascending Vulture' represented by the near-by constellation Aquila. Nevertheless, the Harp has certainly had its place in the sky much longer than the Vulture and it is supposedly depicted on certain Egyptian obelisks as an emblem of spring. The Lyre is also portrayed on Roman money.

Principal stars

a Lyr *Vega*, or *Wega* as it was sometimes called in earlier times; mag 0.1, a brilliant blue-white. It is among the brightest stars in the sky, and was the first star ever to be photographed – on an early daguerreotype plate in 1850. It was well known to the Romans by the name of Lyra, and marked the beginning of their autumn when it set in the morning sky.

At one time it was the Pole Star, and owing to precession it will be Polaris again in approximately 11,500 years from now; by far the most brilliant of the whole series of stars which take their turn. Vega has a mag 10 companion, but it is not a binary member. This faint star is located 1' away, but it is extremely difficult to observe owing to the overpowering brightness of the primary. It is often claimed that a 2-in. telescope and a keen eye will detect it, but it really requires a 3- or 4-inch refractor to be sure of seeing it.

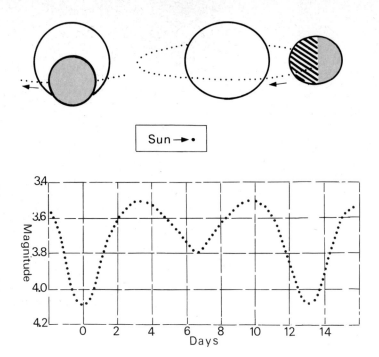

β Sheliak, Shelyak or Shiliak, various Arabic names for Lyra; mag 3.4, blue-white. It is also a variable star, mag range 3.4–4.3; the light variations are due to the mutual eclipse of two unequally large bright bodies very close to one another and ellipsoidal in shape (owing to tidal distortion between them). The system is an extremely interesting one, and some authorities believe that there may be present more than just the two large bodies. The light variations are subject to two unequal minima (3.8 and 4.1) separated by two equal maxima (3.4) over a cycle of 12.9080 days (see fig. 27). These variations were first detected by Goodricke, in 1784, by simple naked-eye observation. It is of great interest that, since discovery, the period of light variation has been lengthening at a rate of two minutes per annum, so that the minima in the 1970's occur approximately 38 days earlier than if the period had been constant since 1784.

γ Sulafat – another name for the whole constellation; mag 3.3, blue-white.

δ¹, δ² Wide naked-eye double; mags 5.5, irregular variable 4.5–6.5, blue-white, orange-red. Delta (δ¹) is also a spectroscopic binary, period 245 days.

ζ Mag 4.1, also a wide double; mags 4.3, 5.9, both white, dist 43″. The primary is also a spectroscopic binary. A fine object for 2-in. telescopes.

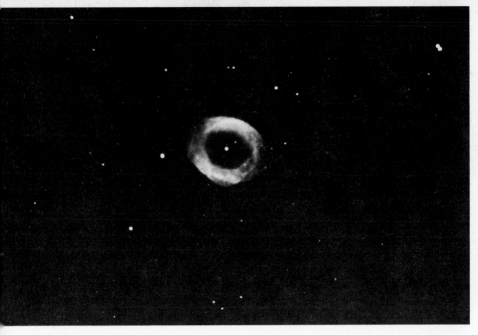

27 *Opposite: explanation of the brightness variations and light curve of β Lyrae.*
28 *Above: the Ring nebula M57 in Lyra.*

Deep-sky objects

ε^1, ε^2 Lyr Mags 4.6, 4.9; a double double system. The principal double are 207″ dist, and some keen-eyed observers have claimed to have separated them with the naked eye. To the ordinary eye, however, they appear as an irregular or elongated star. An opera glass will readily show them separately. With a 2-in. telescope, and a fairly high power, each star is revealed as a separate binary pair (mags 4.6, 6.3, dist 2.9″; 4.9, 5.2, dist 2.3″; both yellow) – a fact first noted by the Jesuit Father, Christian Mayer, in 1779.

Between the two pairs are a number of fainter stars, the brightest of which is a test for a 2-in.; other fainter stars require at least a 6-in. telescope to be sure of seeing them, although many keen-sighted nineteenth-century amateurs claimed to have observed them with far less.

R   Variable star; mag range 4.0–5.0, period 50 days, orange-red. Wholly observable with naked eye, but binoculars show reddish tint to best advantage.

M 56 (NGC 6779) Globular cluster; mag 8.2, dia 2′. Object for 2-in. telescope or 12×60 binoculars. Can be glimpsed with 7×35's when atmosphere is very transparent. In a 3-in. telescope it appears like a small telescopic comet.

M 57 (NGC 6720) Planetary nebula; mag 9.3, dia 83″ × 59″. In spite of faintness can be seen as a hazy star with 2-in. telescopes. It has a ring form which has given rise to it being nicknamed 'the Ring Nebula' (see fig. 28). In a 3-in. telescope it appears just like a miniature smoke-ring. Its strange appearance is due to a ring of low-density gas blowing off from a central star; this emits very intense ultra-violet energy that causes the gas to fluoresce. To observe the central star visually requires a very large telescope.

Lyrids. Meteor shower; swift-moving meteors originating from a radiant point 5° south-west of Vega near the star κ Lyrae. Activity reaches maximum on 19 and 20 April each year, but they are also visible to a lesser degree between the period 5 April to 10 May. The orbits of these meteors show that they have some genetic connection with the orbit of the comet 1861 I.

Note. Within 10° of Vega, three new stars have flared up from obscurity within the past 50 years. The last occasion was in 1963, when a nova was found independently by two amateur observers: the famous American comet hunter Leslie Peltier, who spotted it with the naked eye, and a Swede called Elis Dahlgren, using 10 × 50 binoculars. Both observers were so familiar with the pattern of Lyra's stars that they immediately noticed the intruder.

OPHIUCHUS, *the Serpent Bearer* (Oph)

The constellation Ophiuchus (pronounced off-i-ukus) lies exactly in mid-heavens, being situated halfway between the north and south poles and between the vernal and autumnal equinoxes. Although the ecliptic passes within its southern borders, it is not included among the traditional zodiacal groups. On older maps the group was intermixed with nearby Serpens, but nowadays they are recognized as separate constellations.

Although the configuration covers a large area of the heavens, it is not a prominent one to the casual, roving eye, although it is well endowed with telescopic objects. It can be located by extending a line from the Northern Crown to the 1st-magnitude star Altair (*a* Aquilae); about halfway along, and a little to the south, is Ras Alhague (*a* Ophiuchi).

Mythology

The older astronomers who named the group imagined that they saw the figure of a giant grasping a writhing serpent (Serpens) with his hands, and thus the name Ophiuchus is derived from two Greek words meaning 'the man who holds the serpent'. The early Romans knew it by the name Serpentarius.

Traditional legend says that the figure represents the celebrated physician Aesculapius, son of Apollo, who was instructed in the healing art by Chiron the Centaur, and the serpent is either an emblem of prudence and sagacity or symbolizes his skill in healing the bite of the reptile. To the Persians it was known as 'Eve and the Serpent'.

Principal stars

α Oph *Ras Alhague*, 'the Head of the Serpent Charmer'; mag 2.1, white.
β   *Cebalrai*, 'the Heart of the Shepherd'; mag 2.9, yellow-orange.
γ   *Muliphen* (?); mag 3.7, white.
δ   *Yad* (or *Yed*), 'in the Hand'; mag 3.0, orange-red.
ζ   Mag 2.7, blue.
η   Mag 2.6, white; a very close binary system, mags 3.2, 3.7, dist 0.5"; beyond reach of ordinary telescopes.
κ   Mag 3.4, yellow-orange.
θ   Mag 3.4, blue.

Deep-sky objects

λ Oph Binary system; mags 4.2, 5.3, dist 1.1", period 133 years, white. The separation is now increasing, but it requires a 4-in. refractor to split them.

ρ   Binary; mags 5.2, 5.9, dist 3.2", both blue. Located 3° north of Antares (α Scorpii) and is rather low down for observers in northern temperate latitudes. In the field background is a large, diffuse, obscuring nebula.

τ   Binary; mags 5.0, 5.7, dist 2", both yellow.

70   Binary; mags 4.3, 6.0, dist 1.8"–6.7", period 88 years, yellow and orange. The pair is now closing until 1991.

36   Binary; mags 5.3, 5.3, dist 4.0", period 549 years, both yellow-orange dwarf stars.

U   Eclipsing Algol-type variable; mag range 5.8–6.5, period 1.6773 days, blue. Actual major light variation takes place over interval of 5 hours. Ideal subject for study with binoculars.

Y   Cepheid-type variable (or pulsating star); mag range 6.9–7.8, period 17.11 days, yellow-white; another binocular variable.

X   Long-period variable; mag range 5.9–9.2, period 335 days, orange-red. Can be followed throughout range with 2-in. telescope or 12 × 60 binoculars.

RS   A recurrent nova and one of the most interesting explosive, or eruptive, stars in the sky; mag range 5.3 (?)–11.5, period very irregular, blue.

    It first came to notice with an outburst in 1898, after which it rapidly faded back to mag 10. It brightened again in 1933, 1958, and in 1967. On the latter occasion it was independently co-discovered by three observers: an English amateur, an American amateur and a German professional astronomer. This is a star which should be included on the list of every observer, for one day he may have the good fortune to be first with an independent discovery of a flare-up.

Before 1850, four bright novae were known to have occurred in Ophiuchus. The first one was seen in AD 123; the second in 1230; the third one, popularly known as 'Kepler's Star', in 1604. This latter star, however, was probably discovered by his pupils Mostlin or Brunowski, but Kepler wrote a book about it. It was no ordinary nova but the type known as a supernova, of which only three are known to have occurred within our own galaxy. It became as bright as Jupiter, but later gradually faded back to complete obscurity. Its location is near ξ Ophiuchi, and no surviving star has been observed in this position. However, a nebulous remnant has been photographed which is heavily obscured and is about 4 magnitudes fainter than the Crab Nebula remnant of AD 1054 (see M 1, p. 161). The fourth nova was discovered in 1848 by the celebrated British astronomer J. R. Hind, from an observatory in Regent's Park, London. Nowadays one could hardly imagine discovering a new 4th-magnitude star from such an unlikely location. Although it quickly faded, Hind's star is still visible and is slightly variable over a mag range 12.2–13.0.

Ophiuchus is very rich in globular star clusters, six of which are Messier objects and relatively bright, deep-sky objects. Although they are at low altitude for observers in north temperate latitudes, they may all be observed with 8×30, 10×50 or 12×60 binoculars. In small binoculars they appear as nebulous stars having very much the appearance of a typical telescopic comet without a tail.

M 9 (NGC 6333) Globular cluster; mag 7.3, dia 2.4'.
M 10 (NGC 6254) Globular cluster; mag 6.7, dia 8.2'.
M 12 (NGC 6218) Globular cluster; mag 6.6, dia 9.3'.
M 14 (NGC 6402) Globular cluster; mag 7.7, dia 3.0'.
M 19 (NGC 6273) Globular cluster; mag 6.6, dia 4.3'.
M 62 (NGC 6266) Globular cluster; mag 6.6, dia 4.3'.

SAGITTA, *the Arrow* (Sge)

An insignificant and inconspicuous group in the northern heavens, but one of the forty-eight constellations of the ancients. It is situated south of Cygnus in the plane of the Milky Way, midway between Albireo (β Cygni) and Altair (α Aquilae). None of its naked-eye stars have recognized Arabic names, and it contains no star brighter than magnitude 4.

Mythology

There are two main legends concerning the Arrow. One Greek story says that the constellation owes its origin to one of the arrows with which Hercules killed the vulture that continually gnawed the liver of Prometheus when Jupiter punished Prometheus for his impiety. The other legend, according to Eratosthenes, is that it is the arrow with which Apollo destroyed the Cyclopes.

In lesser-known stories it has often been named 'the Arrow of Cupid'. Julius Schiller called it 'the Spear', or the 'Nail of the Crucifixion'.

Principal stars

a Sge Mag 4.4, yellow-white.
β Mag 4.5, yellow.
γ Mag 3.7, orange-yellow.
δ Mag 3.8, orange-yellow; a spectroscopic binary.

Deep-sky objects

ε Sge Double; mags 5.7, 7.7, dist 91″. Very easy for 2-in. telescopes or 12 × 60 binoculars.
θ Double, probably a true binary system; mags 6.3, 8.4, dist 12″, white and yellow. Another 8.3 mag star, dist 70″.
13   Double; very faint companion; mag 5.6, 12, dist 70″. Requires at least 8-in. telescope, but with binoculars the primary star is worth observing for its fiery orange colour.
U   Eclipsing variable of the Algol type; mag range 6.4–9.0, period 3.3806 days, a yellow spectrum superimposed over a blue-white primary. With 8 × 30 binoculars it can just be glimpsed at minimum if the star has been first identified at maximum.
M 71 (NGC 6838) Globular cluster; mag 8.7, dia 6′. Just visible with 12 × 60 binoculars. Easy with 3-in. telescopes.

SAGITTARIUS, *the Archer* (Sgr)

The ninth constellation of the Zodiac. As seen from north temperate latitudes, the group just hovers above the southern horizon and can only be distinctly recognized on moonless, transparent nights. However, since it lies in the direction of the centre of the Milky Way, it is very rich in binocular and telescopic objects.

It is best located by projecting a line from Deneb (a Cygni) through Altair (a Aquilae), and the group will be found just above the horizon as an extension of this line.

On the Dendera zodiac, the group is drawn with wings and two heads.

Mythology

In many stories this sign represents the outlines of a centaur, a mythical animal which is half horse and half man, and which was probably first suggested by seeing a man at a distance on horseback.

One Greek story says that the Centaur is in memory of Chiron, the son of Saturn, who first taught horsemanship. This story also relates that he excelled in the science of astronomy, and was greatly skilled in the healing art, but that his premature death was brought about by a wound from an arrow dipped in the blood of the Lernaean hydra. One other story is that Sagittarius commemorates a famous hunter by the name of Crotus. It has also been suggested that the Greek name for the Archer is symbolical of the shooting corn, its blades discharged like arrows from the soil.

On certain Babylonian and Persian monuments, the asterism was marked as 'the Giant King of War', probably personifying their archer god of war. On Indian zodiacal signs it was a horse, but many Indian constellations were copies of those of the West.

During the Middle Ages, when the influence of astrology was great, Sagittarius was generally considered to be a lucky sign.

Principal stars

α Sgr *Rukbat*, 'the Archer's Knee'; mag 4.1, blue-white. A relatively faint star to have the designation α. It lies very far south for northern observers and cannot be observed in latitudes higher than 50° N.

β^1, β^2 *Arkab* and *Urkab*, 'the Tendon Joining the Calf and the Heel'. A wide naked-eye double; mags 4.3, 4.5, blue-white, white; β^1 is also a telescopic double, mags 4.3, 7.1, dist 28". Ideal object for 2-in. telescopes but too far south to be seen above 50° N.

γ *Al Nasl*, 'the Head of the Arrow'; mag 3.1, yellow; also a spectroscopic binary.

δ *Media*, 'Middle of the Bow'; mag 2.8, yellow. It has a faint 14.5 mag companion, dist 26".

ε *Kaus Australis*, 'the Southern part of the Bow'; mag 1.9, blue-white.

ζ *Ascella*, 'the Armpit of the Figure'. A beautiful binary system; mags 3.4, 3.6, dist 0.2–0.8"; a very close pair with a period of 21 years. An object for 6-in. telescopes.

η Mag 3.2, orange-red; double star with companion, mag 9.2, dist 3.6".

θ Mag 4.4, blue.

ι Mag 4.2, yellow.

λ *Kaus Borealis*, 'the Northern Part of the Bow'; mag 2.9, yellow.

μ An eclipsing variable star of the Algol type; mag range 4.0–4.2, period 180.45 days. There are also two fainter companions, mag 9.5, 10.0.

ξ Mag 3.6, yellow.

o Mag 3.9, yellow.

π Mag 3.0, yellow-white.

ρ Mag 3.9, white.

σ *Nunki*; mag 2.1, blue-white.

φ Mag 3.3, blue-white.

Deep-sky objects

54 Sgr Double; mags 6.0, 7.5, dist 45", yellow and blue. Ideal object for 2-in. telescopes.

W   Cepheid-type variable; mag range 4.8–6.0, period 7.5947 days, yellow-white. Can be studied with opera glasses or binoculars.

Y   Cepheid-type variable; mag range 5.4–6.5, period 5.7733 days, yellow-white. Opera glasses or binocular star.

X   Cepheid-type variable; mag range 5.0–6.1, period 7.0122 days, yellow-white.

AQ   Irregular variable; mag range 6.6–7.6, brilliant red. A beautiful object in binoculars: the red tint is very noticeable.

    Note. There are no less than 15 Messier objects within Sagittarius, all of which are visible with small telescopes and 12 with binoculars.

M 8 (NGC 6523) Gaseous nebula; mag 6.8, dimensions 60′ × 35′. The 'Lagoon nebula' – so named from its appearance in long-exposure photographs.

M 17 (NGC 6618) Gaseous nebula; mag 7.0, dimensions 46′ × 37′. The 'Omega nebula', since in long-exposure photographs it resembles the Greek letter Ω.

M 18 (NGC 6613) Open star cluster; mag 7.5, dia 12′.

M 20 (NGC 6514) Gaseous nebula; mag 6.9, dimensions 30′ × 30′. The 'Trifid nebula'.

M 21 (NGC 6531) Open star cluster; mag 6.5, dia 10′.

M 22 (NGC 6656) Globular cluster; mag 5.9, dia 17′.

M 23 (NGC 6494) Open star cluster; mag 6.9, dia 25′.

M 24 (NGC 6603) Open star cluster; mag 4.6, dia 4′.

M 25 (IC 4725) Open star cluster; mag 6.5, dia 40′.

M 28 (NGC 6626) Globular cluster; mag 7.3, dia 5′.

M 54 (NGC 6715) Globular cluster; mag 7.0, dia 2′.

M 55 (NGC 6809) Globular cluster; mag 7.0, dia 10′.

M 69 (NGC 6637) Globular cluster; mag 8.9, dia 3′.

M 70 (NGC 6681) Globular cluster; mag 9.6, dia 2.5′.

M 75 (NGC 6864) Globular cluster; mag 8.0, dia 2′.

Scorpius, *the Scorpion* (Sco)

The eighth sign of the Zodiac, and one can easily imagine a scorpion from the chance configuration of its principal stars.

    In north temperate latitudes the group is very low in the southern heavens, and part of it will be below the observer's horizon. It lies due south of Ophiuchus, with Sagittarius and Libra on either side. However, in spite of its low altitude the group is a prominent one and can easily be located by the iridescent flashes of Antares, which dominates a compact group of bright stars, six of them brighter than the 3rd magnitude.

    Mythology

At various ages in history, this sign has been represented by different symbols, such as a snake or a crocodile, but more commonly a scorpion. The Dendera planisphere depicts it in the form of the latter.

In classical Greek mythology the constellation is represented by the animal which killed Orion at the command of Juno. In Egyptian folk-lore the Scorpion was positioned in that part of the heavens where the Sun was at the time of annual maladies and fevers, for it was assumed that the scorpion was the cause of these complaints.

Throughout the ages astrologers have always coupled the planet Mars with the sign of the Scorpion. In the Hebrew Zodiac, the sign is allotted to Dan. In Roman times, the appearance of a great comet within the constellation was supposed to portend a plague of reptiles or insects, and in many instances locusts were cited.

Principal stars

a Sco *Antares*, 'the Rival of Mars' – chiefly, it is thought, because of its brilliant, fiery reddish hue. However, another view is that its name may be derived from the Arabic *antar*, 'to shine'. It has also been nicknamed 'the Scorpion's Heart'. It formed one of the four royal stars of Persia that acted as guardians of the heavens; in ancient Egypt it represented the goddess Selket and many temples were orientated towards both its rising and setting points. Mag 1.2, orange-red.

Antares is a red supergiant and one of the largest stars yet measured, being 370m. miles in diameter. It is also a beautiful double system, mags 1.2, 6.5, dist 1.2″. The companion is a very blue star, but by contrast with the red primary it often appears to be green – a common subjective phenomenon experienced by double-star observers.

β   *Graffias* or *Grappine*, 'the Crab or Scorpion', for both descriptions were interchangeable in former days. A triple group, mags 2, 8.5, 4, dist 0.9″, 13″. The primary star is also a spectroscopic binary, period 6.82 days.

γ (*σ* Lib) see Deep-sky objects.

δ   *Dschubba*, 'the Forehead'; mag 2.5, blue.

ε   Mag 2.4, yellow.

ζ¹, ζ² Mags 4.9, 3.7, blue and orange; a wide double for observers with opera glasses and binoculars. Supposedly observable with the naked eye as a double, but certainly not for average eyes.

η   Mag 3.4, white.

θ   Mag 2.0, yellowish-white.

λ   Mag 1.7, blue.

μ¹, μ² Mags, 3.1, 3.6, both blue; a naked-eye double.

υ   Mag 2.8, blue; also a spectroscopic binary.

Deep-sky objects

ν Sco A quadruple system, very similar to ε Lyrae (p. 103); mags: A^1 star 4.3, B^1 6.5, dist 42″; mags: A^2 star 6.9, dist 1.3″, B^2 star 7.7, dist 2.2″. Requires a 4- to 6-in. telescope although A^1 and B^1 can be split with a 2-in.

ζ A triple system; mags 4.8, 5.1, dist 0.2″, mag 7.2, dist 7.5″. The two brighter members have a period of 44.5 years and are both yellow stars. The fainter 7.2 mag star has a very long period, but is definitely a dynamical member of the system.

σ Double; mags 3.1, 7.8, dist 20″, both yellow; fine object for 2-in. telescopes.

ω^1, ω^2 Wide naked-eye pair just south of β Scorpii; mags 4.1, 4.6, blue and yellow.

RR Long-period variable; mag range 5.0–12.2, period 279.5 days; orange-red. In same wide field with M 62, a globular cluster; mag 6.6, lying south over the border in Ophiuchus.

   Note. Scorpio is extremely rich in star clusters, many of which can be seen through small instruments.

M 4 (NGC 6121) Globular cluster; mag 6.4, dia 14′.

M 6 (NGC 6405) Open cluster; mag 5.5, dia 25′.

M 7 (NGC 6475) Open cluster; mag 3.2, dia 1°; contains a very rich star field, but unfortunately is very far south for northern observers.

M 80 (NGC 6093) Globular cluster; mag 7.7, dia 3.3′. In small telescopes looks like a faint comet, halfway between α and β. In 1860, a star of mag 7 suddenly blazed forth, almost blotting out the rest of the cluster with its light, but, like all novae, it faded back into obscurity.

SCUTUM (SOBIESKII), *Sobieski's Shield* (Sct)

Formed by Hevelius in the seventeenth century from seven un-formed 4th-magnitude stars between Serpens Cauda, Aquila and Sagittarius, in honour of John III Sobieski, King of Poland.

   Mythology

The principal stars are intended to represent the coat of arms of the house of Sobieski. The Polish king distinguished himself by meeting and resisting the Turkish march on Vienna in 1683. The Turks were turned back at Kalenburg, and the sign of the cross was emblazoned on his shield to commemorate this heroic deed.

   In ancient China the group formed part of Tien Pien, 'the Heavenly Casque'.

   Principal stars

α Sct Mag 4.1, yellow-orange.

β Mag 4.5, yellow; spectroscopic binary, period 834 days.

γ Mag 4.7, white.

δ Mag 4.5, slightly variable, yellow-white; a double system, companion, mag 10.0, dist 53″. Also a spectroscopic binary.

Deep-sky objects

R Sct An RV Tauri-type variable: mag range 4.7–7.8, period 144 days, yellow-orange. A good subject for binocular study.

M 11 (NGC 6705) Compact cluster; mag 6.3, dia 10′; containing about 200 stars; fan-shaped with bright star at apex, some nebulosity also visible with small telescopes. Splendid object in binoculars.

M 26 (NGC 6694) Open cluster; mag 9.3, dia 9′; faintish, but 2½-in. telescopes and 10 × 80 binoculars show it readily.

Note. Some fine sweeping of the Milky Way can be had with wide-angle binoculars in this region of the sky. Also worth watching carefully for possible novae.*

SERPENS, *the Serpent* (Ser)

Although in the past it was often grouped with Ophiuchus, this constellation was one of the forty-eight asterisms of the ancients. Nowadays, it is split into two parts, Serpens Cauda and Serpens Caput, lying on either side of Ophiuchus.

In a similar way to Draco, another constellation associated with a long sinuous body, the stars of Serpens wind over a considerable portion of the heavens. The traditional head of the Serpent lies just below, and to the east, of Corona Borealis, while the tail extends to the borders of Aquila.

Mythology

In legend the group is very closely related to nearby Ophiuchus, 'the Serpent Bearer'. The origin of Serpens, however, is uncertain. It may date to the Babylonian sun-god Marduk, but by Greek and Roman times it was universally known in its serpent form, and in later Arabic astronomy represented a snake.

In Greek folk-lore, both Ophiuchus and Serpens symbolized Aesculapius, the ship's doctor of the Argonauts' voyage in search of the Golden Fleece. He was supposedly the first doctor, and the story concerning him relates that one day, in the house of a friend, he killed a snake. But to his astonishment, another immediately glided into the room carrying a magical herb in its mouth which immediately revived its fellow creature. The result was that Aesculapius took a portion of the herb and soon learnt the use of it for healing the sick and restoring the dead.

* On 31 July 1970, G.E.D. Alcock discovered his third nova, a mag 6.9 star, in Scutum.

Principal stars (*Serpens Caput*)

α Ser *Unukalhai*, 'the Neck of the Snakes'; mag 2.7, yellow-orange.
β   Double; mags 3, 9.3, dist 31″, blue and yellow. The visibility of the companion is a severe test for 2-in. telescopes. Only the Chinese appear to have named this star, under the title 'Chow'.
γ   Mag 3.9, yellow-white.
δ   A splendid binary; mag 3.9, mags 4.2, 5.2, dist 4.0″, both yellow-white. The separation is gradually increasing, but the period of revolution must be very long.
ε   Mag 3.7, white.
κ   Mag 4.3, orange-red.
μ   Mag 3.6, white.

Principal stars (*Serpens Cauda*)

ζ Ser Mag 4.6, yellow-white.
ξ   Mag 3.6, white.
η   Mag 3.4, yellow.
θ   Double, probably binary system; mags 4.5, 5.4, dist 22″, both white.

Deep-sky objects (*Serpens Caput*)

Σ 1919 Double; mags 6.1, 7.0, dist 24″.
Σ 1931 Double; mags 6.0, 7.5, dist 13″.
R   Long-period variable; mag range 5.6–14.0, period 357 days, orange-red.
M 5 (NGC 5904) Globular cluster; mag 6.2, dia 12′. In small instruments appears very much like a small telescopic comet. An old friend to 'comet-sweepers' in the morning sky.

Deep-sky objects (*Serpens Cauda*)

59   Double (and variable) system); mags 5.3, 7.8, dist 4.0″, yellow and white; brighter component is also an irregular (?) variable star, mag range 5.2–5.5. There are also two invisible components (spectroscopic binaries), so that there are a total of four stars involved in this system. Useful work on estimating the mag variation can be done by observers with 2-in. telescopes.
M 16 (NGC 6611) Open star cluster; mag 6.4, dia 25′. Easily seen in 8 × 30 binoculars.

VULPECULA, *the Little Fox (and Goose)* (Vul)

One of the least conspicuous and least-known star configurations in the northern heavens. However, owing to its close proximity to the more prominent groups of Cygnus and Aquila, it is easily found, lying about halfway between Deneb (α Cygni) and Altair (α Aquilae).

The constellation is devoid of distinctive naked-eye stars, and none is brighter than 4th magnitude. Although a little dull at first glance to the unassisted eye, the main body of the figure lies directly in the plane of the Milky Way so that myriads of richly-strewn star fields are revealed in even the most primitive field glasses.

Mythology

The origin and history of Vulpecula is comparatively modern; it dates from the seventeenth century when Hevelius arranged a new constellation out of the unformed stars of the ancients.

It is fairly unusual in the sense that it contains no named stars – probably because none was sufficiently bright to warrant this rank. Nevertheless, *a* Vulpeculae may at one time have masqueraded under the name of Anser ('the Goose'). To be strictly accurate, Hevelius formed two constellations here, 'the Fox' *and* 'the Goose', and the atlas of Flamsteed shows both depicted, but in modern times the Goose is generally omitted. It is of interest that Hevelius was persuaded in his choice of the Fox by the fact that the neighbouring constellation, Aquila (the Eagle), should have a suitable companion of the same rapacious and greedy nature.

Principal stars

a Vul (Anser?); Mag 4.6, orange-red. Located 3° south of Albireo (*β* Cygni). It forms a widely separated double, designated by the Flamsteed numbers 6 and 8. Opera glasses will readily split them.

13   Mag 4.5, white; a very close binary, mags 4.6, 8.0, dist 0.8″. Requires 6-in. telescope.

Deep-sky objects

T Vul Cepheid-type variable star; mag range 5.2–6.4, yellow-white, period 4.44 days. Ideal for binocular study.

M 27 (NGC 6853) The famous 'Dumb-bell Nebula', so called because of its appearance in the telescope; mag 7.6, dia 480″ × 240″. A planetary nebula consisting of rarefied gas illuminated from a mag 13.4 central star. Its form is readily visible with 8 × 30 or 7 × 35 binoculars. The central star requires at least an 8-in. telescope.

NGC 6940 Open star cluster; mag 8.2, dia 20′. Requires a dark, perfectly transparent sky to be seen with binoculars. Contains approximately 100 stars.

Nova Vulpeculae 1968. In recent years one of the most interesting objects in Vulpecula has been the nova discovered by the Peterborough schoolmaster, G. E. D. Alcock. It was spotted at 3 a.m. on Easter Monday morning 1968, when he was conducting a routine sky patrol with his 15 × 80 prismatic binoculars. This was the second nova to be discovered by Alcock during a nine-month period – his first being one discovered in Delphinus on 26 July 1967.

When first observed by Alcock, the nova in Vulpecula was mag 5.6. Next night it reached 5.1 and the following night it was easily visible to the naked eye, shining at a magnitude of approximately 4½. Unlike Nova Delphini, the second nova faded rapidly, as is usual with a fast-type nova, and in January 1971 its magnitude was fainter than 14.5.

Nova Vulpeculae 1968 is located very close by the position of the mysterious nova of 1670, and at first it was thought to be a new outburst of this spectacular star of Flamsteed's day. Few reliable observations exist of the 1670 star, and for many years there has been considerable doubt among astronomers as to its exact position as recorded by Picard, which is now preserved in Lemonnier's *Histoire Céleste*. The new nova is in a position 8' to the south of the 1670 one. During the last century, the famous English observer J. R. Hind searched for remnants of the 1670 outburst, but failed to recognize it. Later the eagle-eyed American E. E. Barnard and the Englishman Steavenson also tried. A final attempt was made in 1938 by Humason, using photographs taken with the large reflectors at Mount Wilson in conjunction with an examination of spectrograms of stars in the near vicinity taken with the same instruments – but this again did not lead to any positive identification. If the 1670 nova is the same star as that of 1968, and its position was correctly catalogued, the only explanation left for the discrepancy in position (after allowing for precession) would be due to a large proper motion of the star, and this seems a most unlikely explanation. Another convincing piece of evidence against associating the two outbursts is that the 1968 nova is one of what we call the fast type: that is, it shows a very rapid rise and rapid fall in brightness. The 1670 nova, after brightening to mag 3.0, took two years to sink back beyond naked-eye visibility. At least the 1968 nova has now been identified on the Palomar Sky Survey plates as a star of photographic mag 17.0 – prior to its modern outburst.

Pulsar. Located 3° south of a, at a position angle of 148°. These strange objects, discovered in 1968 by Cambridge University Mullard Radio Observatory, have been given the name of pulsars because of the characteristic series of radio wave pulses which, in this particular example, last for 0.3 second and are repeated every 1.337 seconds, exactly. Some astronomers consider that these objects are the long sought-after neutron stars which were predicted theoretically some years ago.

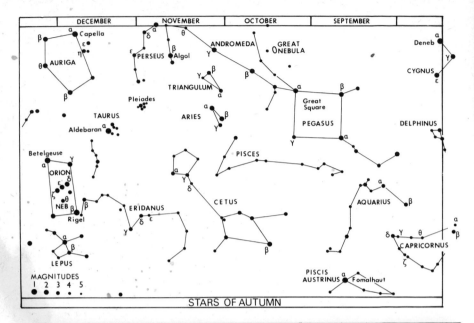

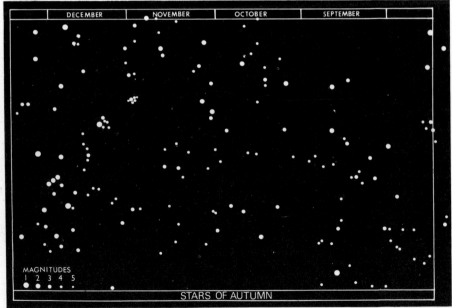

29 Stars of autumn (see note on p. 53). To locate the less conspicuous constellations and for individual star recognition refer to charts, pp. 194–214.

CHAPTER 8

Stars of autumn
September, October, November

Refer to fig. 29 at required month and time.

The Cross of Cygnus has now shifted well into the western sky, and prominent in the southern sky is Pegasus, which in legend was the winged horse ridden by Bellerophon. The 'Square' of Pegasus is easily recognizable as it is delineated by the stars α (Alpheratz), β (Scheat), γ (Algenib) and α (Markab). The two α's are due to the fact that one of the stars at the north-east corner, Alpheratz, is actually the α star of Andromeda – the adjoining constellation – but it is a convenient star to include in Pegasus and so assist easy recognition.

Within the boundary of Andromeda lies what is called the Great Nebula. Actually it is the nearest island universe and is similar to our own Milky Way (Ch. 5). The Great Nebula in Andromeda can just be glimpsed with the naked eye on a transparent, cloudless and moonless night as a faint misty blob, but, of course, it requires a long photographic exposure to bring out all the detail shown in fig. 30.

Continuing a line east of Andromeda, we find Perseus (partially circumpolar), which lies almost directly overhead during the late autumn evenings. It is easily located halfway between the 'W' of Cassiopeia and the striking 1st-magnitude white star Capella (α Aurigae). Alpha, or Algenib, is the brightest member of the constellation and is situated in an area which is richly strewn with naked-eye stars. Beta, or Algol, is sometimes called the Demon star since it was discovered by the older astronomers to be variable in brightness.

Returning to a view of the southern aspect, if the sky is transparent, the observer will see low down, just above the horizon, the bright 1st-magnitude star Fomalhaut, the α star of Piscis Austrinus (the Southern Fish).

Among the northern circumpolar groups, the Great Bear (Ursa Major) is now in its most easily recognizable position, immediately below the north celestial pole, and Cassiopeia has now adopted the distorted letter 'M' configuration high above.

ANDROMEDA, *the Chained Lady* (And)

Part circumpolar above 50° N and remains above north temperate horizons for most of the year. Best located either from Perseus to the east or from Pegasus west of it. Actually *a* Andromedae is a star 'borrowed' by Pegasus in order to create the distinctive 'Square', and is the star located at its north-east corner.

Mythology

Andromeda was the beautiful daughter of Cepheus and Cassiopeia, King and Queen of Ethiopia. According to Greek mythology, her mother boasted that she was fairer than Juno and the Nereids. For this offence, Neptune dispatched a sea-monster to ravage their coasts, and Andromeda was ordered to be exposed to the monster as a sacrifice. To this end she was chained to the rock to await its arrival, but Perseus came across her in the nick of time and changed the monster into stone.

Both the constellation and its legend are very old and probably date back to the civilizations of the Euphrates. The legend was very firmly established by the first century AD, when Josephus wrote that both the links of Andromeda's chain and the bones of the sea-monster might easily be seen in the star configurations!

The Arabian astronomers represented the constellation as a seal with a chain round its neck to which it was connected with one of the fishes. In Julius Schiller's biblical reforms it assumed the form of Sepulchrum Christi.

Principal stars

a And   *Alpheratz*, 'the Head of the Woman in Chains'; mag 2.2, blue-white; also an optical double, faint companion, mag 11.5, beyond the reach of small telescopes. The primary is also a spectroscopic binary, period 97 days. The larger member is 175 times more luminous than the Sun.

β   *Mirach*, 'a Girdle', forms 'the side of the Chained Woman'; mag 2.4, orange-red.

γ   *Alamac*, derived from the Arabic name for a small predatory animal similar to a badger; mag 2.9, white. It forms one of the most beautiful doubles in the sky (but probably not a true binary); companion star mag 4.8, white, dist 10″. Alamac itself forms a binary pair, mags 5.4, 6.6, dist 0.4″.

δ   Mag 3.5, yellow-orange; a faint optical companion, mag 12.5, dist 28″.

ζ   Mag 2.8, yellow; also a spectroscopic eclipsing binary.

v   Mag 4.4, blue-white; spectroscopic binary. Located near the famous Great Nebula in Andromeda, see below.

π   Mag 4.4, blue-white; a wide optical double, companion mag 9.0, dist 36″. Primary is also a spectroscopic binary.

Deep-sky objects

56 And Double; mags 5.8, 6.0, dist 3′. Just resolved with 8 × 30's.

R   Long-period variable; mag range 5.0–15.3, period 408.5 days, orange-red. At maximum brightness plainly visible to the naked eye, but at minimum requires a 12-in. telescope to even glimpse it.

W   Long-period variable; mag range 6.5–14.3, period 397.05 days, orange-red.

30 The Great Nebula M31 in Andromeda.

M 31 (NGC 224) Spiral galaxy, the 'Great Nebula in Andromeda' (see above); plainly visible to the naked eye as a 4th-magnitude (4.8) hazy spot and undoubtedly the nebula longest known to mankind, for there are numerous references to it in different historical periods. Even in 8 × 30 binoculars, by using averted vision, its length can be traced out to nearly 4°, or eight times the diameter of a naked-eye full moon. It is one of the nearest of the island universes – a vast spiral structure at a distance of 1.6 million light-years, with a diameter of 75,000 light-years. In 1885 a new star, or supernova, of mag 7 appeared in it, but by 1890 this had faded to mag 16 and nowadays it cannot be identified.

M 32 (NGC 221) Elliptical galaxy; a galaxy closely related to M 31, and lying in the same field of view with low-power instruments. It cannot be seen in small binoculars, but a 2-in. telescope will reveal it as a hazy star-like object; mag 8.5, dia 1.5'.

NGC 752 Open cluster; mag 7.0, dia 45'. Easy object for binoculars.

Andromedids. Meteor shower; at maximum activity approximately 14 November each year and appears from a radiant point near, and north of, γ Andromedae. This shower has a very interesting history and has been traced back to AD 524. The greatest displays occurred in 1872 and 1885, and these occasions are thought to be connected with the disintegration of Biela's Comet, whose orbit closely resembles that of the meteoroid particles. However, there is no direct evidence – only circumstantial indications – that this comet is now defunct. In point of fact, the material which gave rise to the great meteor displays of 1798, 1830 and 1838 had been travelling far *in advance* of the comet itself. In recent years, owing to secular changes in the meteor orbits, there has been little activity, for the Earth now appears to pass only through the outer, less dense, edges of the stream formation. However, the situation may be different in the future, and it is always worth watching just in case a great meteor storm should occur again, as happened with the Leonids in 1966 (p. 83).

AQUARIUS, *the Water Bearer* (Aqr)

The eleventh of the zodiacal groups. Not a conspicuous constellation, and contains no star brighter than magnitude 3, but it has its fair share of interesting binocular and telescopic subjects. It has a large, straggling configuration and almost overwhelms its neighbour Capricornus.

The group is best located in northern latitudes by projecting a line due south of the Pegasus 'Square'. If the night sky is transparent, it can be traced out *above* the 1st-magnitude star Fomalhaut (a Piscis Austrini).

Mythology

The constellation is a very ancient one, and is represented on early Babylonian tablets as a person pouring water from a bucket or urn which he holds on his shoulder. The Arabs later portrayed it as a mule with two water barrels, and indeed all civilizations have in some way connected it with water or liquid in various forms, ranging from rain and great floods to wine.

In Chaldean astronomy it occupies that part of the sky which they called the 'Sea'. It is curious that in Toltec and Aztec mythology the constellation was the god Quetzalcoatl, who came to them from the eastern seas.

Another story makes it represent Deucalion, who was placed in the sky after the celebrated deluge of Thessaly, which supposedly occurred in 1503 B C. Yet another tale tells us that it is in memory of Cecrops, who came from Egypt to Greece and who built Athens. (He is also said to have improved and polished the manners of the Athenians and to have introduced the olive.)

In Greece, Aquarius was also a symbol of Zeus the creator, who poured water to activate the seeds of life buried in the cold earth. It was a famous sign with the old astrologers, and Sadalmelik (α Aquarii) was considered an extremely lucky star.

Principal stars

α Aqr *Sadalmelik*, 'the Lucky One of the King'; mag 3.2, yellow.

β   *Sadalsund*, 'the Luckiest of the Lucky'; mag 3.1, yellow.

γ   *Sadachbia*, 'the Lucky Star of Hidden Things or Hiding Places', but the name can also be interpreted as simply 'the Tent'; mag 4.0, white. Also a spectroscopic binary.

δ   *Skat*, 'a Wish'; mag 3.5, white.

ε   *Al Bali*, 'the Good Fortune of the Swallower'; mag 3.8, white.

ζ   Mag 3.7, yellow-white; it marks the centre of the traditional urn figure. A binary system discovered in 1777, mags 4.4, 4.6, dist 1.9″, both yellow-white, period 361 years. It is also suspected that there may be an invisible 'dark' star connected with this pair.

η   Mag 4.1, blue-white.

θ   *Ancha*, 'the Hip'; mag 4.3, yellow.

κ   *Situla*, a Latin term for water-jar or bucket, and although faintish for a principal star, it is important owing to the derivation of its name; mag 5.3, yellow-orange.

λ   Mag 3.8, orange-red. Marks the first star of the mythical water stream depicted in classical portrayals of the constellation.

Deep-sky objects

ψ² Aqr Double; mags 4.5, 8.5, dist 50″, yellow and blue. A beautiful object for 2-in. telescopes.

53   Optical double; mags 6.4, 6.6, dist 5″, both yellow.

69   Double; mags 6, 9, dist 28″.

94   Double (binary?); mags 5.6, 7.6, dist 13″, yellow and blue. Ideal for 2-in. telescopes.

T   Long-period variable; mag range 6.7–14.0, period 202 days, orange-red.

R   Long-period variable; mag range 6.7–11.6, period 386 days, orange-red.

M 2 (NGC 7089) Globular cluster; mag 6.3, dia 8′. A bright, easy object for binoculars, having the appearance of a nebulous star. With small telescopes it has been described as 'a heap of glittering fine sand'.

NGC 4628 Planetary nebula; the 'Saturn nebula', so called owing to its immediate telescopic similarity to a hazy depiction of the famous ringed planet; mag 8.4, dimensions 44″ × 26″. Can be seen with 2- to 2½-in. telescopes with magnifications of × 50 or greater.

M 72 (NGC 6981) Globular cluster; mag 9.8, dia 2′. A faint object for small telescopes, and requires 3-in. aperture to identify it.

δ *Aquarids*. Meteor shower; observable every year between 15 July and 10 August and at peak about 29 July, from a radiant point near the star δ Aquarii. At maximum activity upwards of 40 meteors per hour may be seen, which produce long trails and are relatively slow-moving. There is some genetic connection between this meteor shower and another known as the Arietids.

ARIES, *the Ram* (Ari)

The first sign of the Zodiac, the point where, in a highly significant period of ancient history, the Sun was located at the time of the spring equinox. Nowadays, owing to precession, this point has shifted into Pisces although the vernal equinox is still, by tradition, referred to as the first point in Aries. This represents the zero point from which the celestial co-ordinate Right Ascension is measured.

Apart from the star Hamal, Aries is not a particularly prominent group, but it is easily located by bisecting a line connecting the 'Square of Pegasus' and Aldebaran (α Tauri).

Mythology

To the Greek poets, this was a constellation which was closely associated with the Argonauts and symbolized the ram which bore the golden fleece which the expedition set out to seek.

One version of the story relates that Ino, Queen of Thebes and stepmother of Phryxus and Helle, wished to rid herself of the children of the new marriage – she is commonly acknowledged as the prototype wicked stepmother of more modern folk tales.

The gods fortunately took pity on the children and created a supernatural ram to carry them to the protection of Æetes, King of Colchis. However, during the flight, the rapid motion of the ram made Helle giddy; she slipped off its golden back, plunged into the waters of the straits dividing Europe from Asia and was drowned. These straits later became known as the Hellespont to perpetuate her memory. Her brother, Phryxus, arrived safely at his destination and straightaway sacrificed the golden ram to Mars and presented its fleece to Æetes, who guarded it with fire-breathing bulls, and a dragon which never slept. It remained there until Jason sailed in the *Argo* to capture it.

Aries is also associated with the fabulous Phoenix, a sacred bird of the Egyptians which was believed to have built its own funeral pyre and then thrown itself into the flames, from which a young phoenix was reborn.

Among the old astrologers, it was one of the dreaded signs, indicating a passionate and violent temper, and consequently formed the 'House of Mars'. Pliny wrote that if a comet appeared within the borders of Aries, it portended great wars and widespread mortality.

Principal stars

α Ari *Hamal*, 'the Head of the Sheep'; mag 2.2, yellow-orange. An important star in ancient times and at least eight Greek temples were orientated towards it – particularly those commemorating Zeus and his daughter Athene.

β   *Sheratan*, 'a Sign'; mag 2.7, white. A spectroscopic binary, period 107 days.

γ   *Mesarthim*; mag 4.0, white. A binary of long period; mags 4.8, 4.8, both white, dist 8″. This was the first double-star system discovered, by the Englishman Robert Hooke while following the comet of 1664. He remarked: 'I took notice that it consisted of two small stars very near together; a like instance to which I have not else met with in all the heavens.'

δ   *Botein*, 'the Belly'; mag 4.5, yellow-orange.

ε   Mag 4.6, white. Binary system, mags 5.2, 5.2, dist 1.5″. Requires at least a 3- or 4-in. telescope to split them.

41   Mag 3.7, blue-white; this star has no Greek designation.

Deep-sky objects

π Ari Triple system, probably physically connected; mags 5.3, 8.4, 10.5, dist 3.1″ and 25″; the faintest member is a difficult object even for 6-in. telescopes. The brightest member is also a spectroscopic binary, period 3.85 days.

14   Triple system; mags 4.9, 8.5, 7.7, distances 93″ and 105″, white, blue and blue. A fine object for 2-in. telescopes.

λ   Double; mags 5, 8, dist 38″, white and blue. Well within range of 2-in. telescopes.

30   Double, probably *not* a binary system; mags 6.1, 7.1, dist 39″, both white. Object for 2-in. telescopes.

U   Long-period variable; mag range 6.4–15.2, period 370 days, orange-red.

CETUS, *the Whale (or Sea-Monster)* (Cet)

This is the most extensive of constellations and occupies an area of sky 50° in length and 20° in breadth, yet has no star brighter than the 2nd magnitude.

To twentieth-century eyes, the configuration suggests a lounge chair rather than a whale, with the back of the chair leaning towards Orion. It lies south of Aries and Pisces, and west of Eridanus, in what is a comparatively barren area of the sky for naked-eye observers. However, it contains an interesting red variable star, the first of the long-period variables ever detected by man.

Mythology

As depicted in its traditional constellation figure, Cetus is a very peculiar-looking whale indeed compared with the marine creature known to zoologists. He has the head of a dinosaur and the fore-flippers of a walrus – and in some maps he is depicted like the great bull elephant seal of the southern hemisphere, of which the ancients could have no knowledge. He probably assumed the figure of a whale as a matter of convenience, as legend says that he was the largest animal of the sea, but in many tales he was the sea-monster sent by Neptune to devour Andromeda in the classical Perseus legend. However, it is of interest that the name of Cetus, as an asterism, was formed long before the time of Perseus.

Another legend states that he represents the animal sent by Neptune to plague the country of Laomedon, King of Troy. On the celestial maps of biblical reformers, it was natural that he should be depicted as the whale which swallowed Jonah. But the whale tradition has strong connections with Roman times when, according to one story, a whale was washed ashore measuring 40 feet in length, with vertebrae 6 feet in circumference. In former days, whales were plentiful in Mediterranean waters.

Principal stars

α Cet *Menkar*, 'the Nose', inappropriately named since it depicts the Whale's open jaws; mag 2.8, orange-red.

β *Diphda*, 'the Southern Branch of the Tail'; mag 2.2, yellow-orange. In ancient China it was known as Too Sze Kung, or 'the Superintendent of Earthworks'.

γ *Al Kaff al Jidhmah* (but this name rightly belongs to *all* the group of stars that depict the Whale's head); mag 3.6, white; a double system, mags 3.7, 6.4, companion yellow-white, dist 3.0". Possibly a true binary pair of long period.

δ Mag 4.0, blue-white.

ε Mag 5.0, yellow-white; a close double, mags 5.7, 5.7, dist 0.1" (1959).

ζ *Baten Kaitos*, 'the Whale's Belly'; mag 3.9, yellow-orange; with χ Ceti, mag 4.8, yellow-orange, forms a wide naked-eye double.

η   *Deneb* or *Dheneb*; mag 3.6, yellow-orange; forms an easy optical double, companion star, mag 9.5, dist 3.5′.

θ   Mag 3.8, yellow-orange.

ι   *Deneb Kaitos*; mag 3.7, yellow-orange.

Deep-sky objects

66 Cet   Double system; mags 6.0, 7.8, dist 16″, yellow and blue. A moderate test object for 2-in. telescopes.

o   Mira, 'the Wonder'; long-period variable star first noticed by Fabricius in 1596, who thought he had found a new star or nova. It was seen again by Bayer in 1603, and it was named Mira by Hevelius in 1660.

Although its magnitude normally ranges 1.7–9.6, over 331 days, its maximum brightness is often no greater than magnitude 3 or 4. However, in 1779, at maximum, it became a brilliant 1st-magnitude star. It possesses a wonderful reddish tint, and is an ideal subject for naked-eye study, being visible for upwards of six months. Towards maximum it gains brightness quite rapidly and then slowly dies away again. At maximum it is 1,400 times more luminous than at minimum, and its outbursts are thought to be due to great explosive surges of hydrogen gas.

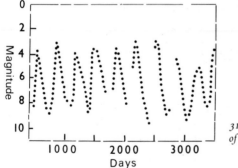

31 *The light curve of Mira (o Ceti).*

In 1923, Aiken, using the giant Lick 36-in. refractor, discovered a bluish companion star, mag 10.1, dist 1″, invisible to all but one or two telescopes in the world.

T   An irregular variable; mag range 5.4–6.9, orange-red. An excellent star for opera glass or binocular study. A period of 157 days is often quoted for the star, but is not yet confirmed and more observations are required.

W   Long-period variable; mag range 6.5–14.5, orange-red, period 316 days. At maximum visible for long intervals with binoculars.

χ   Easy binocular double; mags 4.8 and 7.5.

Lacerta, *the Lizard* (Lac)

A small constellation introduced by Hevelius in the seventeenth

century, lying between Cygnus and Andromeda, and containing
no star brighter than the 4th magnitude.

Mythology

When formed by Hevelius, it was also given the alternative name
of Stellio, a newt found along the Mediterranean coasts. Before
Hevelius' time there also existed a separate constellation known as
the Sceptre and Hand of Justice, formed by Royer in 1679. A
century later Bode formed another constellation in memory of
Frederick II, King of Prussia, naming it Frederici Honores, but
nowadays both these groups go unrecognized.

Part of the present-day Lacerta formed the ancient Chinese
constellation of the Flying Serpent.

Principal stars

α Lac Mag 3.8, white.
β   Mag 4.6, yellow-orange.
4   Mag 4.6, blue-white.
5   Mag 4.6, yellow-orange.

Deep-sky objects

8 Lac Multiple system; two brighter members, mags 6.0, 6.5, dist 22″.
     There is also a star, mag 10.2, dist 28″ and one of mag 8.5, dist 66″.
     With a 3-in. telescope all stars are well seen.
NGC 7243 Open star cluster; mag 7.4, dia 20′. Can be picked up as a
     faint haze with 8 × 30 binoculars when the atmosphere is trans-
     parent.

PEGASUS, *the Winged Horse* (Peg)

A prominent constellation and easy to identify because of the
'Square' configuration of four of its brighter members. Pegasus
appears due south for northern observers at midnight during
September, and because of its distinctive grouping, forms a key
constellation from which to seek out the less arresting neighbouring
constellations.

An interesting feature is that the star Alpheratz, which forms
the north-east corner of the 'Square', is actually borrowed from
the nearby constellation of Andromeda and is common to both
groups. That is why we read in Aratus' classical poem:

> Close and above her head the wanderer's steed
> With hoof and wing exerts a double speed.
> So close they meet, one brilliant star they share;
> Its body it adorns, and decks her hair,
> His side and shoulder with three others graced
> As if by art at equal distance placed.

Mythology

The figure of a winged horse was well known in pre-classical times, for the wings are represented on a horse's figure on various Euphratean tablets and vases. It is also depicted on the coins of Corinth, about 500–430 B C. Pegasus is believed to be derived from the Phoenician words, *pega* and *sus*, meaning the bridled horse used as the figurehead of a ship, and this could account for it being the only part of the winged horse which is visible. However, the Greek poets, in their legends, considered that the unseen part of the horse was merely hidden by clouds.

For northern observers the mythical horse figure is inverted, which has given rise to the theory that the constellation was evolved by a people who lived in the south. Yet this cannot be reconciled with other ideas (pp. 11–13) on the origin of the constellations.

The popular legend concerning the Winged Horse is one which involved it with the legend of Perseus' conquest of the Gorgons. The story relates that Pegasus was created from the blood of Medusa after she was slain by Perseus. Immediately after his birth, he flew to Mount Helicon and established his home. Later, striking the earth with his hoof, he accidentally opened the sacred fountain called Hippocrene. He became a favourite of the Muses and was later tamed by Neptune, who gave him to Bellerophon to conquer the Chimaera. When the monster was successfully destroyed, Bellerophon tried to fly to the abode of Jupiter, but Pegasus, at the instigation of Jupiter, threw him and continued the flight alone to become a permanent constellation in the heavens.

In Julius Schiller's biblical reforms it was transformed into the Archangel Gabriel.

Principal stars

α Peg *Markab*, Arabic for a saddle, or a general term for anything that is to be ridden upon. However, it has also been designated *Matn al Fara*, 'the Horse's Withers' or 'Shoulders'; mag 2.6, blue-white. Nowadays, still quite important as a navigation star.

β *Sheat*, a modern name given by Tycho Brahe, meaning 'Upper Part of the Arm'. An earlier name was *Menkib*, from the Arabic *Mankib al Farm*, 'the Horse's Shoulders'. An irregular variable star, mag range 2.4–2.8, a red giant, and a splendid object to study by naked-eye observation.

γ *Algenib*, 'the Wing' or 'the Side'; mag 2.9, blue-white.

δ *Alpheratz* (α Andromedae) is shared with Andromeda and is borrowed to form the 'Square of Pegasus'; mag 2.2, blue-white; also a spectroscopic binary.

ε   *Enif*, 'the Nose'; mag 2.5, yellow-orange; also two companions, mags 11.5, 8.8, distances 81″ and 140″.

ζ   *Homan*, 'the Lucky Star of the Hero'; mag 3.6, blue-white.

η   *Matar*, 'the Fortunate One'; mag 3.1, yellow; a spectroscopic binary, period 818 days. There is also a faint mag 10 companion visible only with 6-in. telescopes.

θ   Mag 3.6, white.

λ   *Sa'd al Bari*, 'the Good Luck of the Excelling One'; mag 4.1, yellow.

μ   Mag 3.7, yellow.

Deep-sky objects

π¹ and 27 Peg Wide binocular double; mags 4.4, 5.7, white and yellow.

1   Optical double; mags 4.5, 8.5, dist 37″.

3   Optical double; mags 6, 7.4, dist 39″. Fine object for 2-in. telescopes.

AG   Irregular variable; mag range 6.9–7.6, blue-white; of a class known as quasi-nova type stars, about which little is understood. A good binocular star, and regular observations provide a useful programme for amateurs.

R   Long-period variable; mag range 6.9–13.5, period 377 days, orange-red.

M 15 (NGC 7078) Globular cluster; mag 6.0, dia 7′. Appears as a nebulous star in 8 × 30 binoculars.

PERSEUS (Per)

In latitudes 50°–55° N, this constellation is partially circumpolar. It is located in one of the brighter parts of the Milky Way, in a position between the conspicuous 'W' of Cassiopeia and the striking 1st-magnitude white star Capella (α Aurigae).

Mythology

> Her [Andromeda's] feet point to her bridegroom Perseus
>   on whose shoulder they rest.
> He in the north-wind stands gigantic.
> His right hand stretched towards the throne
> Where sits the mother [Cassiopeia] of his bride
> As one bent on some high deed.
> Dust-stained he strides over the floor of heaven.

(Aratus)

Thus Perseus is a member of what the older astronomers once called the Royal Family of constellations. In the past he has also been nicknamed 'the Bearer of the Demon's Head', and in this role he is associated with one of the best-known and most romantic

Greek legends. Briefly, the story relates that Perseus was returning through the air from his conquest of the Gorgon Medusa when he came across Andromeda, chained to a rock and waiting to be devoured by a sea-monster. Perseus turned the monster into stone by showing it the Gorgon's head, and rescued Andromeda who later became his wife. After his death he was transformed into a constellation and was depicted in the heavens with an upraised sword and holding the severed head of Medusa. The nineteenth-century writer Charles Kingsley wrote a full and exciting account of the entire legend.

Principal stars

α Per *Algenib* or *Marfak*, 'the Side'; mag 1.9, yellow-white. Located in an area which even to the naked eye is richly strewn with stars.

β *Algol*, 'the Demon Star', is the best-known object in the entire constellation. It is an eclipsing variable star and one of a kind of which over a thousand are known to exist within the Milky Way. There is some doubt about who first discovered its variations. Hipparchus first mentioned it about 150 BC, and later Ptolemy, but they simply called it a 2nd-magnitude star, without remarks. It was also mentioned by Al Sufi, the Persian astronomer who revised Ptolemy's magnitudes, but he called it a red star which the present-day Algol is certainly not. Some authorities think it strange that the Arabs called it Al Gol (or El Ghoul), the spirit or demon, if at least some suspicion of its variable nature had not been aroused.

The official discovery is credited to Montanari in 1667, but he did not make any note of the times when the light variations took place. The periodic nature of the variations was first recognized in 1783 by the deaf-mute John Goodricke, who established by careful naked-eye observation that once every 2 days 20 hours and 49 minutes Algol underwent a conspicuous fading from magnitude 2.2 to magnitude 3.5 which lasted eight or nine hours. Goodricke also supposed (correctly) that the phenomenon was due to the interposition of a large body revolving round Algol, but it was not until a hundred years later that Vogel, using a spectroscopic technique, proved the idea to be correct.

However, the story does not end there, for F. W. A. Argelander announced in 1885 that the period had shortened by six seconds since the time of Goodricke's discovery. In recent years Algol has been investigated by many famous astronomers, and it turns out to be a system composed of at least four stars. The times of minimum light are advanced or retarded as the eclipsing pair are nearer or further away from us during their slow orbital motion round the centre of mass of the group. However, in spite of intensive research on Algol's mysterious variations, the problem is not yet fully solved. Some observations reveal that the eclipsing pair undergo unpredictable changes, and it is difficult to give a definite explanation as to the reasons why.*

γ Mag 3.1, yellow-white, with a white spectroscopic binary companion.

δ Mag 3.1, blue-white.

ε Mag 3.0, blue-white; binary system, companion, mag 8.1, dist 7″. Visible with 2-in. telescopes.

ζ Mag 2.9, blue-white; binary system, companion, mag 9.4, dist 13″. Visible with 2½-in. telescopes. The primary star is also a spectroscopic binary, period 1.765 days.

η Mag 3.9, yellow-orange; a wide optical double, companion, mag 8.6, blue, dist 28″. The companion is also a very close binary but can only be split with large apertures.

μ Mag 4.3, yellow; a spectroscopic binary, period 283.3 days.

Deep-sky objects

ρ Per A semi-regular variable; mag range 3.2–3.8, orange-red, period 50 days (?). Located close by Algol, and is an ideal star for either naked-eye or binocular observation.

GK (Nova 1901) In modern times the constellation has been host to three 'new' stars, the most important being Nova Persei 1901, one of the brightest novae of the twentieth century. It was discovered by Dr Thomas Anderson, a Scottish recluse and amateur astronomer, who had previously discovered Nova T Aurigae in 1892. It reached magnitude 0.2 and then slowly sank back to obscurity. However, shortly afterwards its spectrum showed all the characteristics of a typical planetary nebula, which led to the discovery of a connection between the two classes of object.

In recent years the nova has hovered about mag 13, but occasionally it shows signs of rapid variability. In 1965, it rose to mag 10.5 for a short period and surges to mag 12 are fairly common. Any observer equipped with an 8-in. reflector should observe this star on every possible occasion – since one day it may erupt in a similar spectacular way as the recurring novae T Coronae Borealis and RS Ophiuchi. Even if without telescopic aid, observation of this area is still useful as it may catch a repeat of the spectacular 1901 outburst.

NGC 869 and 884 Two clusters – the famous 'double cluster', or the 'Sword Hand of Perseus'; mags 4.4, 4.7, dia both 36′; over 300 stars in each group. Both visible to the naked eye as a nebulous smudge. With opera glasses the double nature is easily resolvable, and with binoculars they are a fine object to view. In small telescopes an orange-red star is visible in NGC 884.

* A recent view provides only 3 stars in the system and period changes are attributed to exchange or ejection of matter between them.

M 34 (NGC 1039) Open cluster; mag 5.5, dia 18′; about 80 stars in
group. A fine object for 8 × 30 binoculars.

Perseids. Meteor shower; the radiant points of two major meteor
showers are located within Perseus. The more important of the
displays is 25 July–17 August each year, from a point approximately between χ and η Persei, and giving 10–50 high-velocity
meteoroids per hour at maximum in early morning. In the
Middle Ages the shower was known as 'the Tears of St Lawrence',
after the saint whose feast was celebrated on 10 August. During
the nineteenth century it was shown that the Perseids follow the
orbit of Comet 1862 III, which has a period of 122 years.

The meteor shower has been traced back to AD 830, when it
probably first began to cross the Earth's orbit. The problem of
the origin of both meteor showers and comets is a very controversial one, and there are many aspects of their origin and nature
which are guaranteed to spark off lively debates between theorists.

PISCES, *the Fishes* (Psc)

The twelfth and last zodiacal sign lies at the point where the
ecliptic, or path of the Sun, crosses the equator in the first part of
the year. This point is called the vernal equinox since it marks the
beginning of the spring season.

Although the constellation contains no bright or distinctive
stars, it occupies a considerable area of the sky. It is bounded by
Andromeda to the north and by Aries and Triangulum to the east.
It can readily be located by first searching out the 'Square' of
Pegasus and then projecting a line through β and γ Pegasi.

Mythology

The classic tale told about the fishes is that Venus and Cupid were
one day on the banks of the Euphrates and became greatly alarmed
at the sudden appearance of a terrible giant called Typhon. They
cried out to Jupiter for help. He transformed them into fishes, and
they took to the river to escape. Later Minerva wished to commemorate the event and so placed the two fishes among the stars.

Maps depicting figures of the two fishes always show them
with their tails tied together with a cord.

Principal stars

α Psc *Al Rischa*, 'the Cord', marks the knot in the cord which unites the
two fishes; mag 3.9, white; also a binary system, mags 4.3,
5.2, dist 2.5″, both white. Requires at least 3-in. telescope to split
them.

β *Fum al Samakah*, 'The Fish's Mouth'; mag 4.6, blue-white.

γ Mag 3.9, yellow.

δ Mag 4.6, yellow-orange.

ε Mag 4.5, yellow.

ζ· Mag 5.2, white; also a double, mags 5.8, 6.5, dist 23″, companion yellow-white. Brighter component is also a spectroscopic binary, period 9.1 days.

η Mag 3.7, yellow; also a 11.0 mag companion, dist 1″; difficult object for even 6-in. refractors.

ρ and 94 Together form naked-eye pair; mags 5.3, 5.6, yellow-white and yellow-orange.

Deep-sky objects

ψ¹·Psc Double; mags 5.6, 5.8, dist 30″. For 2-in. telescopes.

77 Double; mags 6, 7, dist 33″.

  Note. Because of the general sparseness of background stars, Pisces, being a zodiacal constellation, is an ideal area for locating minor planets. Familiarity with the general field stars round ζ, ε and δ Piscium will often lead to trapping a brighter minor planet near its opposition time.   •

PISCIS AUSTRINUS (or AUSTRALIS), *the Southern Fish* (PsA)

A small constellation south of Aquarius and dominated by the brilliant 1st-magnitude star Fomalhaut, which, although it rises only 8° above the horizon at the latitude of London, is a prominent object low in the southern sky during clear autumn evenings.

Mythology

In Greek legend it shares the same one as the Northern Fishes. Aratus' classical poem describes the figure as a fish lying on its back, and in this manner it is depicted in old constellation figures, some of which show the fish drinking from a stream. In Egyptian times the emblem of the fish represented the sea.

Principal stars

α PsA *Fomalhaut* or *Fum al Hut*, 'the Fish's Mouth'; mag 1.3, white. Generally the only star of the constellation that can be seen well from northern temperate latitudes, it is a prominent object in a comparatively barren part of the sky. Owing to its low position in the sky for northern observers it will often appear to flash with a red tint, but this is simply due to atmospheric scintillation and physically the star is of a pure white variety.

β Mag 4.4, white. Although nowadays this star has no general name, in the past it was often called, and confused with, Fomalhaut. Also a double, mags 4.4, 7.8, dist 30″; a fine object for 2-in. telescopes.

γ Mag 4.5, white; a telescopic double, mags 4.5, 8.5, dist 4.2″. Object for 3-in. telescopes.

δ Mag 4.3, yellow; double, mags 4.3, 10.5, dist 5.3″, both yellow.

ε Mag 4.2, blue-white.

Deep-sky objects

h 5356 Wide double; mags 6, 7.2, both yellow-white, dist 85″. Also
the fainter member is another telescopic double, mags 7.2, 8.0,
dist 3.0″.

TRIANGULUM, *the Triangle* (Tri)

Sometimes among the constellation figures it is represented by two
triangles. The larger figure is the more ancient one, dating back to
pre-classical times, while the smaller figure was introduced in the
seventeenth century by Hevelius, who called it Triangulum Minor.

The group lies south-east of Andromeda, north of Aries and
west of Perseus. In modern times the smaller triangle is no longer
recognized.

Mythology

The Greek poets believed it was Jupiter who assigned the island of
Sicily a place in the heavens under the figure of a triangle. Another
source, however, states that the large Triangle owes its origin to
someone who wished to represent the figure of the Nile Delta in
the sky and then nicknamed it Deltoton. The Jewish astronomers
named it Shalish, after the name of a musical instrument with a
triangular shape.

Principal stars

α Tri *Caput Trianguli*; mag 3.6, yellow-white. Also a spectroscopic
binary, period 1.73 days.
β   Mag 3.1, white; a spectroscopic binary, period 31 days.
γ   Mag 4.1, white; forms a naked-eye triple with δ Tri (mag 5.1,
yellow) and 7 Tri (mag 5.3, white).

Deep-sky objects

6 Tri Binary system; mags 5.0, 6.4, dist 4″, yellow and blue. A 2-in.
telescope with a high power will just split them. Each star is also a
spectroscopic binary with periods of 14.7 and 2.2 days.
R   Long-period variable; mag range 5.4–12.0, period 266 days,
orange-red. Visible with naked eye at maximum.
M 33 (NGC 598) Spiral galaxy; mag 6.7, dimensions 60′ × 40′. One of
the nearer galaxies, at a distance of 2.3m. light-years and receding
from the Milky Way at 100 miles per sec. It is best observed with
low magnification and even in large telescopes appears pale and
ill-defined. With wide-field 8 × 30 binoculars it is easily visible
and particularly noticeable when the sky has cleared after a rain-
storm.

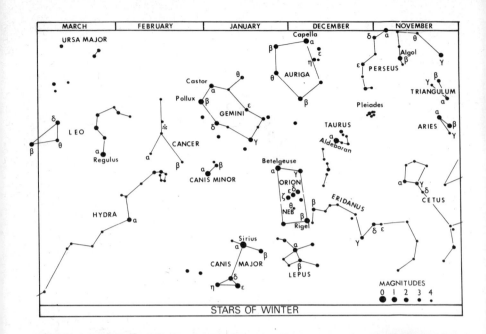

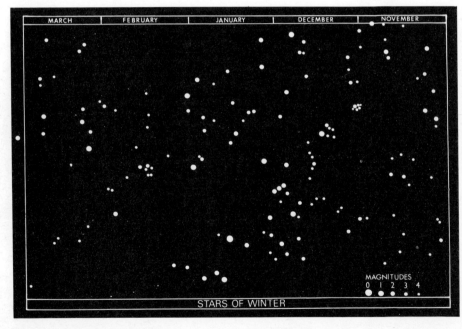

32 Stars of winter (see note on p. 53). To locate the less conspicuous constellations and for individual star recognition refer to charts, pp. 194–214.

CHAPTER 9

Stars of winter
December, January, February

Refer to fig. 32 at required month and time.

To the observer facing southwards, the most prominent winter constellation is Orion, which dominates the southern heavens. It is easily recognizable because of the three distinctive bright stars almost exactly in line which are supposed to identify the ancient hunter's waist belt. North of this belt, and a little east (left), is the 1st-magnitude reddish star Betelgeuse (α Orionis), marking the right shoulder of this mythical hunter. In complete contrast, below the belt and to the west (right) is another 1st-magnitude star, stark blue-white in colour, called Rigel (β Orionis). Orion is a unique constellation in that it is the only one in the northern hemisphere to contain two very prominent 1st-magnitude stars.

Still facing south, if we extend the line from Orion's belt downwards and to the left, we find Sirius, the Dog Star (α Canis Majoris). Sirius is a brilliant and dazzling pure white star which may occasionally appear to flash with a reddish or even a greenish tinge, but this is purely an atmospheric effect owing to its low altitude. It has the honour of being the brightest visible star in the entire heavens, and in consequence it cannot possibly be overlooked. In tropical countries, when Sirius rides high in the sky, one occasionally hears claims that its light is sufficiently bright to cast a perceptible shadow.

Above Sirius, to the left of Betelgeuse, is Canis Minor (the Little Dog). Procyon, its brightest star, is another 1st-magnitude one, and in ancient times it was nicknamed 'the Precursor Dog' since it appears in the dawn sky shortly before the rising of Sirius.

To the north (above) Orion and to the east (left), lies the constellation of Gemini (the Twins). Its two brightest stars are Castor and Pollux (α and β); β is a bright 1st-magnitude one, α is 2nd magnitude.

Returning to Orion, and looking above him to the right, we locate the distinctive 1st-magnitude yellowish-orange star Aldebaran – which is the α star of Taurus, the Bull, and marks exactly the mythical bull's eye. A little further to the right will also be

33 The Pleiades (see fig. 37, p. 159, to identify the principal stars).

spotted the well-known naked-eye cluster of stars called the Pleiades, lying in the shoulder of the bull. Seven stars form its main pattern, but generally only six can be seen with average unaided eyesight. However, with a small telescope or binoculars, at least a hundred will be seen. Yet another prominent star of winter, which will be overhead, is Capella, the *a* star of Auriga, the Charioteer. In northern temperate latitudes Capella is really to be included among the circumpolar stars, so it can be observed throughout the year, but it reaches its highest, most brilliant position during the winter months.

Facing north, looking towards the circumpolar stars, the Great Bear (Ursa Major) will be lying tipped vertically on its long tail, high in the north-east, while Draco, the Dragon, is sprawling its long, sinuous body immediately across the northern heavens.

Auriga, *the Charioteer* (Aur)

In north temperate latitudes it is part circumpolar, being located midway between Perseus and Ursa Major. Previously some of the fainter members of the constellation, bordering Gemini and Lynx, were identified with a separate constellation, Telescopium Herschelii, formed by the Abbé Hell in 1781, which was intended to perpetuate the name of Herschel and the form of the instrument by which he discovered the planet Uranus in 1781. None of these stars was brighter than the 5th magnitude, and the constellation was soon forgotten by the majority of astronomers.

Mythology

There are a number of conflicting stories about this group, but the one generally quoted is that it is intended to depict a young man with a goat which he holds on his arm. This story has also been identified with Amalthea, a daughter of Melissus, King of Crete, who with her sister Melissa fed Jupiter with goat's milk during his infancy. Yet much doubt hangs over the history of this goat and her kids. In earlier stories, and in depictions on Assyrian tablets, Auriga is represented by the chariot, which later became four- or two-wheeled carts pulled by an assortment of animals – even including a zebra.

One of the chariot legends is that it was Boötes who invented the vehicle, and that Auriga was Myrtilus, the son of Mercury, charioteer to Oenomaus, King of Pisa in Elis. This man was reputed to be so skilful in the management of horses that he trained all the steeds of his master to become the swiftest in all Greece.

The Arab astronomers called the entire group 'Guardian of the Pleiades'.

Principal stars

α Aur *Capella*, 'the Little She-Goat'; mag 0.2, yellow. The fourth-brightest star in the heavens and the second-brightest after Vega in the northern hemisphere. In latitudes above 50° N it is circumpolar. In chemical composition it closely resembles our own Sun, but it is much more massive and 80 times more luminous. Many temples were orientated towards it in the past, and in England it used to be nicknamed 'the Shepherd's Star'. Capella is also a spectroscopic binary with a period of 104 days.

β *Menkalinan*, 'the Shoulder of the Rein Holder'; mag 2.1, white. A spectroscopic binary, both stars white and of equal mass, about twice the size of the Sun.

γ *El Nath* (β Tauri); a star common to both Auriga and Taurus; mag 1.8, blue-white.

δ Mag 3.9, yellow.

ε *Al Ma'az*, 'the He-Goat'; a variable star, mag range 3.7–4.5, yellowish-white, period 9,883 days. A spectroscopic binary of the Algol type. An ideal variable for naked-eye study.

ζ   An eclipsing Algol-type variable; mag range 5.0–5.6, yellow-orange and blue-white, period 972 days. Another naked-eye variable.

η   Mag 3.3, blue-white.

θ   Binary systems; mags 2.7, 7.2, dist 3″, white and yellow. An object for 3-in. telescopes.

ι   Mag 2.9, yellow-orange.

Deep-sky objects

λ Aur Optical double; mags 5, 9, dist 2′. Just visible with 2-in. telescopes.

14   Double; mags 5, 7.5, dist 14″. Brighter star is also a spectroscopic binary.

M 36 (NGC 1960) Open cluster; mag 6.3, dia 12′. An open group of some 60 stars ranging from mags 8 to 13. Easy with 8 × 30 binoculars or even opera glasses when the constellation is almost overhead.

M 37 (NGC 2099) Open cluster; mag 6.2, dia 20′. Consists of about 150 stars with an orange-red one near the centre. Easy with minimum optical aid.

M 38 (NGC 1912) Open cluster; mag 7.4, dia 20′. About 100 stars in a cruciform grouping. Visible with 8 × 30's.

RT   A Cepheid variable; mag range 5.4–6.6, period 3.7 days, yellowish-white. A star suitable for opera glass or binocular study.

AE   An irregular variable; mag range 5.4–6.1, greenish-white. An interesting star of which more observations are required. Another ideal binocular subject.

UU   A semi-regular variable; mag range 5.1–6.8, period 3,400 days (?), a deep orange-red. Worth following for unusual behaviour.

T   Nova 1892; discovered by the Scottish amateur astronomer, Dr T.D. Anderson, with opera glasses. It rose to mag 4.1 and is now about mag 15.8, requiring a 15- to 18-in. telescope to observe it. However, the area is worth watching regularly in case the star flares up again, as has happened with other similar novae.

   Note. The area of sky enclosed by the polygon of bright stars which forms the main part of the constellation is rich in glorious star fields, and some fine views can be obtained on dark, transparent evenings, using binoculars.

CANCER, *the Crab* (Cnc)

The group contains no star brighter than the 4th magnitude, yet it is easily found owing to its close proximity to Leo. A line extended from Capella (*a* Aurigae) through Pollux (*β* Gemini) indicates the direction.

Cancer is the fourth sign of the Zodiac and is symbolized by the number 69 turned sideways ♋; but although this form is generally used to symbolize a crab, the zodiac of Dendera shows a beetle.

Mythology

Classical legend tells us that Cancer was the animal sent by Juno to annoy Hercules during his combat with the Lernaean Hydra, and which took hold of the great warrior's foot. However, there is some confusion, for the Greeks, after copying the sign, represented it by two asses – to perpetuate the animals which helped Jupiter in his victory over the giants.

Julius Schiller depicted the group as representing Saint John the Evangelist. In Chaldean and later Platonist philosophy, Cancer symbolized the 'Gate of Man' through which their souls descended from heaven to enter the human form; while Capricorn represented the gate through which they ascended again after earthly death.

Principal stars

α Cnc *Acubens*, 'the Claws', mark the southernmost claw of the mythical crab; mag 4.3, yellowish-white. Also a double, a faint 11th-mag companion, dist 11″.

β *Al Tarf*, 'the End' – of the southern foot; mag 3.8, yellow.

γ *Asellus Borealis*, 'the Northern Ass Colt'; mag 4.7, white. The Asses of Ptolemy are now popularly known as the Donkeys (including δ Cancri). The Arabs also knew them as the Two Asses, after two asses which were engaged in the contest of the Gods with the Giants.

δ *Asellus Australis* (see also γ Cancri); mag 4.2, yellow.

ζ *Tegmine* (or *Tegman*?); mag 4.7, yellow. A triple system; ζ^1 and ζ^2 mags 5.1, 6.0, dist 6″, yellow. ζ^1 mags 5.7, 6.0, dist 1″, yellow. ζ^2 mags 6.3, 7.8, dist 0.2″, yellow. The 6.0 mag star in ζ^1 is also a spectroscopic binary, period 18 years.

ι Mag 4.2, yellow; a wide and beautiful double (long-period binary?), mags 6.6, 4.2, dist 31″, white, yellow. Fine object for 2-in. telescopes.

Deep-sky objects

R Cnc Long-period variable; mag range 6.1–11.9, period 361 days, orange-red.

X Semi-regular variable; mag range 5.9–7.3, period approximately 165 days (?), very deep-tinted orange-red. Visible through entire range with 8×30's.

RS Semi-regular variable; mag range 5.5–7.0, period 253 days (?), orange-red. Another ideal star for binocular study.

M 44 (NGC 2632) The famous Praesepe, or Beehive Star Cluster,

34 The Praesepe or 'Beehive' star cluster M44 in Cancer.

which is readily visible to the naked eye as a nebulous spot. In Bayer's maps it forms the star ε Cancri. Also known as 'the Manger' from which the two asses (γ and δ Cancri) fed. This was one of the first objects which Galileo observed with his newly developed telescope; he was surprised and delighted that (in his telescope) it consisted of no fewer than 36 separate stars.

It was well known in ancient times and often used as an aid to primitive weather forecasting.

... A murky manger with both stars [γ and δ]
Shining unaltered is a sign of rain.

Aratus

The cluster is a splendid object for observers equipped with opera glasses and binoculars; mag 3.7, dia 95' (three times the diameter of the Moon). With 10 × 50's, approximately 75 stars can be counted.

M 67 (NGC 2682) Open star cluster; mag 6.1, dia 15'. Easily visible as a nebulous spot in binoculars. With small telescopes an orange and a red star can also be distinguished.

CANIS MAJOR, *the Greater Dog* (CMa)

A group easy to locate, for it contains Sirius, the brightest visible star in both hemispheres, and in addition it lies just a few degrees south-east of the distinctive configuration of Orion. A line extended from the Pleiades through the three bright stars of Orion's belt points directly towards it, but generally there is no mistaking the dominant, brilliant white star Sirius which, because of its low altitude for observers in northern temperate latitudes, appears to scintillate or twinkle violently, particularly on the cold, frosty nights of mid-winter.

Mythology

The Greeks had many legends to account for the origins of this group. One story relates that it was named in honour of the hunting dog given by Aurora to Cephalus, which was the swiftest member of the species then known. In order to test the animal, it was matched against a fox, then thought to be the fleetest animal of all. The result of the contest was a draw, and it is said that Jupiter rewarded the dog by placing him among the stars to make him immortal. The Egyptians considered it the most important constellation in the sky, and their god Anubis was represented with a dog's head.

Principal stars

α CMa *Sirius*, the brightest star in the sky; mag −1.37, colour brilliant white. Its name is derived from the Greek *seirios*, 'sparkling' or 'burning', but this term was often applied to any bright object in the sky. The Australian aborigines knew it as an entire constellation to itself, calling it 'Eagle'. To the Hindus it was a Rain God. The earliest astronomers, the Chaldeans, termed it 'the Star of the Dog' and it is the only star known with absolute certainty in Egyptian records, for its hieroglyph, a dog, often appears on monuments and temple walls in the Nile area. According to Lockyer, there were seven Egyptian temples orientated to the rising of Sirius, and in the so-called architecture of orientation, the temples were constructed so that at the rising or setting of Sirius, the starlight reached the inner altar. In the Egyptian calendar, when Sirius appeared in the morning sky before sunrise it announced that the annual flooding of the Nile was about to begin – so originated the association with Sirius of the terms Dog Star and Dog-days which we still use today. But it must be remembered that the terms are associated with the star only, and not with the constellation as many suppose. The term 'Dog-days' is simply the reckoning in days from the time of the heliacal rising of Sirius. In remoter times, the Dog-days started four days after the summer solstice and lasted until 14 September. At the present time they begin on 3 July and continue till 11 August. It can therefore be seen that the Dog-days of modern times have no reference to the rising of Sirius – or any other star – because the time of their rising is permanently affected by the precession, or backwards movement, of the equinoxes. They have reference only to the summer solstice, which does not change its position in respect to the seasons.

The Phoenicians called it 'the Barker', and in Hebrew science it was known as 'Sitior the Nile Star'.

Sirius is 8.6 light-years away from the Earth. It is twenty-seven times as bright as the Sun and twice its diameter. On dark, moonless nights in tropical regions, it can be seen to cast a perceptible shadow, and even at midday, in bright sunshine, it can be picked up with opera glasses *if one knows exactly where to look*. The older astronomers thought that the star had some strange ability to change colour quickly, but this effect is an atmospheric one, due to the phenomenon known as scintillation, and is noticed particularly when Sirius is low in the sky. As Tennyson wrote:

The fiery Sirius alters hue,
And bickers into red and emerald.

Sirius has a companion star with some very interesting characteristics. As long ago as 1834, the German astronomer Bessel was convinced that the motion of Sirius was subject to regular variations which were brought about by an invisible body revolving round it. From the deviations some astronomers predicted where the companion should lie, but although intensive searches were made, no object was seen. However, in 1862 it was finally discovered by Alvan Clark, the famous American telescope maker, who was engaged in testing his new 18½-in. objective to check its figure. Nowadays, when the companion is favourably situated, it can often be glimpsed with a 6-in. refractor; such is the difference in observing circumstances when a body is *known* to exist somewhere in the field of vision.

Sirius 'B', as it is called, varies in its distance from the primary star from 2″ to 11″ during its orbital period of 48 years. In the present era it reaches its widest separation in 1974. As a star it is only 1/10,000 as bright as Sirius and shines with an apparent mag of 8.4. Its diameter is only three times that of the Earth, but it is 250,000 times more massive, and its density is 36,000 times greater. One cubic inch of Sirius 'B' material weighs as much as a ton on Earth, and in spite of its diminutive diameter of 26,000 miles it contains more material than the Sun (864,000 miles).

β   *Murzim*, 'the Sirian Announcer' – a name given by the Arabs because its own appearance heralded the immediate rising of Sirius; mag 2.0, blue-white. In the figured maps of the constellation it marks the right foot of the Dog.

γ   *Muliphen* (or *Mirza*); mag 4.1, blue-white. There is some reason to suppose that this star has varied in brightness since ancient times.

δ   *Wezan*, derived from *Al Waza*, 'weight', as the star appears to have difficulty in rising; mag 2.0, yellow. It has a totally unconnected mag 7.5 companion star, approximately 3' dist, which can readily be picked up in opera glasses.

ε   *Adara* or *Undara*, derived from the Arabic *Al Adhara*, 'the Virgins'; mag 1.6, blue-white. There are many other name variations given to this star. Also a double, mags 1.6 and 8.0, dist 7.5".

ζ   *Furud*; mag 3.1, blue-white.

η   *Aludra*; mag 2.4, blue-white.

Deep-sky objects

M 41 (NGC 2287) Open cluster; mag 4.6. A cloud of minute stars about $\frac{1}{2}°$ in dia which is just visible to the naked eye 4° south of Sirius as a small nebulous spot. There is an orange-red star near the centre which can be picked out with binoculars.

v^1 CMa Double; mags 5.8 and 7.9, yellow, white, dist 17.5".

μ   Double; mags 5.2 and 8.0, orange-red, dist 3". It requires at least a 2-in. telescope.

R   Eclipsing Algol-type variable; mag range 5.9–6.7, white, period 1.14 days. This variable can be followed with opera glasses, using nearby stars to compare brightness.

    Note. For observers who wish to see a good example of colour contrasts between nearby stars, using binoculars, compare θ Canis Majoris (yellow-orange) with ε Canis Majoris (blue-white).

CANIS MINOR, *the Little Dog* (CMi)

A constellation easy to locate, being south of Gemini, west of Hydra and north-east of Canis Major. In a similar fashion to the Greater Dog the group is dominated by one bright star, Procyon, which with Betelgeuse and Sirius forms an almost equilateral triangle. Another method to locate it is by extending a line from the three stars of Orion's belt towards Sirius and raising a perpendicular line which will then pass through Procyon.

There is an old star recognition rhyme which goes as follows:

Orion's belt from Taurus' eye
Leads down to Sirius bright;
His spreading shoulders guide you east,
'Bove Procyon's pleasing light.

Mythology

The various legends about the Little Dog are very diverse. The Greek poets supposed it was intended as one of the hounds which belonged to the pack of Orion, but others say that it is the faithful Moera, which belonged to Icarius and after the death of his master threw himself down a well in his despair.

The Egyptians recognized it as a companion to the Great Dog – which had great significance in predicting the inundation of the Nile. On some early Arab maps it is represented by a tree.

Principal stars

α CMi *Procyon*; mag 0.5, yellow-white; the eighth-brightest star in the heavens. Also a binary star which was discovered in a similar fashion to the binary nature of Sirius. In 1840, Bessel noted some irregularities in its proper motion, but the companion star proved very elusive and was not discovered until observed by Schaeberle with the great 36-in. refractor of the Lick Observatory in 1896. Companion, mag 9.5, dist 4.3″, period 40 years.

β *Gomeisa*; mag 3.1, blue-white.

γ Mag 4.6, yellow-orange; also a spectroscopic binary, period 389 days.

Deep-sky objects

14 CMi Binocular triple: mags 6, 8, 9, dist 85″ and 117″; not physically connected. Well seen in 8 × 30's.

ERIDANUS, *the River* (Eri)

An extremely long constellation extending some 60° in length, beginning from a point near the celestial equator, south of Taurus, and then winding southwards to declination minus 58°. Most of the group really forms a southern hemisphere constellation since only half of its entire length can be seen from northern temperate latitudes. Except for Achernar (α Eridani) (which can only be seen in the southern hemisphere) it contains no star brighter than the 3rd magnitude – yet it contains some 300 stars visible to the naked eye.

It can best be located by starting close by Rigel (β Orionis) and following the stars depicting the winding river as it twists southwards as far as the observer's northern latitude will allow him to continue.

Mythology

Although the Milky Way does not pass through the constellation, in mythology it has often been associated with ideas of the same kind, i.e. a river of Heaven. The classical Greek story-theme of the group is that of the daring youth Phaethon who asked his father Phoebus Apollo to give some incontestable proof of his tenderness; Phoebus swore a great oath by the River Styx that he would grant his son whatever he wished, and Phaethon at once demanded permission to drive the chariot of the Sun. He set off, but during the journey the horses lost confidence in their inexperienced driver and left the usual track. For this infringement Jupiter struck Phaethon from the skies with a thunderbolt (or meteorite), and he fell into the River Eridanus, or the Po. His sisters, who mourned his unhappy end, were not spared either, and Jupiter changed them into poplar trees to live along the banks of the river.

The Egyptians used the constellation to typify the Nile, and yet other legends connect it with the great deluge and Orion. It was called Fluvius by the Romans, and it has also been identified as a fabled stream which ran into the oceans from north-western Europe, or Homer's ocean stream which flowed around the Earth.

Principal stars

α Eri *Achernar*, 'the End of the River'; mag 0.6, blue-white, the ninth-brightest star in the sky. It lies only 32° from the south celestial pole and therefore cannot be seen from northern temperate latitudes. Intrinsically a much bigger star than the Sun and at least 200 times as luminous.

β   *Cursa*, 'the Chair or Footstool of the Central One'; mag 2.9, white. The brightest star of the constellation visible from the north. Easily located since it is situated 3° northwest of Rigel (β Orionis).

γ   *Zaurac*, 'the Bright Star of the Boat'; mag 3.2, orange-red. There is a 10th-magnitude companion, dist 50″.

δ   Mag 3.7, yellow-orange.

ε   Mag 3.8, yellow-orange.

ζ   Mag 4.9, white; also a spectroscopic binary.

η   Mag 4.1, yellow-orange.

θ   Mag 3.2, white; also a fine binary system, mags 3.4, 4.4, dist 8.2″, both white. In earlier times also called Achernar.

o¹   Mag 4.1, yellow-white.

o²   Mag 4.5, yellow-orange.

τ²   *Angetenar*, 'the Bend in the River'; mag 4.8, yellow-orange.

145

The designation τ is remarkable in that it defines nine separate stars in this constellation, lying close by the northern boundary of the constellation Fornax.

τ^1 Mag 4.6, yellow–white.

τ^3 Mag 4.2, white.

τ^4 Mag 3.9, orange–red; double, mags 3.9, 9.8, dist 6″.

τ^5 Mag 4.3, blue–white; a spectroscopic binary.

τ^6 Mag 4.3, yellow–white.

τ^7 Mag 5.0, white.

τ^8 Mag 4.8, blue–white.

τ^9 Mag 4.7, white; a spectroscopic binary.

Deep-sky objects

55 Eri Double; mags 6.7, 6.8, dist 9.3″, yellow and yellowish-white. Fine object with 2-in. telescope.

32 Double; mags 4.9, 6.3, dist 7.0″, yellow and white. Object for 2-in. telescope.

GEMINI, *the Twins* (Gem)

The constellation is the third in order of the twelve zodiacal groups and one of the oldest known to mankind. Among the Babylonian boundary stones, there is a picture of a young crescent Moon, horns pointed straight up, and near it two stars (see fig. 35). Thousands of years ago the spring equinox was situated in Gemini, so that at this period Castor and Pollux would have shone close to the new spring Moon. The boundary stones also give us the year of the king's reign and shows them to have been set between 1200 and 1500 BC. Such a combination of the Moon and these two stars will not recur for some 20,000 years.

Gemini can be located outdoors by projecting a diagonal line through δ and β Ursae Majoris towards Sirius (a Canis Majoris): the Twins are approximately halfway between. Although it is above the horizon in north temperate latitudes for most of the year (autumn, winter and spring months), the constellation is best seen in the clear, cold frosty skies of January and February, when at midnight it rides high in the southern sky.

If there were such things as league tables or divisions for star groups, then Gemini would surely be in the premier one, since apart from its brilliance and importance as a zodiacal group, it is also rich in historical associations.

Mythology

Fair Leda's twins, in time to stars decreed,
One fought on foot, one curbed the fiery steed.

35 Babylonian boundary stone depicting Castor and Pollux close to a new spring moon.

The constellation is considered to have had its origin in the classic story of the twin sons of Jupiter and Leda which the stars Pollux and Castor represent. However, there is some evidence to suppose that the constellation bore the name 'the Twins' before it had been agreed which particular pair of brothers they represented. Castor and Pollux were regarded by both Greeks and Romans as the patrons of navigators, and this is referred to in *Acts* 28: 11.

Principal stars

α Gem *Castor*; mag 1.6, white; a binary system, mags 2.0 and 2.9, both white, dist 1.9″. This is one of the first double star systems to be recognized as a true binary pair as against a chance optical configuration, by Sir William Herschel in 1802 – although it was Bradley, the third Astronomer Royal, who first drew attention to their angular change of approximately 30° between the years 1718 and 1760. The period of one complete revolution is 420 years, and in recent years they have closed position, so that at least a 3-in. telescope is required to split them. In 1895, it was discovered that the fainter member (mag 2.9) is also a spectroscopic binary, with a period of 2.9 days. And again, a few years later the brighter star (mag 2.0) was also found to be a spectroscopic system, period 9 days. To make it even more interesting and complicated it was also found that a faint reddish-coloured star of mag 9, at a distance of 73″, was also a member of the system, and, additionally, was itself an eclipsing binary with a period of one day. Thus Castor can be considered to be a rather unusual sextuple star system.

β   *Pollux*; mag 1.2, the other twin and of a yellow-orange tint (in contrast with the whiteness of Castor). It has a number of faint optical companions which are difficult objects to observe with small instruments, but they are definitely not members of a binary system. Pollux with Castor forms a useful celestial measuring rod, for the two stars are approximately $4\frac{1}{2}°$ apart.

γ   *Almeisan*, 'the Proudly Marching One'; mag 2.2, a brilliant white star situated close by the galactic equator. The area around is strewn with myriads of minute stars, and in binoculars the spectacle is breathtaking. Very close by this star, the famous Halley's Comet was first detected by Max Wolf of Heidelberg on 11 September 1909, as a tiny photographic smudge, when last the comet returned to the Sun after its 75 years' journey in space.

δ   *Wasat* or *Wesat*, 'the Middle'; mag 3.5, white; an optical double, mags 3.5 and 8, dist 6.8″. Can be used as a test object for a 2-in. telescope with moderate magnification (× 50–60). It lies practically on the ecliptic plane, and it was near δ Gem that the planet Pluto was first detected and recognized as the ninth planet in February 1930, by Clyde Tombaugh, a one-time farm boy and amateur stargazer who had recently become a professional astronomer. This discovery was the result of an intermittent 23 year photographic search for a new outer planet by the staff at Lowell Observatory, Arizona.

ε   *Mebsuta*, 'the Outstretched'; mag 3.2, yellow; double, mags 3.2, 9.5, dist 2′. Easy for 2-in. telescopes.

ζ   *Mekbuda*; an ideal star for binocular study, being both a double and a variable star, mag variations 3.7–4.5, yellow. The companion is mag 7 at a distance of $1\frac{1}{2}′$. The primary star is a Cepheid-type variable, period 10.1535 days, first detected by Julius Schmidt in 1847.

η   *Propus*; another double/variable combination, mags 3.2–4.2, orange-red; companion star, mag 9, period 230 days. Its variable nature was another of Schmidt's discoveries (1865). Its light variations are erratic: it is classified among semi-regular variables and is a very suitable object for study with the naked eye or wide-field binoculars. It was near η Gem that Sir William Herschel accidentally discovered the planet Uranus on 13 March 1781 – the first planet to be discovered by the aid of telescopes.

θ   Mag 3.6, white.

κ   Mag 3.7, yellow; binary system, mags 3.7, 8.5, dist 7″.

λ   Mag 3.7, white; binary system; mags 3.7, 11.3, dist 10″.

μ   Mag 3.2, orange-red. Double, mags 3.2, 9.8, dist 122.5″.

ξ   Mag 3.4, yellow-white.

R Gem Long-period variable; mag range 5.9–14.1, orange-red, period 370 days. Of similar kind to Mira (*o* Ceti) and can be glimpsed with the naked eye at maximum brightness, but at minimum it requires a telescope of at least 12-in. aperture. When making identification, care must be taken not to confuse it with 44 Gem, another star close by.

M 35 (NGC 2168) Open cluster; mag 5.3, dia 40′; possibly the most exquisite sight in the entire constellation, lying north of *η* Gem. It can be glimpsed with the unassisted eye by using averted vision, and it appears as a nebulous smudge if the sky is sufficiently dark and transparent. But even the simplest optical aid reveals its splendour, and in opera glasses – or binoculars – it has been likened to 'a piece of frosted silver over which a twinkling light is playing'. With small telescopes the region presents a gorgeous field – strewn with stars ranging in brightness from mags 9 to 16, covering an area a little larger than that presented to the naked eye by the full Moon.

Geminids. Meteor shower; this occurs annually about 13 December. The radiant point (which moves eastwards 1° per day) lies close to Castor at shower maximum. Under favourable conditions, perhaps fifty or more (but often less) swift-moving meteors may be seen every hour. The Geminids, as they are called, are of considerable interest, for the orbit described by the meteoroids round the Sun is smaller than any other known meteor stream. Its period is only 1.65 years, and they approach the solar surface to within 0.14 a.u. during the course of their highly eccentric paths. They also appear to originate from extraordinarily dense particles which tend to be slowed down (or decelerated) far less in the Earth's atmosphere than most other meteoroids. Although they may be associated with a comet, no object of this kind has yet been observed with the same orbital characteristics.

Note. Before leaving Gemini, mention must be made of the possibilities of observing minor planets, or asteroids. Since the constellation is zodiacal, many asteroids pass through it from time to time and are often accidentally picked up by variable-star observers who can readily spot a stranger in their familiar star fields. Equipped with a small telescope, say of 2- to 4-in. aperture, a surprisingly large number of these miniature planets can be spotted at their closest approach to the Earth, and even prismatic binoculars will enable the observer to see a score or more. However, to be certain of their correct identification, it is necessary to consult a specialized star atlas which depicts stars down to mag 9, or lower; and also to consult their ephemerides (or predicted places), which can be found in a number of annual astronomical handbooks generally obtainable at public reference libraries.

Lepus, *the Hare* (Lep)

The group forms a small constellation lying immediately south of Orion and presents a distinctive pattern of stars at approximately the same altitude as Sirius and situated some 20° to the west of it.

An old rhyme gives directions as follows:

> Orion's image, on the south has four stars – small but fair;
> Their figure quadrilateral points out the timid Hare.

Mythology

The origin of the Hare and its significance are obscure. Although it contains no particularly bright stars, with a little imagination one can actually trace out the figure it is supposed to represent.

Probably one of the best explanations as to its significance is the idea that it is connected with the great devastation wrought in Sicily by hares in early times, and therefore a convincing configuration of stars fortuitously close by Orion was placed in that position to be forever chased by the Hunter. Had not Orion been close by, it seems doubtful that a separate constellation would ever have existed.

In early Egyptian astronomy it was included in the Boat of Osiris, and to the Chinese it was a shed. In the biblical representation created by Julius Schiller, it was portrayed as Gideon's Fleece.

Principal stars

α Lep *Arneb*, Arab name for the whole group; mag 2.7, yellow-white; also a 9.5 mag companion, dist 35″. The primary member is a giant star with a diameter nine times that of the Sun.

β *Nihal* – a collective name which includes all the brighter stars near by; mag 3.0, yellow. Also a binary system, mags 3.0, 11, dist 2.4″. Requires a 6-in. telescope to detect the faint companion.

γ Mag 3.8, yellow-white; also a wide double, mags 3.8, 6.4, dist 95″. Just within binocular range; companion star a striking orange-yellow colour.

δ Mag 3.9, yellow.

ε Mag 3.3, orange-yellow.

ζ Mag 3.7, white.

η Mag 3.8, yellow-white.

θ Mag 4.7, white.

μ Mag 3.3, white.

Deep-sky objects

κ Lep Double; mags 4.5, 7.3, blue-white, dist 2.3″. An object for 3-in. telescopes.

R Long-period variable; mag range 5.5–10.7, red, period 436.43 days. Also known as 'Hind's Crimson Star', named after the

150

British astronomer who discovered it and described it as '. . . of the most intense crimson, resembling a blood drop on the background of the sky'. The deep-red colour is very apparent in small binoculars when the star is at maximum brightness.

M 79 (NGC 1904) Globular cluster; mag 8.4, dia 3.2'. Just visible in 10 × 50 binoculars as a faint hazy star, but its low position in the sky makes it a difficult object for northern observers.

LYNX, *the Lynx or Tiger* (Lyn)

A rather dull, uninteresting group to the naked eye, but containing some interesting telescopic objects. It can be located halfway between Castor and Pollux, in Gemini, and the distinctive 'bowl' of Ursa Major.

Mythology
A modern constellation, introduced by Hevelius to 'organize' stars in a part of the sky left unformed by the ancients.

Each after each, ungrouped, unnamed, revolve.

(Aratus)

But why Hevelius chose the lynx to represent this insignificant part of the heavens is not known for certain, and his later retort that one should be lynx-eyed to see it, must have been a wry afterthought. However, there is an early reference to it in 1624 by Bartschius, son-in-law of Kepler, which refers to the region as 'spots on the Tiger'.

Principal stars
α Lyn Mag 3.3, orange.
38   Mag 3.8, white; also a double, mags 4.0, 5.9, dist 3".
2   Mag 4.4, white.
15   Mag 4.5, yellow; very close binary system, mags 4.9, 6.1, dist 1".
21   Mag 4.5, white.
10 (UMa) Mag 4.1, yellow; very close binary, mags 4.3, 6.2, dist 0.6". Owing to the revision of constellation boundaries in 1930, this star is now in Lynx.

Deep-sky objects
19 Lyn Double; mags 5.3, 6.6, dist 15"; object for 2-in. telescopes.
20   Double; mags 6.6, 6.8, dist 15".
R   Long-period variable of the Mira type; mag range 6.5–14.8, period 378 days, deep-red tint.
Y   Irregular variable; mag range 6.9–7.4, period 250 days (?), orange-red; can be observed throughout its light variations with 8 × 30's.

MONOCEROS, *the Unicorn* (Mon)

Although the Milky Way extends across the constellation, it is rather a dull area of the heavens for the naked-eye observer. However, the region is rich in telescopic objects, some of which are visible with small instruments.

Mythology

Another of the modern constellations adopted by Hevelius on his maps, but it was first introduced by Bartschius, Kepler's son-in-law, to fill a large vacant field between Canis Minor and Orion. Some antiquarians, however, claim to trace its origin to a much earlier period, and it is supposedly represented on a Persian sphere.

Principal stars

α Mon Mag 4.1, yellow-orange.
β   Mag 3.9, blue-white; also a triple system, mags 4.7, 4.6, 5.6, dist 7.4″ and 2.8″. A beautiful object for 2½-in. telescopes.
γ   Mag 4.1, yellow-orange.
δ   Mag 4.1, white.
ζ   Mag 4.4, yellow.

Deep-sky objects

8 (ε) Mon Double system; mag 4.3, white; mags 4.5, 6.5, dist 13″. Object for 2-in. telescopes; some fine sweeping for low-powered instruments in this region of the sky.

S   An irregular variable; mag 4.7, greenish-white. A very hot star. Little is known about its range of light variation and therefore it is an important star for amateurs to observe and estimate at regular intervals. Best seen with opera glasses or wide-angle binoculars.

T   Cepheid variable; mag range 6.3–7.8, yellow, period 27.018 days. Can be followed through entire cycle with 8×30 binoculars and easy to locate 7° east of Betelgeuse (α Orionis).

U   Pulsating variable (RV Tauri type); mag range 6.1–8.1, yellow, period 92.26 days. Another binocular variable.

M50 (NGC 2323) Open star cluster; mag 6.9, dia 16′. Can be seen as a hazy star with opera glasses, and a bright array of stars become visible with binoculars, including an orange-red one about 7′ south of the centre.

NGC 2353 Open star cluster; mag 5.3, dia 20′, containing about 20 stars. Visible with the smallest instruments.

NGC 2244 Open star cluster; mag 6.2, dia 40′. The cluster is involved in both dark and luminous gaseous clouds, and the whole object is best seen in small wide-angle instruments.

NGC 2301 Open star cluster; mag 5.8, dia 15′. A very loose cluster of about 60 stars, but well seen in small instruments and low powers.

ORION, *the Hunter* (Ori)

This constellation is undoubtedly one of the most beautiful in the entire heavens and is so prominent that even the most dilatory of stargazers will never forget its configuration once it is seen. The Hunter is generally represented by the figure of a man having a sword suspended from his girdle and attacking the Bull (near by) with a huge club held in his right hand. The left hand holds the skin of a lion which serves as a shield. Three bright stars of the 2nd magnitude, almost in a straight line and spaced equidistantly, form the belt or girdle. Some authorities refer to them as the Three Kings and others as Jacob's Staff, Rod or Rake. If a line is projected beyond these three prominent stars, to the east it points to Sirius, and to the west to the yellow-orange Aldebaran (the eye of the Bull) and the Pleiades.

Mythology

The name Orion is thought to be derived from Vraanna, meaning 'the Light of Heaven'. According to ancient fable, Orion was a man of gigantic stature and greatly celebrated as a hunter. On the island of Crete he accompanied Diana and Latone to the chase, and then died by the bite of a scorpion which the earth produced under his feet as punishment for his vanity in bragging that there did not exist an animal that he could not conquer. After his death, and at the request of Diana, he was placed among the stars in a position directly opposite that of the Scorpion so that he would never be seen in the sky with his enemy.

Principal stars

α Ori *Betelgeuse*, Arabic for 'the Armpit of the Central One'; mag 0.7, twelfth-brightest star in the sky, and its orange-red colour makes it a very conspicuous object in winter skies. Betelgeuse is also interesting because it belongs to the family of stars known as Red Giants, having a diameter of 300m. miles. It is also an irregular variable and fluctuates in the mag range 0.3–1.1. A check comparison for brightness can be made using Aldebaran (α Tauri), a star of comparable brightness and of the same colour type.

β *Rigel*, 'the Left Leg of the Giant'. A brilliant bluish-white double, mags 0.3 and 8.0, dist 9.1″.

γ *Bellatrix*, 'the Female Warrior', traditionally marks the giant's left shoulder. Mag 1.7, blue-white. In ancient astrology it was said that all women born under its influence would be lucky and loquacious.

δ *Mintaka*; mag 2.5, greenish-white, the first of the 'belt' stars. Also a double, companion, mag 6.8, dist 53″.

ε *Alnilam*; mag 1.8, greenish-white. The middle star of Orion's belt.

ζ   *Alnitak*; mag 2.1, blue-white; a double system, mags 2.1, 4.2, dist 2.4″. The lowest star of the belt. In the past, the three belt stars were often called by the group name of 'String of Pearls'. In 1807, the University of Leipzig conferred on them the new name of 'Napoleon', while incensed Englishmen, on hearing the news, decided on the alternate title of Nelson. Neither name appears on modern star maps.

η   *Saiph*, which represents the sword; mag 3.4, bluish-white; also a triple system, mags 3.5, 5.0 and 5.0.

θ   Mag 4.6, greenish-white; marks the sword scabbard and also the 'mouth' of the nebula M 42 (see under Deep-sky objects). Theta is one of the most beautiful multiple systems in the entire sky and is composed of four giant stars which form a distinctive trapezium, individual mags 6, 7, 7.5 and 8. Well seen with 2-in. telescopes.

ι   Mag 2.9, greenish-white; double star, mags 2.9, 7.4, companion white, dist 11.4″. The brighter member is also a spectroscopic binary, period 29.2 days.

κ   Mag 2.2, bluish-white; a bright star but, surprisingly, possessing no known Arabic name other than Saiph, which really belongs to η.

λ   Mag 3.7, greenish-white; a double, mags 3.7, 5.6, companion, blue-white, dist 4.5″.

τ   Mag 3.7, blue-white.

Deep-sky objects

M 42 (NGC 1976) Gaseous nebula; the famous Great Nebula in Orion which is visible in transparent, dark skies to the unaided eye, appearing exactly in the position of θ Ori as a misty star. This is one of the most attractive objects in the entire heavens. Even with opera glasses a greenish tinge is readily detectable, and with prismatic binoculars its fan-shaped form can be easily seen. The multiple star θ Ori is immersed completely, and in a small refractor the star can be resolved into its four main components which form a trapezium shape. With small instruments, and with the eye averted, the delicate outline of the greenish-coloured nebula can be traced over a large area of the field. No photograph can depict the natural beauty of this glowing cloud of gas which is thought to be one of the actual birthplaces for stars. Although its peculiar misty nature was detected by the ancient observers, it was rediscovered telescopically in 1618, by an astronomer called Cysatus.

M 78 (NGC 2068) Gaseous nebula; mag 8.3, dia 8′ × 6′. On the clearest nights can be glimpsed with 10 × 50 binoculars.

U   Long-period variable; mag range 5.2–12.9, orange-red, period 373 days. At maximum brightness it is well within naked-eye visibility.

PUPPIS, *the Stern or Poop* (Pup)

This group was originally part of the great constellation of
Argo Navis, which lay mostly in the southern hemisphere and
had a total length of 75°. In modern times this great ancient sprawl
of stars was divided into four separate constellations: Carina,
the Keel; Vela, the Sails; Puppis, the Stern; and Malus, the Mast.
However, the latter constellation is nowadays represented by the
southern group of Pyxis.

Puppis is not particularly well observed from the northern
temperate zone, and never rises much above the southern horizon,
yet when a bright nova appeared there in 1942, it was discovered
independently by a keen-eyed Welsh fisherman when the new
star was only 4° above the horizon – a remarkable feat for naked-
eye observation.

The part of the constellation which is visible to observers
in the north temperate zone lies immediately east of Canis Major
and can be roughly located by projecting a line from Orion's
Belt through Sirius and then an equal distance beyond.

Mythology

Argo was the name of the famous ship which carried Jason and his
fifty-four Argonaut companions to Colchis in Thessaly about
1263 B C when they ventured after the Golden Fleece. The vessel is
reputed to have employed fifty oars, and on her prow she carried a

piece of the speaking oak of Dodona, to guide and warn its crew.

Different authorities give different sources for the legend. One version states that the Grecian fable is founded upon an earlier Egyptian traditional tale which referred to the preservation of Noah and his family during the Flood.

With another version it symbolizes the first ship to sail the oceans, which, long before Jason's time, carried Danaos and his fifty daughters from Egypt to Rhodes. Sir Isaac Newton became intrigued with the origin of this ship and actually persuaded himself that it dated from forty-two years after King Solomon, or about 940 B C. Newton's general work on tracing the origin of the constellations proved to be far less definitive than his work on gravity.

Principal stars

Owing to the constellation becoming a separate entity in modern times, the designations for the brighter stars do not follow the usual pattern.

ζ Pup Mag 2.3, greenish-white.

π   Mag 2.7, yellow-orange.

ρ   Mag 2.9, yellow-white.

ξ   Mag 3.5, yellow; also a double with a mag 13.8 companion, dist 4.6″. Only large telescopes will show it.

τ^1 Mag 2.8, yellow; also a spectroscopic binary, period 1,066 days.

υ   Mag 3.2, blue-white.

Deep-sky objects

2 Pup Double; mags 6.2, 7.0, dist 17″. A beautiful object for small telescopes.

5   Double; mags 5.5, 8.2, dist 2.2″, yellow-white, yellow. Requires a $2\frac{1}{2}$-in. telescope.

k   Double; mags 4.5, 4.6, dist 10″. A bright pair almost equally matched.

L^2 Long-period variable; mag range 3.4–6.2, period 140 days, orange-red. Observable through entire range with opera glasses, but unfortunately too low for observers in north temperate latitudes.

V   Eclipsing variable (β Lyrae type); mag range 4.5–5.2, period 1.4545 days, blue-white. A naked-eye variable, but again too low for some northern observers.

M 46 (NGC 2437) Open star cluster; mag 6.0, dia 24′. An easy object for binocular observers.

M 93 (NGC 2447) Open star cluster; mag 6.0, dia 25′; also includes a variety of objects: a wide double, a triple and two orange-red tinted stars. Well seen in 2-in. telescopes.

Taurus, *the Bull* (Tau)

One of the twelve signs of the Zodiac, and second in order of importance since it depicted the vernal equinox from about 4000 BC to 1700 BC and marked the beginning of the year on ancient zodiacs. The Pleiades star cluster also forms part of this constellation although in early times it was often reckoned as a separate one.

Taurus is easily located lying immediately south of Auriga (sharing one of its stars) and north and west of Orion.

Mythology

The Bull is one of the oldest constellations, and many earlier civilizations have given it considerable importance in forming their mythologies; many references are to be found in Egyptian, Hebrew and Greek sources. The constellation is important also in that it somewhat resembles its animal form, for the yellow-orange star Aldebaran (a Tauri) represents accurately the Bull's eye. In more modern configurations the Indian tribes of South America considered it took the form of a tapir.

In Greek mythology the sign commemorates the animal which bore Europa safely across the sea to Crete, but it had its place as a zodiacal group long before the Greek civilization came into being. The earlier Egyptians worshipped it under the name Apis, and the Persians as Mithra. In north-western Europe it was venerated by the Druids, and when the Sun entered the constellation, they celebrated the pagan festival Tauris. The Romans constructed a temple at Eboracum (York) which was dedicated to Serapis – the incarnate bull – where great bonfires were lit and burnt sacrifices offered to the gods of Earth and fertility.

The five brightest stars, which form the Hyades cluster, are reputed to represent five of the twelve daughters of Atlas, King of Mauretania, and his wife Pleione. Their names were Phaola, Ambrosia, Eudora, Coronis and Polyxo, and they were transformed into stars through the grief they expressed over the loss of their brother Hyas. In earlier times the Hyades were used in astrological predictions and indicated at their rising the imminence of great rains.

The Pleiades cluster represents the other seven daughters of Atlas, sisters to the Hyades. Their names were Alcyone, Merope, Maya, Electra, Taygete, Sterope and Celaeno. Legend tells us that Merope was the only sister who married a mortal, and it is on this account that the star is fainter than the rest. At one time the Pleiades were represented by a hen and her chickens.

α Tau *Aldebaran*, 'the Follower' or 'the Hindmost', because this star follows the Pleiades in their journey round the sky; mag 1.1, yellow-orange. The thirteenth-brightest star in the heavens. Also a double, companion, mag 11.0, orange-red, dist 31"; this faint star is normally beyond any telescope less than 4-in., but some eagle-eyed observers in the nineteenth century claimed to have 'glimpsed' it with 2-in. telescopes.

β   *El Nath*, 'the Butting One', situated on the northernmost tip of the Bull; mag 1.8, blue-white. A star shared with the neighbouring constellation of Auriga and identical with γ Aurigae, lying exactly at the boundary. In this connection one authority puts forward (with tongue in cheek?) the theory that this star gives rise to the expression 'he doesn't know β from a bull's foot', particularly since, in the constellation Auriga, the Arabs called it 'Heel of the Reinholder'. In the past it was an important astrological star, and for those who came under its influence it portended eminence and fortune. To the Hindus, however, it represented the God of Fire.

γ   *Hyadum I* or *Prima Hyadum*, 'the Leading One of the Hyades Cluster'; mag 3.9, yellow. Located at the apex of the V-shape forming the cluster.

δ   *Hyadum II*; mag 3.9, yellow.

ε   Mag 3.6, yellow; Flamsteed called it Oculus boreus, 'the Northern Eye'.

ζ   Mag 3.0, blue-white.

$\theta^1 - \theta^2$ Mags 4.0, 3.6, yellow and white; forms an easy naked-eye double, dist 5.5'. θ^2 is also a spectroscopic binary.

Hyades. This so-called open cluster involves many of the brighter stars forming the group depicted like a capital V turned on its side. Aldebaran marks the upper left hand, ε the right-hand side and γ the apex. This distinctive configuration is not a chance one, and most of the visible stars (except Aldebaran) belong to a group which appear to have the same proper motion in the sky.

Pleiades. They are the most wonderful object in the entire sky to both naked-eye and telescopic observers, and in Aratus' *Phenomenon* they were listed as a separate constellation. They have attracted the attention of man since the earliest times, and they have been mentioned in poetry as far back as Hesiod, who referred to them as the 'Seven Virgins'.

No group of stars figures so largely in myth and legend. Their name is probably derived from the Greek *pleione*, many, which is very similar to the Hebrew name for it, *Kimah*, the Cluster or Heap. The individual names, much used today, are those of the seven daughters of Atlas and Pleione. The group has also been titled 'Hen and Chickens', while some Greek poets spoke of 'Rock Pigeons' or simply 'the Dove'.

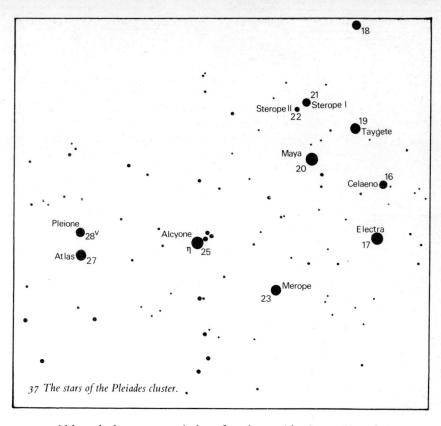

37 The stars of the Pleiades cluster.

Although they are popularly referred to as 'the Seven Sisters', with ordinary eyes only six will be readily counted, and in some eyes lacking normal acuity they present a nebulous haze containing a few bright stars. Nevertheless, observers with good vision have counted up to fourteen when the atmosphere has been particularly transparent.

The outline formed by the cluster is not unlike the Dipper, and it is not surprising that they are often referred to as the Little Dipper. In ancient Greece, many temples were erected in their honour and they were used to herald the equinoctial sun. The Greek farmers reaped their corn when the Pleiades rose at sunrise in May, and ploughed their fields when they set at sunrise in November. Some South American Indians worshipped the cluster and used it to portend cold and rain. The Australian aborigines believed the weather to be totally influenced by them, and held them to be more significant than the Sun. In every primitive mythology, without exception, the influence of the Pleiades can be traced.

η Tau (Flamsteed No. 25) *Alcyone*; mag 3.0, blue-white. The brightest member of the Pleiades group; represents the Atlantid nymph who became the mother of Hyrieus by Poseidon. With opera glasses can also be seen three faint companions which form a triangle.

20   *Maya*; mag 4.0, blue-white. Represents the first-born, and the most beautiful of the sisters.

17   *Electra*; mag 3.8, blue-white. Sometimes known as the lost Pleiad; legend says that she withdrew her light owing to her sorrow at witnessing the destruction of Ilium, founded by her son Dardanos.

23   *Merope*; mag 4.3, blue-white. Also considered as the lost Pleiad, for having married a mortal she hid her face in shame. The star is involved in a faint gaseous nebula, first detected by the comet-hunter Tempel in 1859. Great doubts were cast by subsequent observers as to whether this nebula actually existed,. for it was difficult to observe, being close to Merope. After photography was applied to astronomy, the nebula was proved to exist beyond all doubt. When the sky is transparent, it can be seen with relatively small instruments and I have often observed it with 10×80 binoculars.

19   *Taygete*; mag 4.4, blue-white. A name famous in Spartan legend as the mother of Lacedaemon by Zeus.

16   *Celaeno*; mag 5.4, blue-white. Also considered as the lost Pleiad owing to the difficulty of seeing it with the naked eye.

21 and 22 *Sterope I* and *II*; mags 5.9, 6.5, both blue-white. Forms a wide opera-glass double.

27   *Atlas*; mag 3.8, blue-white; a modern addition to the Seven Sisters, added by Riccioli.

28   *Pleione*; mag 5.0–5.5, blue-white, an irregular variable star suitable for opera-glass study. Another modern addition to the group introduced by Riccioli.

Even with the minimum optical aid the Pleiades cluster is a glorious spectacle; binoculars will show at least seventy members of the group and with long-exposure photographs (see fig. 33) thousands of stars can be counted. The cluster lies about 350 light-years distant and is 12 light-years in diameter.

Deep-sky objects

σ^1, σ^2 Tau Mags 5.2, 4.9, both white. A wide pair of stars 7' dist which, although they can just be observed with the naked eye, are best observed with opera glasses.

φ Double; mags 5.1, 8.7, yellow-orange, yellow-white, dist 52″. Requires a 2-in. telescope.

τ Double; mags 4.3, 7.0, blue-white, dist 1'. A binocular pair.

χ Double; mags 5.4, 8.2, white, dist 20″. Object for 2-in. telescopes.

118   Double; mag 5.9, 6.6, blue-white, dist 5″.

λ Eclipsing Algol-type variable; mag range 3.4–4.3, period 3.9530 days, blue-white. Suitable for observation with opera glasses although naked-eye observations are also possible.

M 1 (NGC 1952) Planetary nebula; the famous Crab Nebula, so called owing to its appearance in large telescopes (fig. 38); mag 8.4,

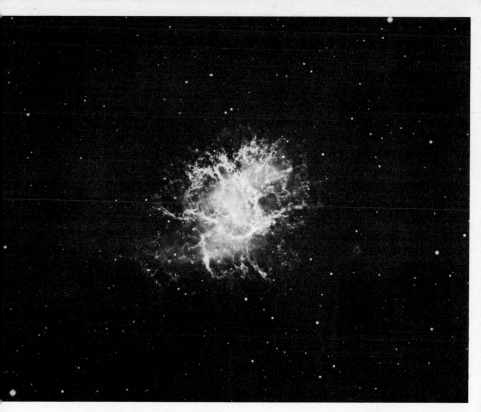

38 The Crab Nebula M1 in Taurus.

dimensions $6' \times 4'$. On transparent nights, can be seen with 8×30 binoculars; easy in 2-in. telescopes. This nebula is now known to be the result of a spectacular supernova explosion which occurred over 900 years ago. The event is recorded in the Chinese chronicles of AD 1054, where it is mentioned as a 'guest star' – a name the Chinese gave to transient celestial phenomena. Some more recent research has revealed that it was actually witnessed by Japanese astronomers some ten days before the Chinese.

In modern times the nebula has been of great interest to astronomers because enormous quantities of X-radiation has been detected emerging from it, and in addition, inside the nebular remnants, has been observed a pulsar – one of a new class of astronomical objects which emit radio pulses at very regular intervals. The M 1 pulsar is particularly interesting in that it was also the first one to be identified in a telescope as a visual object.

At the present time, astronomers do not know for certain what these strange objects actually represent. They are probably superdense, star-like bodies consisting of neutrons packed so tightly together that they give rise to physical phenomena that go beyond the present-day laws of physics.

CHAPTER 10

Stars of the southern hemisphere

Although this book is written primarily for observers in the northern hemisphere, no manual of stars would be complete without a brief reference to the constellations and stars of the southern hemisphere. Also in the modern jet-age it is quite unexceptional for the traveller to find himself suddenly transported to the southern hemisphere to an unfamiliar canopy of stars, and it is for him and the curious northerner who simply demands to know what lies below his immediate horizon that the following guide is included.

In an earlier chapter it was mentioned that the stars surrounding the southern celestial pole were not observed by the original makers of the constellations; and indeed it may be remembered that the fact that ‚they were not known enabled the modern constellation detectives to deduce the makers of the northern constellations.

Probably the first man to produce a major catalogue of southern stars, under his latinized name of Petrus Theodorus, was the Dutch pilot Pieter Dirckszoon Keyser, of Madagascar, in 1595. This catalogue, consisting of some twelve new constellations, was pirated in 1603 by Frederick de Houtman (one of the first voyagers to visit the coast of West Australia), who is said to have received much personal credit. Bayer incorporated the new constellations into his *Uranometria* in 1603, and his example was followed by later astronomers.

Others of the period who made contributions to knowledge of the southern sky included two French astronomers, Richer and Meurisse, who observed from a station at Cayenne and subsequently published a small catalogue of star positions.

Edmund Halley, while still an undergraduate, made a special expedition to St Helena in 1676 in order to study the southern heavens; in 1678 he published a catalogue locating 341 southern stars and, later, a planisphere on which he regrouped some of them, forming a new constellation, Robur Carolinum, to commemorate the oak tree in which Charles II had hidden after the Battle of Worcester.

It was, however, the French astronomer Lacaille who extended the knowledge of the southern stars to equal that of the northern hemisphere. During the years 1751–2, he lived alone near Table Mountain, Cape of Good Hope, and with a telescope of $26\frac{1}{4}$-in. focal length, $\frac{1}{2}$-in. aperture and a magnification of $\times 8$, fixed the position of 10,000 stars and formed fourteen new constellations. For this magnificent work he was called the 'True Columbus of the Southern Skies'.

To a stargazer a first visit to the southern hemisphere is a strange and unforgettable experience. If the journey is made at a leisurely pace by sea, the passage of each day allows the familiar stars of the north to sink lower and lower on the horizon, while unfamiliar configurations, only previously seen on the impersonal printed pages of a star atlas, begin to emerge from the southern skies.

The constellation of Scorpius, which to observers in the northern temperate zone just hovers above the southern horizon, climbs to unfamiliar, brilliant heights, and then one day the traveller sees for the first time the Southern Cross and its famous black coal-sack nebula appearing like a hole in the Milky Way.

Yet, to the stargazer looking for the first time at the region round the southern celestial pole, it will be somewhat disappointing, for the area is entirely destitute of bright stars and the easily recognizable configurations that are common in the north. At the actual southern pole lies the constellation of Octans which was formed by Lacaille in 1752. It contains only one star brighter than magnitude 4, and nearly all its other naked-eye stars are fainter than 5.5. The star designated as the southern Pole Star is σ Octantis, mag 5.8.

Nevertheless, the southern sky as a whole is not completely lacking in interesting objects, for there are two distinctive bodies which have no equal in the northern hemisphere. They are the Magellanic Clouds or Cape Clouds, so called after the navigator Magellan, who was one of the first to observe and comment upon them after his circumnavigation of the globe in 1519. Their correct scientific titles, however, are Nubecula Major, for the larger one, and Nubecula Minor for the lesser one. These clouds are among the most beautiful objects in the entire heavens. They are plainly visible with the naked eye and are also overwhelmingly rich in telescopic objects. They are vast independent stellar systems similar to our own Milky Way and are in fact related to it, being members of what is known as the local group of galaxies. The large cloud lies 150,000 light-years away, and the lesser 165,000 light-years away. The large cloud contains a star known as S Doradus which is the most luminous individual star known at present, being 400,000 times as bright as the Sun.

The large cloud lies in the constellation of Mensa (formed by Lacaille and named after Table Mountain), and Doradus, the Swordfish, invented by Bayer in 1604, while the small one is in Tucana, the Toucan. But there is no denying that the most famous of all southern constellations is the Southern Cross, or Crux as it is correctly known. Although it is only a very small constellation, it lies in an area completely immersed in the star fields of the Milky Way. At latitude 34° S, it becomes a southern circumpolar constellation and therefore never sets. It contains three 1st-magnitude stars and six others brighter than mag 5. In the Cross configuration the upper and lower stars a and γ have similar right ascensions and can be used, like a and β Ursae Majoris in the north, to indicate the approximate position of the celestial pole, which lies $27\frac{1}{2}°$ from a Crucis. It has also been nicknamed the 'Southern Celestial Clock' since with a little familiarity and respect for the degree of 'uprightness' of the cross as it swings round the polar pivot – advancing four minutes per day – one can readily tell the time of night. Within the Cross also lies the Coal-sack nebula, 8° long and 5° wide, containing only one star visible with the naked eye. This is a vast agglomeration of dust which obscures the light of the stars behind it, and was first noted by the early voyagers about AD 1500.

Nearly 5,000 years ago, the Southern Cross was visible from the shores of the Baltic Sea, but precession carried it out of view. It is now receding once again from the southern polar region so that one day, in the distant future, it will reappear above the European horizons. At the present time one must live no further north than latitude 30° N in order to catch a glimpse of it.

In Ptolemy's time, the Southern Cross formed part of Centaurus, the Centaur, which nowadays surrounds it on three sides. Centaurus has ten stars brighter than the 3rd magnitude and is a large constellation sprawling across 60° of sky. Although it lies very far south, it formed one of the ancient forty-eight constellations, and part of it can just be seen in northern temperate latitudes during the spring months, when the sky is particularly transparent. In mythology the name is supposed to have originated from the sons of Ixion, who were fabulously represented as half men and half horses. One of its stars, α Centauri, is of especial interest. It is the fourth-brightest star in the sky and the second-nearest of our stellar neighbours, lying at a distance of 4.3 light-years. It forms part of a triple system, the first ever discovered in southern skies. The faintest of the three stars, Proxima, is closer to the Earth than any other *known* star, at a distance of 4.2 light-years.

In the legends of the southern stars, Centaurus plays an important role. The South African Bushmen knew α and β Centauri – which are pointers to the Southern Cross – as the 'Two Men That Once Were Lions', and the Australian aborigines knew them as 'Two Brothers' who supposedly speared to death another of their mythical figures.

The constellation forming the Great Ship Argo is nowadays divided up into three different constellations: Carina, Vela and Puppis. The old planispheres depict it as a vessel travelling stern foremost, and in mythology it is closely connected with the legend of the Argonauts and the Golden Fleece. One of the brightest stars of this ancient constellation is Canopus (α Carinae), mag $-$ 0.4, white, and the second-brightest star in the sky after Sirius. It is named after the chief pilot of the fleet of Menelaos who, after returning from the destruction of Troy in 1183 BC, visited Egypt on the way home, but died near Alexandria. At this period of history the star rose only $7\frac{1}{2}°$ above the city, but, nevertheless, was a brilliant object in the clear, transparent skies of the desert.

Many modern authorities consider that the constellations of the southern hemisphere were conceived in the worst possible taste. Their criticism is that the figures selected are utterly inappropriate to their surroundings and unpractical as a means of identifying stars. But although some of these criticisms are justified, the patterns are too long-established to make modern changes, and the contemporary observer has to make the best of it. Yet in practice it is surprising how familiar even the obscure patterns become, and they quickly establish themselves as old friends when the seasonal shifts carry them endlessly round the heavens. The southern observer has also the advantage of better skies, for the climates of the southern hemisphere generally give superior observing conditions and the stars can be seen at their best.

Another of its famous and fascinating stars is η Carinae. Halley, in 1676, classified it as a 4th-magnitude star, but by 1751 Lacaille observed it at magnitude 2. Eighty-six years later Sir John Herschel, during his observing expedition to the Cape of Good Hope in the footsteps of Lacaille to complete the Herschel survey of the heavens, was astonished to find it had brightened to nearly zero magnitude. Then by 1843 it outshone Canopus (α Carinae), at magnitude − 1, and only Sirius rivalled it in the entire sky. However, quite suddenly it began to decline in brightness again, and by 1880 it had faded to magnitude 7, beyond naked-eye visibility. Although it continued to fluctuate slightly, it remained faint for many years and different theories were formed in attempts to explain the star's peculiar variations. In 1933, a nebulous halo was noticed for the first time, and there could be no doubt that the star was responsible for producing it. It has been suggested that some kind of explosion was observed in 1843, and since that time a gaseous halo has moved outwards from the surface of the star at the rate of about 5″ per century. It is certainly not a typical exploding star or nova, and as an object it continues to baffle present-day investigators, who have now had it under close observation for many years.

A short glossary of southern constellations

ANTLIA, *the Air Pump*
A constellation between Hydra and Vela, introduced by Lacaille about 1752.

APUS, *the Bird of Paradise*
A group of stars lying about 13° from the southern celestial pole and situated immediately below the Southern Triangle. Introduced on to star maps by Johann Bayer early in the seventeenth century, but its invention is attributed to Petrus Theodorus.

ARA, *the Altar*
One of the original forty-eight constellations; Ptolemy called it 'the Censor'.

CAELUM, *the Engraving Tool*
Situated between Eridanus and Columba, but its northern part is just visible in latitude 50° N. One of Lacaille's new constellations, whose brightest star is only mag 4.

CARINA, *the Keel (of Argo Navis)*
This is the southernmost part of the ancient constellation of Argo Navis.

CENTAURUS, *the Centaur*
An ancient constellation, included in the *Almagest* of Ptolemy. Depicted on the Farnese globe (p. 15).

CHAMAELEON
A small group which was included in Bayer's maps from observations gleaned from southern voyages. It is located between

Carina and the south celestial pole. In ancient China part of the present constellation was called Seaou Tow – a small dipper.

CIRCINUS, *the Pair of Compasses*

One of Lacaille's new constellations between Centaurus and the Southern Triangle and lying in the plane of the Milky Way.

COLUMBA, *Noah's Dove*

Introduced by Bayer and Royer. Although very much a southern constellation, part of it is observable from north temperate latitudes although probably only α and β Columbae, both mag 3 stars, can be picked out with the naked eye. It lies due south of Orion and Lepus. According to various authorities it was a group towards which Egyptian temples were often orientated.

CORONA AUSTRALIS, *the Southern Crown*

A small, inconspicuous constellation. Although a southerly one, it was among the original forty-eight groups of Ptolemy.

Bayer in his star map depicted Corona as a typical wreath, but without the streaming ribbons of its northern namesake.

CRUX, *the Southern Cross*

Crux Australis is a group of universal attraction to all stargazers when they cross into the southern hemisphere. It is a constellation that never fails to command the attention, and the poetic and literary fancies, of many travellers to southern climes, and since it lies directly in the plane of the Milky Way, it contains many attractive objects, including ten bright open star clusters. From the northern hemisphere it begins to come into view in the latitude of Florida.

DORADO, *the Swordfish*

Introduced as a group by Bayer in 1604, and contains the interesting naked-eye galaxy called Nubecula Major, or the Greater Magellanic Cloud – after Ferdinand Magellan who commanded an expedition which set out to circumnavigate the globe in 1519. It is one of the nearest irregular galaxies, at a distance of 150,000 light-years from the Earth. It also contains the most luminous star in the entire heavens, S Doradus, which is estimated to be almost 400,000 times brighter than the Sun, but it is not such a brilliant object in our skies since it is situated a vast distance away in space.

FORNAX, *the Chemist's Furnace*

Another invention of Lacaille, dated 1752, between Eridanus and Cetus, it lies in a barren part of the southern heavens for naked-eye stars. It is, however, extremely rich in telescopic objects such as extragalactic nebulae, and great numbers have been photographed which swarm together as 'super-clusters', vastly out-numbering the foreground stars of our own Milky Way that lie between.

GRUS, *the Crane*

A Bayer constellation of 1604, between Indus and Phoenix and lying south of the bright star Fomalhaut (α Piscis Austrinis).

HOROLOGIUM, *the Pendulum Clock*

An inconspicuous Lacaille group whose brightest star is only mag 3.8. Located between the most southern part of Eridanus and the groups that form Caelum, Dorado and Reticulum.

HYDRUS, *the Sea Serpent*

A Bayer constellation between Horologium and Tucana. In Schiller's biblical constellations it formed part of Raphael.

INDUS, *the Indian*

A group lying between Grus and Pavo and originated by Bayer on the assumption that its configuration represents a typical American Indian completely naked but with arrows in both hands. Later depictions give the Indian a spear in his right hand. However, Schiller associates the group with Pavo, as the patriarch Job.

LUPUS, *the Wolf*

It was known to the Greeks and Romans as simply the Wild Animal, but it was well known as a separate group long before this time. It lies between Centaurus and Scorpius in a rich region of the sky and encompasses part of the Milky Way.

MENSA, *the Table Mountain*

Originally entitled Mons Mensae and formed by Lacaille to perpetuate the memory of his stay in South Africa in order to survey the southern skies. It forms the mountain immediately behind Cape Town which had witnessed his nightly toils and vigils. The constellation is situated near the southern pole, and although a relatively dull group, it includes part of the rich Nubecula Major cloud overlapping its boundary from neighbouring Dorado.

MICROSCOPIUM, *the Microscope*

Another inconspicuous Lacaille group with few bright stars. Gamma (γ) Mic is mag 4, but the rest are mag 5 and lower. It is formed by neat rectangular borders and is located immediately south of Capricornus between Piscis Austrinus and Sagittarius.

MUSCA, *the Southern Fly*

Introduced by Bayer as Apis, the Bee, but Lacaille changed its designation to the present one in 1752. A small constellation lying immediately south of Crux and containing some fine telescopic objects. Julius Schiller combined it with Apus and Chamaeleon to depict mother Eve.

NORMA, *the Level and Square*

Reconstructed by Lacaille to its present modern form from the earlier configurations of Theodorus and Bayer, who nicknamed it the Southern Triangle. It is a difficult constellation to trace out with the naked eye although it lies in a rich part of the sky.

OCTANS, *the Octant*

Formed by Lacaille in 1752, to commemorate the instrument invented by John Hadley in 1730. It occupies a barren region round the southern celestial pole, and its brightest star is ν Octantis, mag 3.1. It also contains the nearest star to the pole visible to the naked eye, σ Octantis, mag 5.5, which lies about 1° away from the true pole's pivot point.

PAVO, *the Peacock*

A Bayer invention, traditionally the bird sacred to Juno, the immortal Queen of the Heavens; it lies between Telescopium and Octans, and south of Sagittarius.

PHOENIX

Originally represented by a boat and later a figure of young ostriches. It was later changed into a griffin or eagle, and finally became the mythical bird which rose again from its own ashes after destruction by fire. In Julius Schiller's biblical figures it was combined with Grus to depict Aaron, the High Priest. It is located between Eridanus and Grus, south of Fornax and Sculptor.

PICTOR, *the Painter's Easel*

Formerly called Equuleus Pictoris, formed by Lacaille, and lying south of Columba.

PYXIS, *the Mariner's Compass*

Formed by Lacaille out of the mast of the ancient constellation of Argo. For a time it became obsolete as a separate group, but it was resurrected by the American astronomer Gould when he published his famous work *Uranometria Argentina* in 1879.

RETICULUM, *the Net*

A Lacaille rearrangement from an earlier constellation called Rhombus, invented by Isaak Habrecht, lying between Dorado and Horologium.

SCULPTOR, *the Sculptor*

An inconspicuous Lacaille group between Cetus and Phoenix. Although a southern constellation, it can be observed from latitude 40° N.

TELESCOPIUM, *the Telescope*

Formed by Lacaille from a small insignificant star grouping situated between Pavo and Sagittarius. A group not to be confused with the now defunct Telescopium Herschelii, between Lynx and Gemini, formed by the Abbé Hell in 1781 in honour of Sir William Herschel.

Triangulum Australis, *the Southern Triangle*

The southern equivalent of the Northern Triangle, but more prominent as a configuration formed by what are termed 'the triangle stars'. It first appeared in the star maps of Bayer, who borrowed it from Petrus Theodorus of a century earlier. Schiller depicted it as the Three Patriarchs, its three prominent stars representing Abraham, Isaac and Jacob. The group lies between Ara and Circinus.

Tucana, *the Toucan*

A Bayer constellation lying south of Phoenix and formerly called 'the American Goose'. It contains the Nubecula Minor, the lesser Magellanic Cloud – an irregular galaxy and one of the closest to the Milky Way at a distance of 165,000 light-years. The old navigators often termed both the larger and smaller clouds the Cape Clouds.

Vela, *the Sails*

Another of the three groups which were part of the division of Argo Navis when the old constellation was split up. It lies in the plane of the Milky Way and contains a number of irregular banded clouds of absorbing dust. These have the effect of blotting out the stars lying behind them, giving the appearance of holes in the sky, to which the name 'coal-sack' is often descriptively applied.

Volans, *the Flying Fish*

Another Bayer asterism formerly entitled Piscis Volans. It lies between Nubecula Major and Carina, and in Schiller's grouping it depicts, along with Dorado, Abel the Just.

CHAPTER 11
What planet is that?

When the observer has familiarized himself with the general patterns of the constellations, or perhaps when he is in the very process of identifying their principal stars, his eyes may well alight upon a stranger in the group which is not depicted on the chart. First reaction might well be: 'Have I discovered a nova?' It may well be that he has, just as others have done before him. However, before jumping to conclusions, the observer must be certain that the 'new star' is not simply another transient celestial object such as a planet, which anyway would not normally be depicted on a star chart. Mis-identifications are even made occasionally by such veteran sweepers of the sky as G. E. D. Alcock, who often finds a 6th- or 7th-magnitude minor planet in a familiar star field, about which he has little current information at hand. However, like all good observers, he thoroughly checks any 'new' object before announcing a fresh discovery.

The Central Bureau for Astronomical Telegrams, located in Cambridge, Mass., USA, is the organization through which announcements of genuinely new objects, such as novae and comets, are made known to the rest of the astronomical world. Unfortunately, it also receives, among the few genuine reports, numerous other reports of pseudo-discoveries which in many instances turn out to be observations of a well-known bright planet such as Venus or Jupiter, both of which from time to time are particularly striking objects in the sky. False reports cause much waste of time, for all discovery announcements from observers are re-checked by independent sources just in case the object is a genuinely new one, as often happens with comets.

Even professional astronomers occasionally make mistakes, and not long ago a well-known one, whose name shall remain a secret to spare his blushes, announced he had discovered a bright naked-eye comet near the Sun, only to find later it was the planet Venus. Another strange instance occurred in the middle of the nineteenth century – long before the era of flying saucers. At the height of midsummer, some observers reported high-flying telescopic objects, of which, at first, no one could give a satisfactory explanation. However, a casual conversation between an astronomer and a botanical expert soon identified the strange objects: they turned out to be seed-pods carried high into the Earth's atmosphere by thermal currents.

At the end of this chapter is a series of planetary tables for the period 1971–80, which are specially intended for the amateur observer with no access to up-to-date information on planetary positions. By the use of these tables, and the ecliptic charts provided, he can locate, at any time, the position in the sky of any of the major planets. If a stranger is recognized in a star field, or if he simply wants to make a planetary identification, the information can be gleaned from the appropriate column in a matter of seconds and plotted on the chart *in pencil*.

The Planets

The name 'planet' is derived from the Greek word *planetes*, meaning 'wanderer'. Five are plainly visible from time to time with the naked eye – Mercury, Venus, Mars, Jupiter and Saturn – and consequently they were well known to the ancients as wandering stars even before their true nature was realized.

Even to a casual observer, these brighter planets are noticeably different in appearance from the fixed stars. They appear to shine by a much steadier light and this effect is a real phenomenon. The stars twinkle, or scintillate, because they are so far distant from the Earth that their light can be reckoned as an extremely narrow point source. The planets, on the other hand, are much closer, and although we cannot see their discs with the naked eye, their larger apparent diameters make their images less susceptible to displacement by the ever-turbulent atmosphere.

Nowadays we know that, in addition to our own Earth, there are eight major planets in the solar system, three of which – Uranus, Neptune and Pluto – were discovered by the aid of telescopes. There are also thousands of asteroids, or minor planets, which are concentrated between the orbits of Mars and Jupiter, although some of them have orbits which bring them close to the Earth. Probably the asteroids number over 30,000 separate planetoids, ranging from Ceres, with a diameter of 770 km., down to small chunks of rock of less than a metre. In many instances during the history of the Earth, asteroids have fallen as meteorites, some producing sizeable craters.

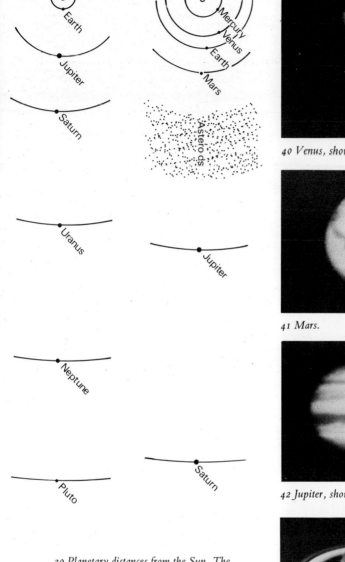

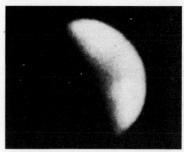

40 *Venus, showing phase form.*

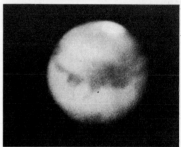

41 *Mars.*

42 *Jupiter, showing cloud belts.*

43 *Saturn.*

39 *Planetary distances from the Sun. The left-hand drawing shows the outer orbits at a quarter of the scale used for the inner planets.*

MERCURY

Mercury has a diameter of 4,840 km., and is the nearest planet to the Sun, taking only 88 days to make one orbital revolution. Since it lies within the Earth's orbit, it can only be observed with the naked eye, shortly after sunset as an evening 'star', or in the early morning before sunrise, depending where the planet is located in its orbit. Its closeness to the Sun makes it a difficult planet to observe in temperate latitudes where long twilight periods occur. The great Copernicus, founder of the Copernican system of astronomy, is said never to have observed Mercury from his native Poland owing to the constant mists arising from the River Vistula. These mists completely blot out from view all celestial objects near the horizon.

With small telescopes very little can be made out of the surface of the planet, apart from the phases it shows (as the Moon does from Earth) owing to it being located within the Earth's orbit. It can be observed telescopically in broad daylight if one knows precisely where to look, and often it is at these times that the best views are obtained, particularly when the planet is high in the sky, away from the effects of turbulent air masses near the horizon. It is generally considered that the surface features of Mercury resemble those of the Moon.

Because of its rapid revolution round the Sun, its movement among the stars can be seen from day to day observation. It can also be easily picked up in daylight, using binoculars, if its precise location is known, and with a little ingenuity on the part of the observer this can easily be accomplished.

VENUS

The next planet in order from the Sun after Mercury again shows the phase-angle effect. Venus is a much larger planet than Mercury; its diameter is 12,610 km., and its orbital period 224 days. Through a telescope we never see any surface markings, for the planet is apparently covered with a thick layer of dense cloud which reflects a considerable amount of light, making Venus one of the brightest objects in the sky. In a similar fashion to Mercury, it is also observed alternately in the evening or morning skies, and at its greatest elongation from the Sun it becomes an unmistakable brilliant object of mag -4.3.

Claims are occasionally made that the phases of Venus can be detected with the naked eye, but, to say the least, this claim is very doubtful. However, a pair of 8×30 prismatic binoculars will readily show them, and with the same instrument Venus can easily be 'swept up' in bright sunlight at midday.

MARS

This is the first planet which lies outside the Earth's orbit, and unlike Venus and Mercury, which only show their dark hemispheres when nearest to the Earth, it presents its entire visible illuminated disc.

Mars has a diameter of 6,860 km. and takes 1.88 Earth years (or 687 days) to orbit the Sun. When visible, it can readily be identified (using the tables) by its predominantly reddish colour – a kind of terracotta, brick-red. Because of its orbital period, it is only observed when close to the Earth (called opposition), once every two years, and then becomes bright as magnitude −2.3. At these times even a 2-in. refractor with × 50 magnification will show the disc. Many years ago the English astronomer Proctor made a series of drawings of the planet with only a 1-in. telescope and an eyepiece of × 100, near opposition time. These drawings showed many of the prominent dark markings and also one of the polar caps. With a modern, good-quality 3-in. refractor and suitable eyepieces of × 100 and × 150, many surface markings are recognizable, and the planet's rotation period of 24 hours is readily apparent.

ASTEROIDS (or Minor Planets)

Although most of these tiny bodies have orbits which keep them between the orbits of Mars and Jupiter, some of them travel round the Sun in ellipses of great eccentricity, which occasionally allow them to pass very close by the Earth. In 1967, the minor planet Icarus passed within 4,258,000 miles, but this planet is so small that even the largest telescope will not show its form, and it was so faint that at least an 8-in. reflector was required to even catch a glimpse of it.

The brighter, larger asteroids such as Ceres (diameter 740 km.), Pallas (diameter 480 km.), Juno (diameter 200 km.) etc., are occasionally just at the extreme limit of naked-eye visibility. They are at these times readily picked up with 8 × 30 prismatics, but their position (in RA and Dec) must be sought from a handbook such as that published by the British Astronomical Association each year, or by consulting the US astronomical monthly periodical *Sky and Telescope*.

JUPITER

This is certainly one of the easiest to identify. It takes twelve years to make one orbit round the Sun and is therefore located in each particular zodiacal constellation for approximately one year's duration. It is the next-brightest after Venus and Mars, and at opposition is mag −2.3 and shines with a steady yellowish light.

By the standards of the other planets it is of a colossal size, having a diameter of 143,640 km. Opera glasses of the Galilean type will show its four brighter moons (supposing that one, or more, is not in transit or passing behind the planet). These four moons were discovered shortly after the invention of the telescope in 1610. History relates that it was Simon Marius who first saw them, nine days before Galileo, using a telescope with a power of ×7. Each of these moons is as large as the Earth and they revolve round Jupiter in regular fashion, similar to our own satellite. If one is interested in where they are to be located in relation to the planet, this information can be gleaned (via reference libraries) from *The Astronomical Ephemeris*.

Even with a small 2- or 3-in. refractor, the disc of Jupiter can be seen to be covered in parallel cloud belts which have irregularities, or spots, and which enable the observer to see the planet rotate in approximately 9 hours 50 minutes. The most famous of the irregularities is called the 'Red Spot', a permanent feature varying in colour (but not often red in spite of its name). A 3-in. refractor will often show it as a large, oval spot on a cloud belt known as the South Tropical Zone. It measures 48,000 km. long and 11,000 km. wide, and is thought to be a solid or quasi-solid mass floating in an ocean of dense gases.

SATURN

To many observers this planet is the most fascinating of all. Almost everyone has heard of the rings of Saturn and even in a small 2-in. telescope they are a wonderful object – and generally one of the first celestial lollipops that the new owner of a telescope views if the planet is visible in the night sky. At their widest phase-angle they are visible with 8 × 30 prismatics. If sought with small instruments, the rings are occasionally invisible. This occurs at regular intervals when the line of sight from the Earth passes through the ring plane. At these times, even with the largest of telescopes, they are lost from view for a day or so.

When Galileo first observed Saturn, he thought he was seeing *three* objects, owing to the inferior optical quality of his telescope. The true nature of Saturn and its system was not resolved until some time later by the seventeenth-century astronomer Huygens, who used a telescope having a focal length of 23 feet. The rings are not solid in the sense of a monolithic mass, but made up of myriads of smaller particles which give the appearance of solidity when they reflect sunlight. Each particle can be considered as a tiny satellite which revolves round the planet in a definite period of time. Probably they once formed a solid body, like the Moon, which came too close to the main body of the planet and was shattered into fragments by tidal forces. Saturn is 110,000 km. in diameter at the poles and 120,000 km. at the equator; it takes 29 years to orbit the Sun and at opposition reaches mag −0.2. Binoculars will often show Titan, the brightest satellite of Saturn, and a 3-in. telescope will show three more. Cloud belts similar to those of Jupiter, but less prominent, are often observed even with small telescopes, and, more rarely, large whitish spots which show that the planet rotates every 10.2 hours.

URANUS

This was the first of the planets to be discovered with the telescope, in 1781 by the German-born British astronomer William Herschel, who systematically examined the heavens with a self-constructed 7-in. reflecting telescope.

It is just a little too faint to be seen directly by naked-eye observation and generally shines at mag 6.0–6.5. A pair of opera glasses will allow it to be picked out from the field stars, and with prismatic binoculars it can be recognized by its characteristic, steady, pale-greenish light. But to make anything of the disc of the planet requires at least a 6-in. telescope. Sometimes with large instruments observers are able to detect faint belts across the planet, similar to those of Jupiter. Uranus has a diameter of 53,400 km., takes 84 years to orbit the Sun, and has a rotation period of 10.7 hours.

NEPTUNE

Discovered in 1846, after observations had shown that Uranus was slightly affected by some unseen body that lay beyond it. At its brightest, it shines at mag 7.7 and unless one has a chart showing stars fainter than say, mag 8.5, it is difficult to locate; although of course it can be located if the position is known, by plotting the field stars (which will include Neptune) from night-to-night observation. After an interval the planet will be identified as the object which has moved relatively to the 'fixed' stars. With a star atlas such as *Atlas Eclipticalis*, depicting stars to mag 9.0, it can be readily identified using 8 × 30 binoculars. Neptune has a diameter of 49,700 km., takes 165 years to orbit the Sun at a distance of 4,493 million km., and rotates in 14 hours.

PLUTO

With Pluto we reach the furthest known planet, at a distance which varies from thirty times the Earth's distance from the Sun to fifty times the distance, since it has a very eccentric orbit of a kind similar to some of the asteroids and comets. It was discovered in 1930 after a prolonged photographic search, lasting many years, conducted by the Lowell Observatory in Arizona. It cannot be seen with small instruments and requires at least a 15- to 18-in. telescope, and is never brighter than magnitude 14.5. Pluto is a small planet and its diameter is not known very accurately, but probably it is of the size of the Earth. It rotates once every 6.3 days, and its orbital period round the Sun takes 248.43 years.

COMETS

These, like the planets, belong permanently to the solar system, and are among the more spectacular transient objects; they are rarely misidentified as a star or planet by even the most inexperienced observer. However, by far the greatest majority of comets are very faint telescopic objects, and some can never be seen visually through even the largest telescopes. These faint comets can only be followed by employing long-exposure, deep-sky photography.

Each year, nevertheless, there are one or two comets which can be observed with binoculars or small telescopes. More rarely, there is a comet which can be seen with the naked eye and which may have a long, spectacular tail. One of these latter comets was Ikeya-Seki 1965, discovered independently by two young Japanese amateurs whose names are now perpetuated by it. Amateurs discover a good many comets and this is a field in which they can play a very important role.

The amateur stargazer should always be on the look-out for the sudden appearance of a spectacular comet. They have very long orbits which often bring them very close to the Sun's surface and then carry them away almost halfway towards the nearest stars. They are at their brightest when near the Sun, in the evening or morning skies, and they may appear at *any* time. Amateurs have discovered bright comets by regularly watching the skies after sunset and before dawn, and indeed many bright comets have been discovered by people totally unconnected with astronomy, simply because they happened to be looking in the right place at the right

44 Arend-Roland Comet, 1957.

time. Such an example occurred in 1961, when an airline hostess discovered a new comet while looking through the aircraft cabin window for the airport lights. Strangely enough, the same bright comet was also found by an airline pilot – a breed of men whose occupation gives them ample opportunities to spot a bright new comet in the morning skies.*

Comets must not be confused with meteors. Although comets do travel with high velocities, the naked-eye observer does not see this directly and a comet can only be seen to shift by night-to-night observations. Meteors, on the other hand, flash brilliantly across the sky and generally last only a second or so before completely extinguishing themselves.

The average comet, when observed through binoculars or small telescopes, shows no tail whatsoever and cannot usually at first glance be distinguished from a star cluster or nebula. Only by watching a suspicious object over a period of some hours, or from one night to the next one, to detect its movement in relation to the background stars, can it then be positively identified. However, some amateur astronomers become so familiar with the brighter nebulae and clusters that they know their position instinctively and a strange new object can be identified at once.

* Another brilliant comet, with a tail 8° long, was spotted by an Air France pilot, Emilio Ortiz, while flying across the Pacific on 21 May 1970.

METEORS

Although meteors are often referred to as 'shooting stars', they have no connection with stars whatsoever. Most meteors are tiny bodies, often smaller than a grain of sand. They are actually small particles literally revolving round the Sun in space like the planets and comets; in fact there is some definite genetic connection between comets and meteors, for often their orbits are practically identical. The ones we observe have orbits which happen to intercept the Earth's orbit, or others which pass sufficiently close by to be attracted by the Earth's gravitational field. They are travelling with such high velocities that when they hit the thick blanket of air surrounding the Earth, the friction of heat created burns them up long before they have opportunity to reach the ground. Occasionally the Earth encounters a swarm of such bodies, which gives rise to a meteor shower or storm. Each year there are a number of such showers when the Earth encounters the orbit of a particular group. The most spectacular of these displays, called the Leonids, occurs on or about 17 November (see p. 83). Sometimes a bright meteor will leave a persistent train or trail which may last for some seconds after the meteor itself has disappeared. In some rare instances such illuminated trains last for many minutes if the upper atmosphere is wind-free.

FIREBALLS

These objects are often called bolides – from the Greek word meaning 'to throw'. They should not be confused with terrestrial

45 Opposite: the Leonid meteor shower in 1966. Turn the figure through 90° anticlockwise and the 'Sickle' shape of Leo can be traced out. The star images are trailed owing to the time exposure of the photograph. The meteoroid paths can all be traced back to a point within the 'Sickle'.

46 Right: zodiacal light.

fireballs or thunderbolts, which are purely local phenomena connected with electrical storms.

A fireball differs from a meteor simply in classification, by the fact that it is brighter than mag -3.5, or (approximately) just a little fainter than Venus at average brightness. These brilliant fireballs are by no means rare occurrences, and regular observation outdoors will allow the stargazer to see a dozen or more each year. Fireballs are produced by pieces of cosmic material larger than that which gives rise to the less brilliant meteors. Often, if the chunk of matter is large enough, it produces an illumination in the night sky which momentarily turns night into day. If the object is larger still, it will not completely burn out during the passage through the atmosphere and will crash to the earth and form a crater. This is then classified as a meteorite, which can produce some very spectacular events including a great deal of frightening noises that are sometimes heard as much as fifteen miles away. The famous crater in Arizona was caused by such an object, and also the event which occurred in Siberia in 1908, where a forest was blasted by a swarm of meteorites. Surprisingly, records reveal that no human being is known to have been killed by the fall of such objects. If residing near an airfield, the observer should be warned about frequent green or red fireballs, which are certainly more likely to be Verey light shots from the pistol of a flight controller!

THE ZODIACAL LIGHT

The ability to see the Zodiacal Light depends very much on the location of the observer. It is more readily seen at different times of the year and is always seen better from the tropics.

The Zodiacal Light is the name given to a 'cone' of light located on or near the ecliptic, on the western horizon after sunset, and on the eastern horizon before dawn. Its origin has been ascribed to a concentration of small meteoritic particles or dust, in the same plane as the planetary orbits, which is rendered visible by sunlight. There is also a second, less conspicuous, component called the Gegenschein, sometimes referred to as the Counter-Glow, which lies at a point in the sky known as the anti-solar point. In addition there is also a possibility of the existence of dust concentrations trapped in orbits round the Earth, of which observations from high-flying aircraft have been reported, but their real nature is very uncertain at the present time.

At certain times of the year the Zodiacal Light is so bright that it has been nicknamed the 'false dawn' and it becomes very brilliant in tropical desert regions.

Aurorae or auroral displays

These are atmospheric disturbances caused by electrically charged particles from the Sun interacting with the magnetic field of the Earth. They take the form of sky glows, often of great brilliance and with rapid movement. Since they are most active near the magnetic polar regions, they can be more frequently observed in high latitudes; although at times of great activity on the Sun they give rise to brilliant displays that are sometimes to be observed near the equator. When observed in the northern hemisphere, they are called Aurora Borealis or Northern Lights, and in the southern hemisphere, Aurora Australis or Southern Lights.

The glows are often brilliantly coloured reds, greens and blues – almost every hue of the rainbow. Although nowadays it is not likely that anyone will mistake auroral activity for any other celestial object, yet in the past it is likely they were often confused with brilliant comets, especially those which the ancients described as being the colour of blood.

Artificial satellites

These objects and their carrier rockets are now extremely common in the sky. Many of the brighter ones can easily be picked out with the naked eye as they drift across the heavens. Some of these are extremely slow-moving objects and may momentarily startle the observer into thinking he has found a nova. Another characteristic is that one may suddenly disappear in mid-sky. This is owing to it passing into eclipse, for, like the planets, they are only rendered visible by reflected sunlight, and being located very close to us, they

47 Above: the Aurora Australis, or Southern Lights.

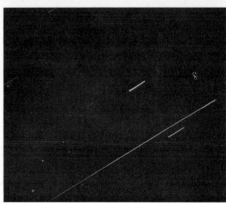

48 Right: photographic trail produced by an artificial satellite.

occasionally enter the Earth's shadow. The reverse phenomenon can be equally startling; suddenly to see a 1st-magnitude object flash into view never fails to increase the observer's adrenaline flow.

With the larger mounted binoculars such as 10 × 80's or 25 × 105's, a greater number of fainter satellites can be picked up, and they are very noticeable with wide-angle instruments during routine comet sweeps. They certainly distract the eye and it is difficult to resist following one, especially if it is 'tumbling', causing rapid changes in light as it revolves in its orbit round the Earth. The light-variation effect is due to varying surface areas periodically reflecting greater or less light in the line of sight of the observer.

Scattered throughout the world there is a very keen band of observers dedicated just to making regular observations of satellites in order to track their ever-changing paths. One British observer always uses a 19-in. reflecting telescope to follow many of the fainter ones – this telescope being almost as large as the one used by William Herschel in the late eighteenth century to discover the faint nebulae. However, it is at least three times shorter in focal length, which makes it much more manœuvrable for rapid changes in elevation.

Space probes

Similar in many respects to the artificial satellites, these differ a little in some instances, such as with the lunar probe Apollo 10, in 1968, when shortly after launch it appeared at times like a naked-eye comet. On this occasion the author's telephone rang continuously for at least two hours while the 'new comet' was spotted shortly after dark, above the south-western British horizon, by a host of keenly dedicated young observers who wished him to confirm their discoveries.

Such phenomena are bound to recur in the future when the activities of various national space programmes gain impetus and increase in frequency. To date such probes have not been seen visually after leaving the vicinity of the Earth, but it could well be different when larger, more powerful vehicles are dispatched, or when orbiting staging posts become established.

Postscript

If you wish to meet other sky-observers like yourself, then join a local or national astronomical society. Don't be afraid of being a beginner; remember we all were at the start. One can glean a great deal of 'inside' knowledge by fraternizing with more experienced observers, and they will also be able to answer those queries that crop up from time to time, and which are never answered satisfactorily in any book.

National astronomical societies catering principally for
amateur observational astronomy:

Canada
Royal Astronomical Society of Canada.
252 College Street, Toronto, Ontario.

USA
The Association of Lunar and Planetary Observers (ALPO).
University Park, New Mexico, 88001.
The American Association of Variable Star Observers (AAVSO).
187 Concord Ave., Cambridge, Mass. 02138.
The American Meteor Society (AMS).
512 North Wynnewood Ave., Narberth, Penn. 19702.

Great Britain
The British Astronomical Association (BAA).
Burlington House, London W.1.
Junior Astronomical Society (JAS).
58 Vaughan Gardens, Ilford, Essex. (In spite of its name, there are
no age limits in this society!)

In addition, there are hundreds of friendly local societies and stargazing groups in Great Britain, the USA and Canada who are happy
to see new members. Addresses can be found at local public libraries
and in Year Books of Astronomy, and they are also often mentioned
in the popular US monthly periodical *Sky and Telescope*.

Table of planetary positions, 1971–1980

The tables provided below enable the observer to locate any of the naked-eye planets on any date between January 1971 and December 1980. The planet positions are tabulated at 10-day intervals and are given in Celestial Longitude, a co-ordinate which is measured in an anti-clockwise direction along the ecliptic to the nearest whole degree. The deep-sky star charts also show the plane of the ecliptic (or apparent paths of the planets and Sun). At the top edge of the deep-sky charts is shown the Celestial Longitude at 10° intervals, to coincide with the equivalent hours and minutes of Right Ascension shown along the bottom edge of the charts. It will be seen that it is a simple matter to convert RA to CL and vice-versa, i.e. 1 hour RA = 15° CL. When the date of observation falls between the tabulated 10-day intervals, a simple fractional estimate will provide a sufficiently accurate position for any planet to be located.

Example: To locate Mars on 3 January 1973, note that the date falls between the entries 28 December 1972 and 7 January 1973. Select the appropriate chart for celestial longitudes 238° and 245° (or alternatively find the correct chart by reference to Table 1 (below), which shows the appropriate CL for the different zodiacal constellations). In pencil, lightly plot both longitudes on the chart on the line of the ecliptic, and then by fractional proportion mark lightly the estimated position for 3 January.

From time to time, all the planets vary slightly in their paths along the ecliptic owing to their different orbital inclinations. But the brighter planets will never be more than 7° north or south of the ecliptic (often much less) and they are still sufficiently close to make recognition easy. It will also be noticed that when a planet is located in that part of the ecliptic south of (below) the Celestial Equator, it will appear much lower in the observer's sky than when it is north of (above) the Celestial Equator. This is an important factor to bear in mind when planning telescopic observations, since a planet low down in the sky will often be greatly affected by atmospheric disturbances, and you will probably have bad 'seeing' (p. 42).

It must also be borne in mind that a planet is often located near the Sun and, therefore, will not normally be visible unless a telescopic search is made in the daytime sky. To assist the observer in deciding whether a particular planet is visible in the night or daytime sky, the position of the Sun is also tabulated at similar 10-day intervals, and this information, when plotted, will provide a guide to the suitability of any planet for observation in the night sky by bearing in mind its angular relationship to the Sun at any given date.

In the particular case of Mercury, whenever the longitudinal distance from the Sun is near to, or greater than, 25° this indicates the most likely occasion when the planet may be spotted with the naked eye, or when it may be easily picked up with binoculars. However, this again depends on the time of year, and the most favourable occasion is when the ecliptic is inclined at the maximum angle to the observer in either the evening or morning skies. In the case of Mars, the middle of the most favourable occasion, when it can be observed through the entire night, is marked with ★.

The list below will assist the observer to quickly locate the zodiacal constellation in which a brighter planet is situated at any particular time by reference to its celestial longitude in the Planetary Tables that follow.

celestial longitude	constellation
0° – 26°	Pisces
26° – 50°	Aries
50° – 89°	Taurus
89° – 119°	Gemini
119° – 140°	Cancer
140° – 174°	Leo
174° – 215°	Virgo
215° – 239°	Libra
239° – 245°	Scorpius
245° – 265°	Ophiuchus
265° – 301°	Sagittarius
301° – 329°	Capricornus
329° – 351°	Aquarius
351° – 0°	Pisces

DATE	SUN	MERCURY	VENUS	MARS	JUPITER	SATURN	DATE	SUN	MERCURY	VENUS	MARS	JUPITER	SATURN
1971 Apr 8	18	34	341	286	246	51	1972 May 12	52	29	91	90	278	67
1971 Apr 18	28	31	353	292	246	52	1972 May 22	61	46	95	97	278	69
1971 Apr 28	37	24	5	297	245	53	1972 Jun 1	71	66	94	103	277	70
1971 May 8	47	23	17	303	244	55	1972 Jun 11	80	89	89	109	276	72
1971 May 18	57	31	29	308	242	56	1972 Jun 21	90	108	83	115	274	73
1971 May 28	66	43	41	314	241	58	1972 Jul 1	99	124	77	122	273	74
1971 Jun 7	76	60	53	318	240	59	1972 Jul 11	109	136	76	128	271	75
1971 Jun 17	85	80	66	320	239	60	1972 Jul 21	119	142	80	134	270	76
1971 Jun 27	95	103	78	322	238	61	1972 Jul 31	128	140	85	141	269	77
1971 Jul 7	104	122	90	323	237	62	1972 Aug 10	138	133	93	147	269	78
1971 Jul 17	114	138	103	324	237	63	1972 Aug 20	147	130	101	153	268	79
1971 Jul 27	123	151	115	323	236	64	1972 Aug 30	157	139	111	160	268	79
1971 Aug 6	133	159	127	320	237	65	1972 Sep 9	167	157	121	166	269	80
1971 Aug 16	143	160	140	315*	237	65	1972 Sep 19	176	176	132	173	269	80
1971 Aug 26	152	153	152	313	238	66	1972 Sep 29	186	194	143	179	270	80
1971 Sep 5	162	147	164	312	239	66	1972 Oct 9	196	210	154	186	271	80
1971 Sep 15	172	154	177	312	240	66	1972 Oct 19	206	225	166	192	273	80
1971 Sep 25	182	170	189	314	242	67	1972 Oct 29	216	239	178	198	274	81
1971 Oct 5	191	189	202	315	243	67	1972 Nov 8	226	249	190	205	276	80
1971 Oct 15	201	206	214	318	245	66	1972 Nov 18	236	253	202	212	278	79
1971 Oct 25	211	222	227	322	247	66	1972 Nov 28	246	241	214	218	280	78
1971 Nov 4	221	238	239	328	249	65	1972 Dec 8	257	237	227	225	282	77
1971 Nov 14	231	252	252	333	251	64	1972 Dec 18	267	246	239	232	284	76
1971 Nov 24	241	264	264	340	253	63	1972 Dec 28	277	259	252	238	287	75
1971 Dec 4	252	269	277	346	256	61	1973 Jan 7	287	274	264	245	289	74
1971 Dec 14	262	259	289	352	258	60	1973 Jan 17	297	290	277	252	291	73
1971 Dec 24	272	252	302	358	261	59	1973 Jan 27	307	306	289	259	294	73
1972 Jan 3	282	259	314	5	263	59	1973 Feb 6	317	324	302	266	296	73
1972 Jan 13	292	272	326	12	265	59	1973 Feb 16	328	342	315	273	298	73
1972 Jan 23	303	286	338	18	267	58	1973 Feb 26	338	356	327	280	300	73
1972 Feb 2	313	302	350	24	269	58	1973 Mar 8	348	358	340	287	303	74
1972 Feb 12	323	319	2	31	271	59	1973 Mar 18	358	349	352	294	305	74
1972 Feb 22	333	337	14	38	273	59	1973 Mar 28	8	345	4	301	306	75
1972 Mar 3	343	356	26	44	274	60	1973 Apr 7	17	350	17	308	308	76
1972 Mar 13	353	12	37	51	276	61	1973 Apr 17	27	0	29	315	309	77
1972 Mar 23	3	16	48	57	277	61	1973 Apr 27	37	14	41	322	310	78
1972 Apr 2	13	10	59	64	278	62	1973 May 7	47	32	54	329	311	79
1972 Apr 12	23	4	69	70	278	64	1973 May 17	56	52	66	336	312	81
1972 Apr 22	32	6	78	77	279	65	1973 May 27	66	75	79	343	312	82
1972 May 2	42	15	86	84	279	66	1973 Jun 6	75	94	91	350	312	83

DATE	SUN	MERCURY	VENUS	MARS	JUPITER	SATURN
1973 Jun 16	85	109	103	357	312	85
1973 Jun 26	94	119	116	4	312	86
1973 Jul 6	104	123	128	10	311	87
1973 Jul 16	114	120	140	16	310	89
1973 Jul 26	123	113	152	22	308	89
1973 Aug 5	133	114	164	28	306	90
1973 Aug 15	142	125	176	33	305	91
1973 Aug 25	152	143	188	37	304	92
1973 Sep 4	162	163	200	39	303	93
1973 Sep 14	171	181	211	40	302	94
1973 Sep 24	181	198	223	40	302	94
1973 Oct 4	191	213	235	38	302	94
1973 Oct 14	201	226	246	36★	302	95
1973 Oct 24	211	235	257	32	303	94
1973 Nov 3	221	236	268	27	304	94
1973 Nov 13	231	224	278	25	305	94
1973 Nov 23	241	222	288	24	306	93
1973 Dec 3	251	232	297	25	308	93
1973 Dec 13	261	246	304	26	310	92
1973 Dec 23	272	262	309	28	312	91
1974 Jan 2	282	278	313	32	314	90
1974 Jan 12	292	294	311	37	317	89
1974 Jan 22	302	311	306	41	319	88
1974 Feb 1	312	328	300	46	321	87
1974 Feb 11	322	341	296	51	324	87
1974 Feb 21	332	340	297	57	326	87
1974 Mar 3	342	330	301	63	329	87
1974 Mar 13	352	327	308	68	331	88
1974 Mar 23	2	335	316	73	333	88
1974 Apr 2	12	346	325	79	335	89
1974 Apr 12	22	1	335	85	337	89
1974 Apr 22	32	18	346	91	340	90
1974 May 2	42	38	357	97	342	91
1974 May 12	51	61	8	103	343	93
1974 May 22	61	80	19	109	345	94
1974 Jun 1	70	94	31	115	346	95
1974 Jun 11	80	102	42	121	347	96
1974 Jun 21	89	103	54	128	347	97
1974 Jul 1	99	97	66	134	348	99
1974 Jul 11	109	94	77	140	348	100

DATE	SUN	MERCURY	VENUS	MARS	JUPITER	SATURN
1974 Jul 21	118	97	89	146	347	102
1974 Jul 31	128	110	101	152	348	103
1974 Aug 10	137	129	114	159	347	104
1974 Aug 20	147	150	128	165	345	105
1974 Aug 30	157	169	139	171	344	106
1974 Sep 9	166	185	151	177	342	106
1974 Sep 19	176	200	163	184	341	107
1974 Sep 29	186	212	176	191	339	108
1974 Oct 9	196	220	188	197	338	108
1974 Oct 19	206	219	201	204	338	109
1974 Oct 29	216	207	213	211	337	109
1974 Nov 8	226	207	226	218	338	109
1974 Nov 18	236	218	238	224	338	109
1974 Nov 28	246	234	251	231	339	109
1974 Dec 8	256	250	264	238	340	108
1974 Dec 18	266	266	276	245	341	108
1974 Dec 28	276	281	289	253	342	107
1975 Jan 7	287	298	301	260	344	105
1975 Jan 17	297	314	314	267	346	104
1975 Jan 27	307	325	326	274	348	103
1975 Feb 6	317	322	339	281	350	103
1975 Feb 16	327	312	351	289	353	102
1975 Feb 26	337	312	4	296	355	102
1975 Mar 8	347	320	16	304	357	102
1975 Mar 18	357	332	28	312	0	102
1975 Mar 28	7	347	41	319	2	102
1975 Apr 7	17	5	53	327	5	103
1975 Apr 17	27	25	65	334	7	103
1975 Apr 27	36	46	76	342	9	104
1975 May 7	46	65	88	349	12	105
1975 May 17	56	78	99	357	14	106
1975 May 27	65	83	110	4	17	107
1975 Jun 6	75	81	120	12	18	108
1975 Jun 16	84	75	131	19	20	110
1975 Jun 26	94	74	140	27	21	111
1975 Jul 6	103	82	148	33	22	112
1975 Jul 16	113	96	155	40	24	114
1975 Jul 26	123	115	160	47	24	115
1975 Aug 5	132	137	162	54	24	116
1975 Aug 15	142	156	160	60	25	117

DATE	SUN	MERCURY	VENUS	MARS	JUPITER	SATURN
1975 Aug 25	151	172	154	66	25	118
1975 Sep 4	161	187	149	72	24	119
1975 Sep 14	171	198	145	77	23	120
1975 Sep 24	181	205	146	82	22	121
1975 Oct 4	190	202	150	86	21	122
1975 Oct 14	200	190	156	90	19	122
1975 Oct 24	210	192	164	92	18	123
1975 Nov 3	220	205	174	93	16	123
1975 Nov 13	230	221	184	92	15	123
1975 Nov 23	240	237	194	89	14	123
1975 Dec 3	251	253	206	87	14	123
1975 Dec 13	261	269	217	83★	14	123
1975 Dec 23	271	285	229	79	14	122
1976 Jan 2	281	300	241	76	15	122
1976 Jan 12	291	310	253	74	16	121
1976 Jan 22	302	304	265	73	18	120
1976 Feb 1	312	294	277	74	19	119
1976 Feb 11	322	296	289	77	21	118
1976 Feb 21	332	306	302	80	22	117
1976 Mar 2	342	319	314	83	24	117
1976 Mar 12	352	334	326	87	27	116
1976 Mar 22	2	352	339	92	29	116
1976 Apr 1	12	11	351	97	31	116
1976 Apr 11	22	32	4	102	33	116
1976 Apr 21	31	51	16	107	36	117
1976 May 1	41	61	28	112	39	118
1976 May 11	51	63	41	117	41	118
1976 May 21	60	58	53	123	44	119
1976 May 31	70	54	65	128	46	120
1976 Jun 10	79	56	78	134	48	121
1976 Jun 20	89	66	90	140	50	122
1976 Jun 30	99	82	102	146	52	123
1976 Jul 10	108	101	114	152	54	124
1976 Jul 20	118	123	127	158	56	126
1976 Jul 30	127	143	139	164	58	127
1976 Aug 9	137	159	152	171	59	129
1976 Aug 19	146	173	164	177	60	130
1976 Aug 29	156	183	176	183	61	131
1976 Sep 8	166	188	189	190	61	132
1976 Sep 18	175	183	201	196	61	133
1976 Sep 28	185	174	213	203	61	134
1976 Oct 8	195	177	225	210	60	135
1976 Oct 18	205	191	237	216	60	136
1976 Oct 28	215	208	249	223	58	137
1976 Nov 7	225	225	262	230	58	137
1976 Nov 17	235	241	274	237	56	137
1976 Nov 27	245	257	286	244	54	138
1976 Dec 7	256	272	298	252	53	137
1976 Dec 17	266	286	309	259	52	137
1976 Dec 27	276	294	321	267	51	137
1977 Jan 6	286	287	332	274	50	136
1977 Jan 16	296	277	343	281	50	135
1977 Jan 26	306	282	354	289	51	134
1977 Feb 5	317	292	3	297	51	134
1977 Feb 15	327	306	12	305	53	133
1977 Feb 25	337	321	19	312	54	132
1977 Mar 7	347	339	23	320	53	131
1977 Mar 17	357	358	25	328	57	131
1977 Mar 27	7	18	22	335	59	130
1977 Apr 6	16	36	16	343	60	130
1977 Apr 16	26	45	10	361	63	130
1977 Apr 26	36	43	7	359	65	131
1977 May 6	46	36	9	7	67	131
1977 May 16	55	34	13	15	69	132
1977 May 26	65	40	20	22	72	133
1977 Jun 5	74	52	28	30	74	133
1977 Jun 15	84	68	38	37	77	134
1977 Jun 25	94	87	48	44	79	135
1977 Jul 5	103	110	58	51	81	136
1977 Jul 15	113	129	69	58	83	137
1977 Jul 25	122	146	80	65	85	138
1977 Aug 4	132	159	91	72	87	140
1977 Aug 14	141	168	103	79	89	141
1977 Aug 24	151	171	114	85	91	143
1977 Sep 3	161	164	126	92	93	144
1977 Sep 13	170	157	138	97	94	145
1977 Sep 23	180	162	150	103	95	146
1977 Oct 3	190	178	162	108	95	147
1977 Oct 13	200	196	175	113	96	148
1977 Oct 23	210	212	187	118	96	149

DATE	SUN	MERCURY	VENUS	MARS	JUPITER	SATURN	DATE	SUN	MERCURY	VENUS	MARS	JUPITER	SATURN
1977 Nov 2	220	229	200	122	96	150	1978 Dec 7	255	252	220	266	129	164
1977 Nov 12	230	244	213	126	95	150	1978 Dec 17	265	245	224	273	128	164
1977 Nov 22	240	259	225	129	95	151	1978 Dec 27	275	253	231	281	128	164
1977 Dec 2	250	272	238	131	93	151	1979 Jan 6	286	266	240	289	126	164
1977 Dec 12	260	278	251	132	92	151	1979 Jan 16	296	281	249	297	125	164
1977 Dec 22	271	269	263	131	91	151	1979 Jan 26	306	297	259	304	123	163
1978 Jan 1	281	261	276	128	89	151	1979 Feb 5	316	313	270	312	122	163
1978 Jan 11	291	267	288	125★	88	151	1979 Feb 15	326	331	281	320	121	162
1978 Jan 21	301	279	301	121	87	150	1979 Feb 25	336	349	293	328	120	162
1978 Jan 31	311	293	313	117	86	149	1979 Mar 7	346	5	304	336	119	161
1978 Feb 10	321	309	326	114	86	148	1979 Mar 17	356	9	316	344	119	159
1978 Feb 20	331	326	338	112	86	147	1979 Mar 27	6	1	328	352	119	159
1978 Mar 2	341	344	351	111	86	146	1979 Apr 6	16	355	340	359	119	158
1978 Mar 12	351	4	3	112	86	146	1979 Apr 16	26	359	352	7	120	158
1978 Mar 22	1	20	16	114	87	145	1979 Apr 26	36	9	3	15	121	158
1978 Apr 1	11	27	28	117	88	144	1979 May 6	45	22	15	23	121	158
1978 Apr 11	21	22	41	120	90	144	1979 May 16	55	39	27	30	123	158
1978 Apr 21	31	15	53	124	91	144	1979 May 26	64	60	40	38	124	158
1978 May 1	41	16	66	128	93	144	1979 Jun 5	74	82	52	45	126	159
1978 May 11	50	24	78	133	95	144	1979 Jun 15	84	102	64	52	128	159
1978 May 21	60	36	90	138	97	145	1979 Jun 25	93	117	76	59	130	160
1978 May 31	69	53	102	143	99	146	1979 Jul 5	103	129	89	66	132	161
1978 Jun 10	79	74	114	148	101	146	1979 Jul 15	112	134	101	74	134	162
1978 Jun 20	89	96	126	153	103	147	1979 Jul 25	122	132	113	81	136	163
1978 Jun 30	98	116	137	159	106	148	1979 Aug 4	131	125	126	87	138	164
1978 Jul 10	108	132	149	165	108	149	1979 Aug 14	141	123	138	94	140	165
1978 Jul 20	117	144	160	171	110	150	1979 Aug 24	151	133	150	100	143	166
1978 Jul 30	127	152	171	177	112	151	1979 Sep 3	160	150	163	107	145	167
1978 Aug 9	136	152	182	183	115	152	1979 Sep 13	170	170	175	113	147	168
1978 Aug 19	146	144	192	189	117	153	1979 Sep 23	180	188	188	119	149	170
1978 Aug 29	156	140	202	196	119	155	1979 Oct 3	190	205	200	125	151	171
1978 Sep 8	165	147	211	202	121	156	1979 Oct 13	199	220	212	131	153	172
1978 Sep 18	175	164	219	209	122	157	1979 Oct 23	209	233	225	136	154	173
1978 Sep 28	185	183	227	216	124	159	1979 Nov 2	219	243	237	141	156	174
1978 Oct 8	195	200	231	222	125	160	1979 Nov 12	229	246	250	146	157	175
1978 Oct 18	205	217	234	229	127	161	1979 Nov 22	240	234	262	151	158	175
1978 Oct 28	215	232	232	237	128	162	1979 Dec 2	250	230	275	155	159	176
1978 Nov 7	225	246	227	244	128	162	1979 Dec 12	260	239	288	158	159	176
1978 Nov 17	235	258	221	251	129	163	1979 Dec 22	270	253	300	161	160	177
1978 Nov 27	245	262	218	258	129	163	1980 Jan 1	280	269	312	164	160	177

DATE		SUN	MERCURY	VENUS	MARS	JUPITER	SATURN
1980 JAN	11	290	284	324	165	160	178
1980 JAN	21	301	301	336	165	159	177
1980 JAN	31	311	318	349	163	158	177
1980 FEB	10	321	335	1	161★	157	177
1980 FEB	20	331	349	12	157	155	176
1980 MAR	1	341	351	24	153	154	176
1980 MAR	11	351	341	36	150	153	175
1980 MAR	21	1	337	46	147	152	174
1980 MAR	31	11	343	57	146	151	173
1980 APR	10	21	354	67	145	150	172
1980 APR	20	30	8	76	147	150	172
1980 APR	30	40	26	84	149	150	171
1980 MAY	10	50	46	89	152	151	171
1980 MAY	20	59	68	92	156	151	171
1980 MAY	30	69	88	92	160	152	172
1980 JUN	9	79	102	87	164	153	172
1980 JUN	19	88	112	80	169	154	173
1980 JUN	29	98	115	75	174	156	173
1980 JUL	9	107	111	74	179	157	174
1980 JUL	19	117	105	77	185	159	175
1980 JUL	29	126	107	83	191	161	175
1980 AUG	8	136	118	91	197	163	176
1980 AUG	18	145	136	99	203	165	177
1980 AUG	28	155	157	109	210	167	178
1980 SEP	7	165	175	119	216	169	179
1980 SEP	17	175	192	130	223	171	180
1980 SEP	27	184	207	141	229	174	182
1980 OCT	7	194	220	152	236	176	183
1980 OCT	17	204	228	164	244	178	184
1980 OCT	27	214	229	176	251	180	185
1980 NOV	6	224	217	188	258	182	186
1980 NOV	16	234	215	200	266	184	187
1980 NOV	26	244	226	212	273	185	187
1980 DEC	6	255	241	225	281	187	188
1980 DEC	16	265	256	237	288	187	189
1980 DEC	26	275	272	250	296	188	189
1981 JAN	5	285	288	262	304	189	190

Charts

Seven charts covering the sky from $+90°$ Declination to $-40°$ Declination depicting all naked eye stars and deep-sky objects described in the seasonal texts, and for use in conjunction with the planet finder tables (pp. 188–92).

NORTHERN STARS

Chart			page
1	RA 00^{h}40^m to 11^{h}20^m — — — —	Dec $+30°$ to $+90°$	194–5
2	RA 8^{h}40^m to 19^{h}20^m — — — —	Dec $+30°$ to $+90°$	196–7
3	RA 16^{h}40^m to 3^{h}20^m — — — —	Dec $+30°$ to $+90°$	198–9

EQUATORIAL AND ZODIACAL STARS

4	RA 21^{h}20^m to 4^{h}40^m	CL 320° to 70°	Dec $+40°$ to $-40°$	200–1
5	RA 2^{h}40^m to 10^{h}00^m	CL 40° to 150°	Dec $+40°$ to $-40°$	202–3
6	RA 9^{h}20^m to 16^{h}40^m	CL 140° to 250°	Dec $+40°$ to $-40°$	204–5
7	RA 16^{h}00^m to 23^{h}20^m	CL 240° to 350°	Dec $+40°$ to $-40°$	206–7

SOUTHERN SKY CHART (principal stars)   208–9

VARIABLE STAR FINDER CHARTS   210–14

In these, each small square represents an area of sky measuring approx. $3° \times 3°$, and shows the position of each variable star by a small circle. The brighter field comparison stars assist identification and enable magnitude estimates to be made.

To observe a particular variable star, find its general location on the relevant deep-sky chart (via the index). Then, using binoculars or a small telescope, first identify the brighter field stars surrounding it. When you go outdoors, remember to allow time for your eyes to become adapted fully to night vision, and when referring to this book, use only a dim light (preferably red).

Remember that long-period variables may be at minimum brightness and therefore beyond range with binoculars or small telescopes.

When a small number appears alongside a comparison star, it refers to its magnitude. The decimal point is omitted to avoid ambiguity, e.g. 93 = mag 9.3.

Generally speaking, the majority of field stars are beyond naked eye visibility. The faintest stars depicted are about mag 10, but in some charts of the brighter variables, the fainter stars are omitted since they are not required for purposes of identification.

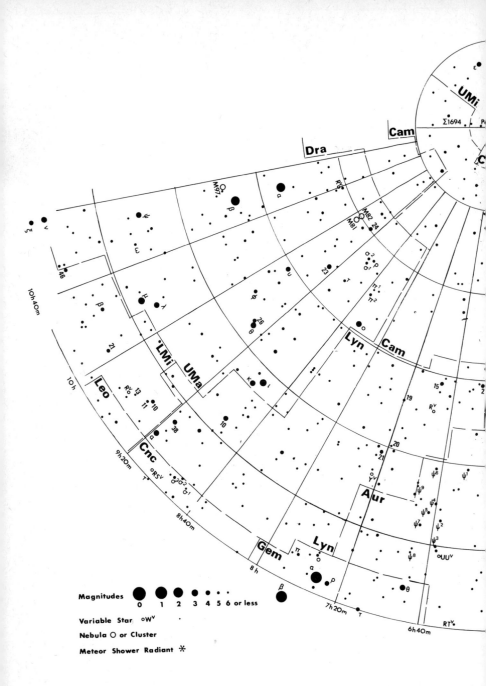

Magnitudes ● ● ● ● ● ● ● 6 or less
0 1 2 3 4 5

Variable Star ○W^V ·

Nebula ○ or Cluster

Meteor Shower Radiant ✳

194

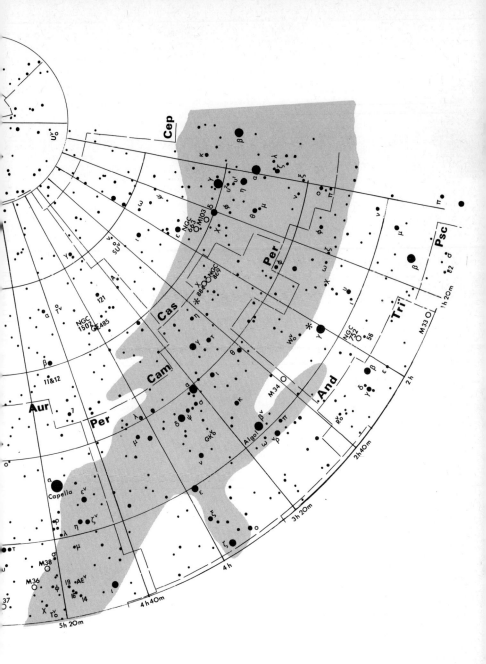

Cep

Per

Psc

Cas

Tri

Cam

And

Aur

Per

Algol

Capella

NGC 1502
NGC 1485
121
11&12

NGC 663
M103
NGC 869
NGC 884

M34

NGC 752
56
M33

M38
M36

19 AE
16 14

5h 20m
4h 40m
4h
3h 20m
2h 40m
2h
1h 20m

195

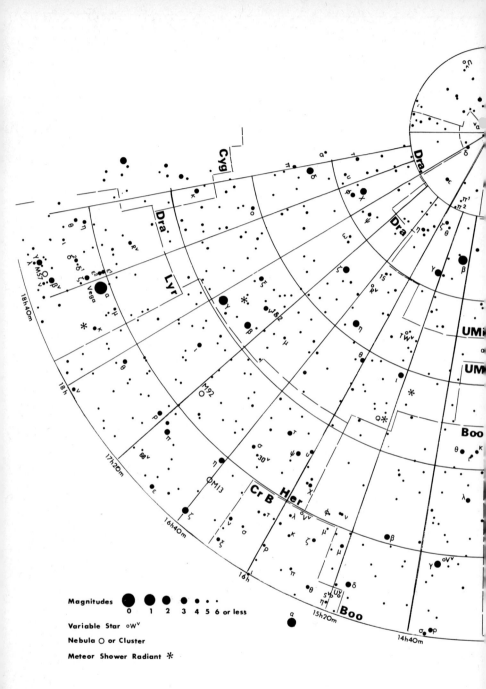

Magnitudes ● ● ● ● · · ·
              0   1   2   3 4 5 6 or less

Variable Star ○W^V

Nebula ○ or Cluster

Meteor Shower Radiant ✳

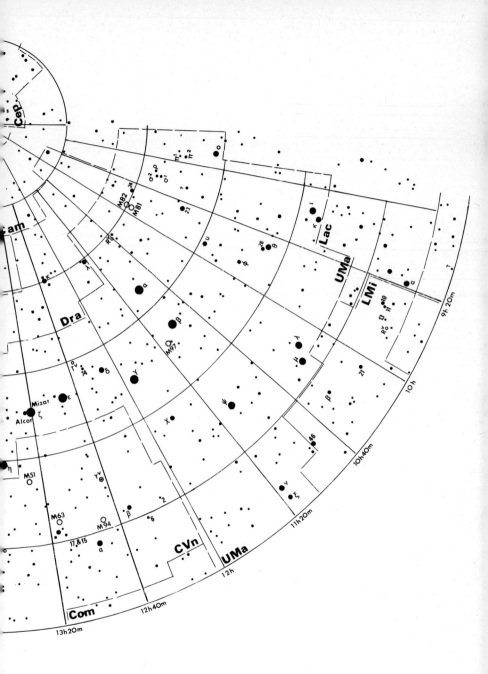

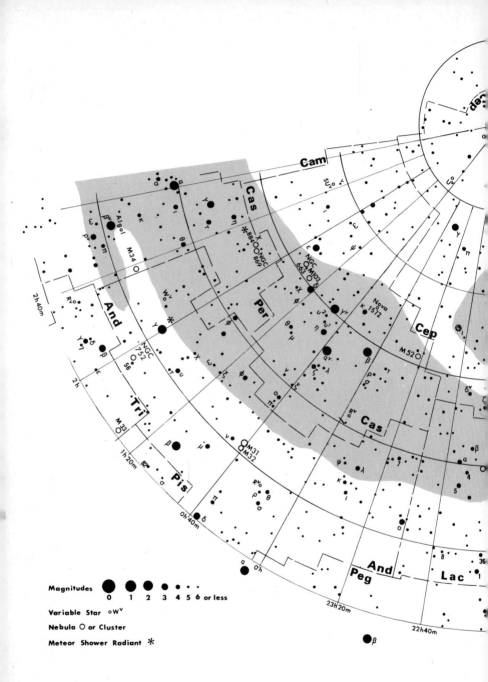

Cam

Cas

Per

Cep

Nova 1572

M52 O

Cas

Algol

M34 O

And

2h40m

NGC 752

Tri

M33

Pis

M31
M32

2h

1h20m

0h40m

0h

And

Peg

Lac

23H20m

22h40m

β

Magnitudes ● ● ● ● ● · · ·
0 1 2 3 4 5 6 or less

Variable Star o W v

Nebula O **or Cluster**

Meteor Shower Radiant *

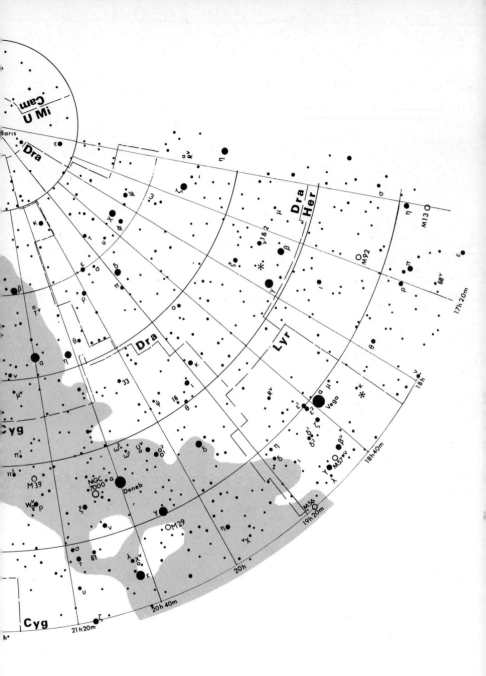

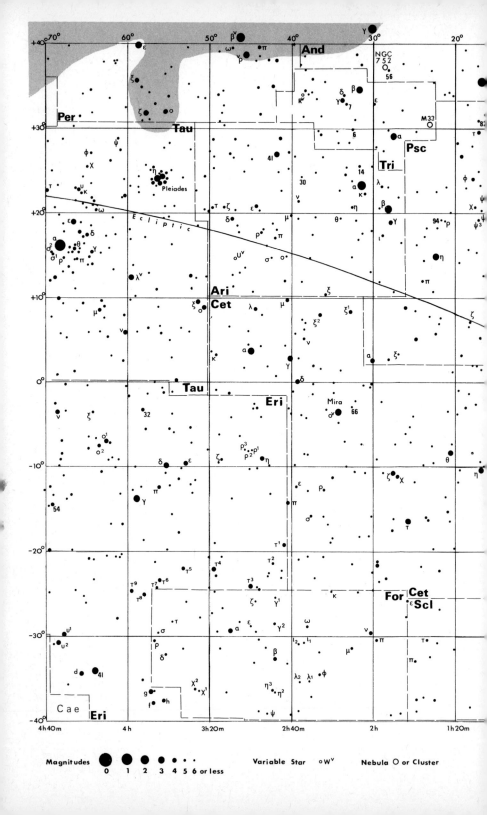

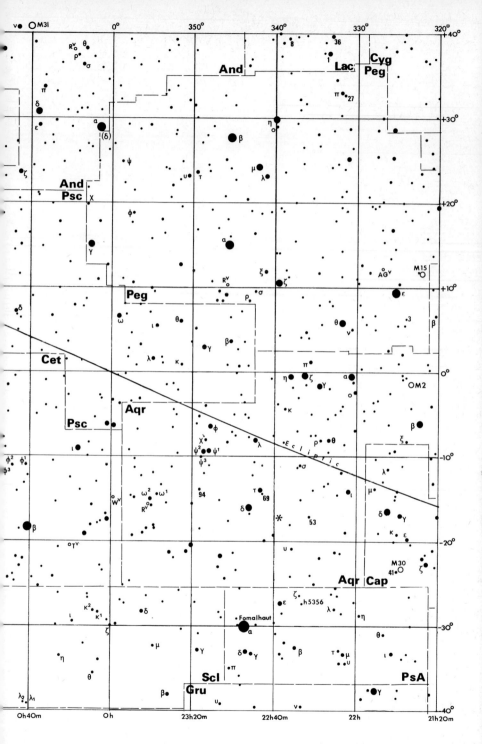

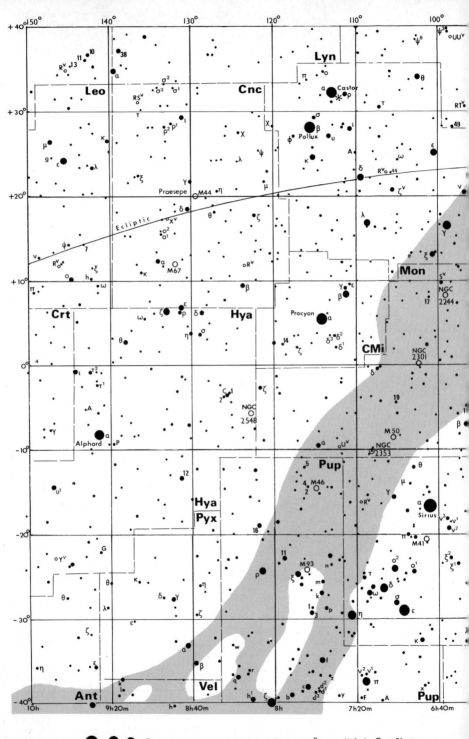

Magnitudes ● ● ● ● · · ·
0 1 2 3 4 5 6 or less

Variable Star ○Wᵛ

Nebula ○ or Cluster

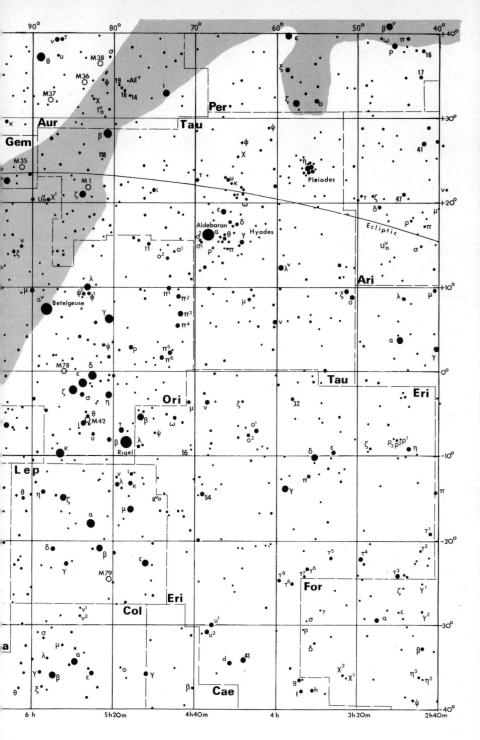

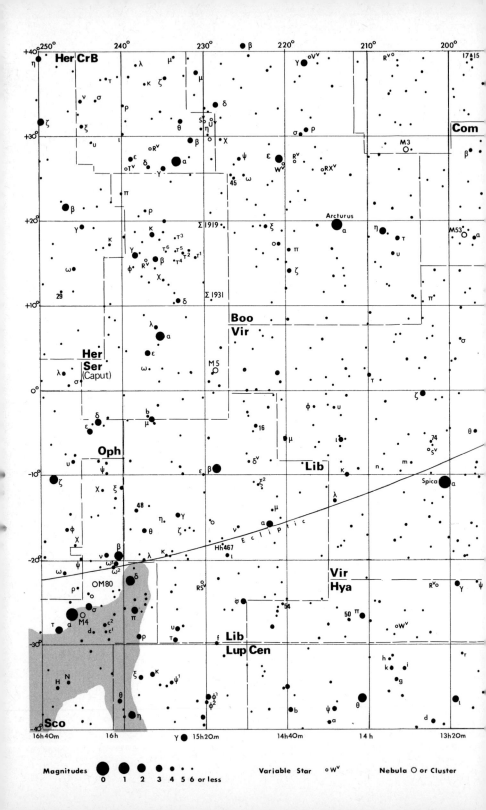

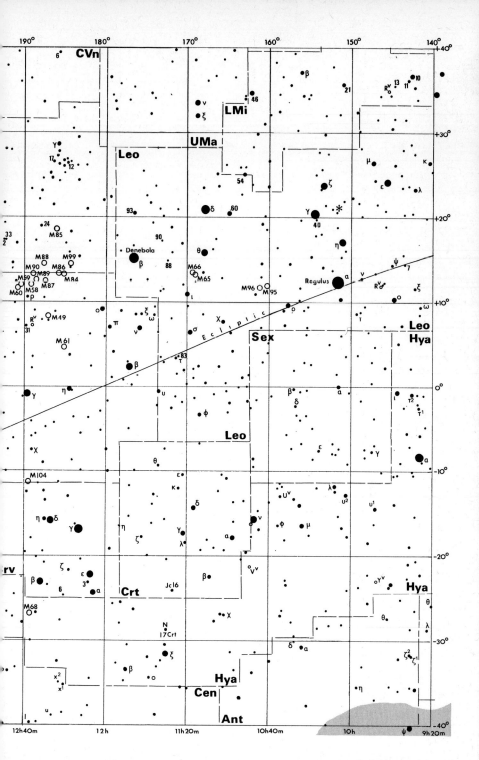

Meteor Shower Radiant ✳

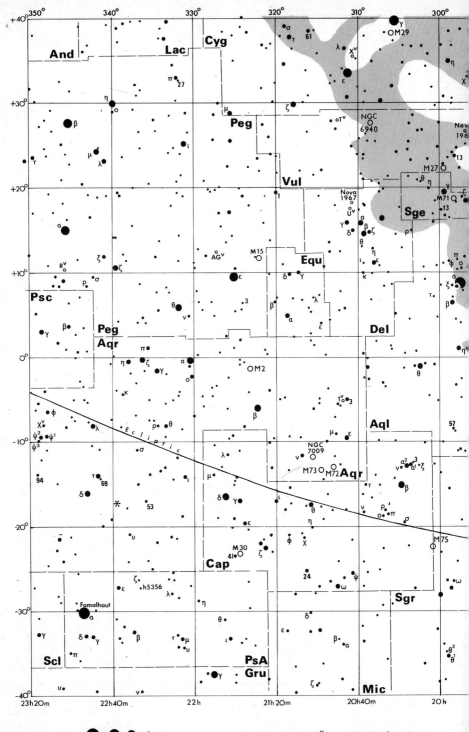

Magnitudes ● ● ● ● ● · · · Variable Star ○wᵛ Nebula ○ or Cluster
0 1 2 3 4 5 6 or less

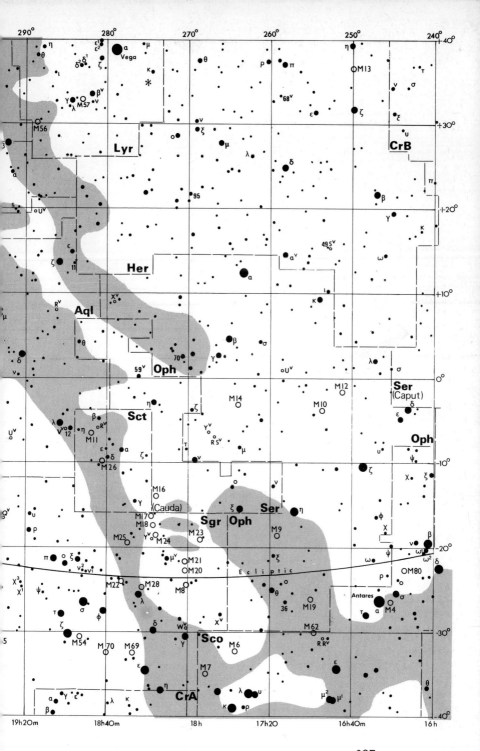

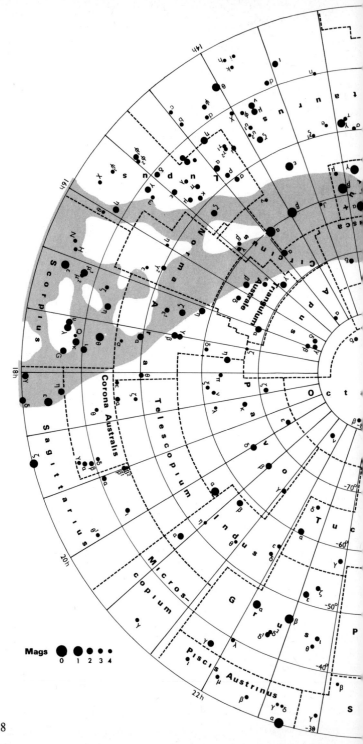

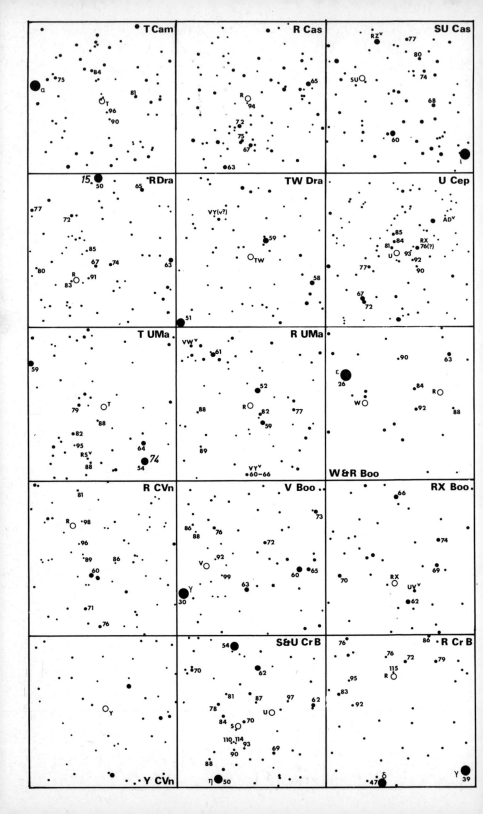

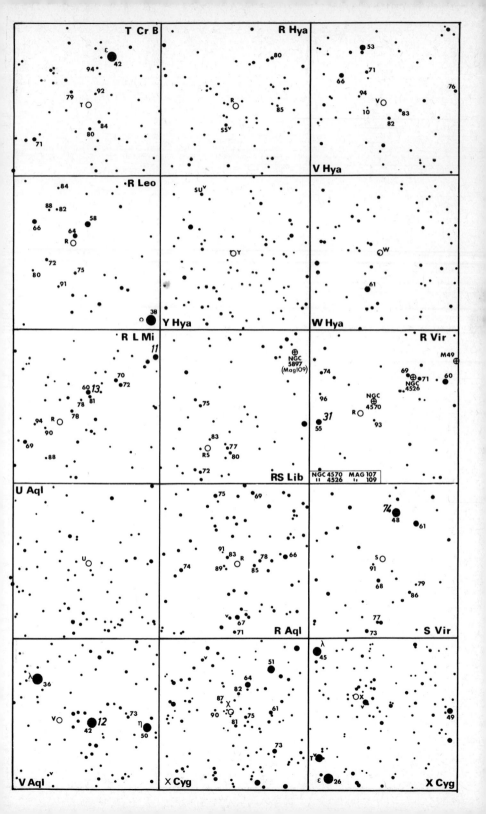

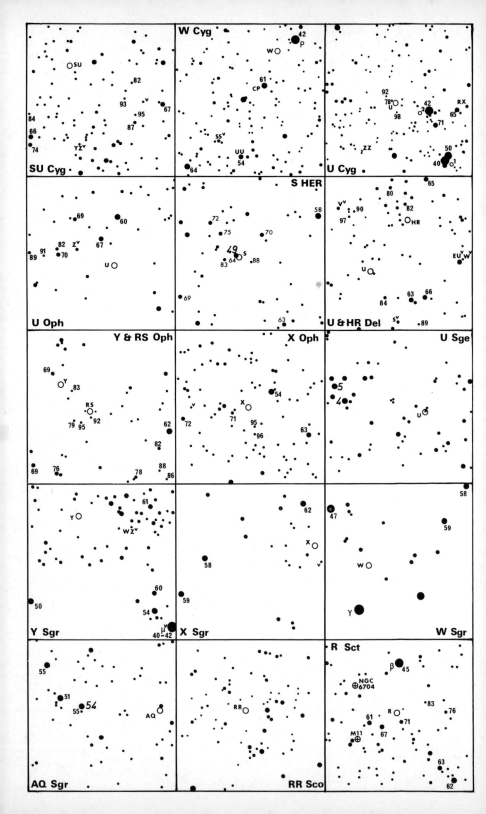

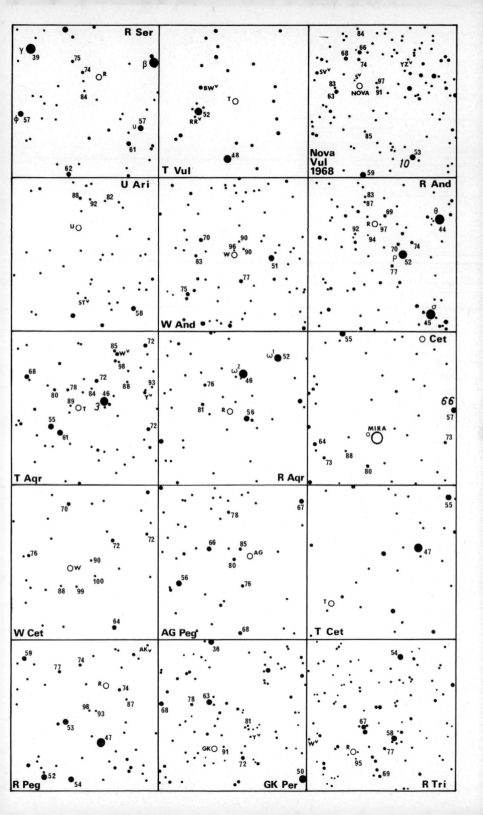

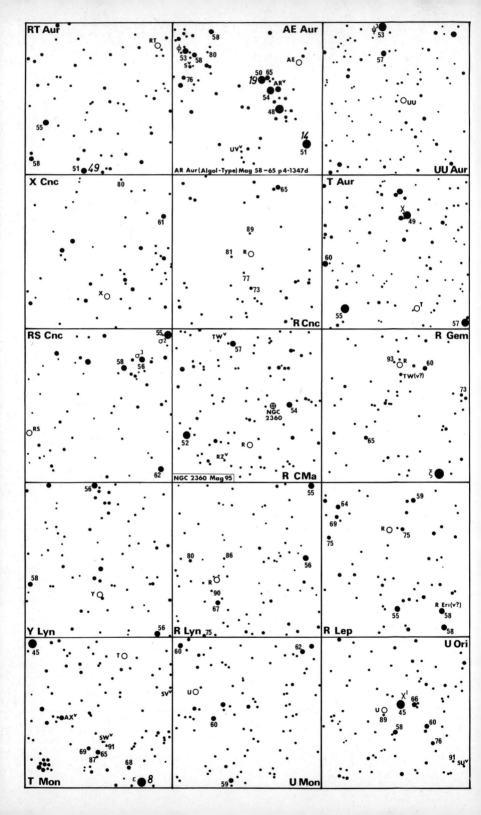

RT Aur

RT

55

58   51 *49*

AE Aur

58
φ
53 58   80
SΦ
76

50 65
19   AR^V
54
48

14
51

UV^V

AR Aur (Algol-Type) Mag 58–65 p 4·1347d

ψ^3
53

57

○ UU

UU Aur

X Cnc

80

61

X ○

R Cnc

65

89

81   R ○

77
73

T Aur

X
49

60

55

○^T

57

RS Cnc

55
σ^2

σ^3
58   56

○ RS

62

R CMa

TW^V
57

NGC
2360

54

52   R ○

RZ^V

NGC 2360 Mag 95

R Gem

93 ○ R   60
TW(v?)

73

65

ξ

Y Lyn

56

58

Y ○

56

R Lyn

55

80   86

56

R ○
90
67

75

R Lep

64
69
75

R ○   75

59

55

R Eri(v?)
58
58

T Mon

45

T ○

SV^V

AX^V

SW^V
91
69   65
87   68

ε
8

U Mon

60

U ○

60

59

62

U Ori

X^1
U ○   45   66
89
58   60
76

91
SU^V

Naked–eye variables

Type Descriptions

SR   Semi-regular stars.
EA   Eclipsing binary stars of Algol-type.
δ Cep   Delta-Cepheid-type variables.
β Lyr   Beta Lyrae-type variables.
Irr   Irregular period stars.
LP   Long period stars.
N   Novae-type stars.
★   Difficult naked-eye object.
†   Naked-eye only at maximum.

Variable	RA 1950.0		Decl 1950.0		Magnitudes MAX	MIN	Period (DAYS)	Type
TV Psc	00h	25ᵐ4	+17°	37′	4.6	5.2	49.1	SR
α Cas	00	37.7	+56	16	2.5	3.1	–	Irr
YZ Cas★	00	42.3	+74	43	5.6	6.0	4.467	EA
γ Cas	00	53.7	+60	27	1.6	3.0	–	Irr
o Cet	02	16.8	−03	12	2.0	10.1	331.48	LP
ρ Per	03	02.0	+38	39	3.2	3.8	50?	SR
β Per	03	04.9	+40	46	2.2	3.5	2.8673	EA
BU Tau★	03	46.2	+23	59	5.0	5.5	–	Irr
λ Tau	03	57.9	+12	21	3.5	4.0	3.9530	EA
ε Aur	04	58.4	+43	45	3.7	4.5	9883	EA
ζ Aur	04	59.0	+41	00	5.0	5.6	972.162	EA
AE Aur★	05	13.0	+34	15	5.4	6.1	–	Irr
α Ori	05	52.5	+07	24	0.4	1.3	2070	SR
η Gem	06	11.9	+22	31	3.1	3.9	233.4	SR
ζ Gem	07	01.1	+20	39	4.3	5.1	10.1535	δ Cep
VZ Cam	07	20.7	+82	31	4.8	5.2	23.7	SR
U Hya	10	35.1	−13	07	4.8	5.8	–	Irr?
R Hya†	13	27.0	−23	01	3.5	10.9	387	LP
δ Lib★	14	58.3	−08	19	4.8	5.9	2.3273	EA
χ Oph	16	24.1	−18	21	4.4	5.0	–	N
α Sco	16	26.3	−26	19	1.2	1.8	1733	SR

Variable	RA 1950.0		Decl 1950.0		Magnitudes MAX	MIN	Period (days)	Type
30 (g) Her★	16h	27m0	+41°	59'	4.6	6.0	80	SR
μ¹ Sco	16	48.5	−37	58	3.0	3.3	1.4463	β Lyr
α¹ Her	17	12.4	+14	27	3.0	4.0	100	SR
μ Her	17	15.5	+33	09	4.6	5.1	2.0510	β Lyr
X Sgr★	17	44.4	−27	49	5.0	6.1	7.0122	δ Cep
β Lyr	18	48.2	+33	18	3.4	4.3	12.9080	β Lyr
R Lyr	18	53.8	+43	53	4.0	5.0	50	SR
χ Cyg†	19	48.6	+32	47	2.3	14.3	406.66	LP
η Aql	19	49.9	+00	53	3.9	5.1	7.1766	δ Cep
o¹ Cyg★	20	12.1	+46	35	4.9	5.3	3803	EA
P Cyg	20	15.9	+37	53	3.0(?)	6.0(?)	–	N
T Cyg★	20	45.2	+34	11	5.0	5.5	–	Irr
μ Cep	21	42.0	+58	33	3.6	5.1	–	SR
δ Cep	22	27.3	+58	10	3.9	5.0	5.3663	δ Cep
β Peg	23	01.3	+27	49	2.4	2.8	–	Irr
ρ Cas	23	51.9	+57	13	4.1	6.2	–	Irr
R Cas†	23	55.9	+51	07	4.8	13.6	430.93	LP

Except for the brighter members, variable stars are generally denoted by Roman capitals beginning with R and then continuing alphabetically through to Z in order of discovery. When the number of variables in a constellation increased to more than nine, the letters were doubled, i.e. RR, RS etc. to ZZ. Later the entire alphabet (excepting J) was used: AA, BC etc. Nowadays *new* variable stars are denoted by a number preceded by V, thus V350 Sco means the 350th variable star in Scorpius.

Indexes

INDEX OF STARS

Some of the names are only rarely encountered nowadays, but they are included as they often occur in literature and in the older star atlases. Stars shown on a map but not mentioned in the text are shown thus: 204m. Italic figures indicate main reference. Alternative names in italics.

ACHERNAR α Eri 144, *145*
ACHERNAR θ Eri *see* Acamar
ACHIRD η Cas 56
ACRAB β Sco *see* Graffias
ACUBENS α Cnc *Sertan 139*
ADARA ε CMa *Undara 143*
ADHAFERA ζ Leo *82*
AIN ε Tau *see* Oculus boreus
ALAMAC γ And *118*
ALARAPH β Vir *see* Zavijara
AL BALI ε Aqr *Albali 121*
ALBIREO β Cyg 96, 106, 114
ALCAID η UMa *see* Benetnasch
AL CHIBA α Crv *Alchita 78*
ALCOR 80 UMa 63
ALCYONE η Tau 157, *159*
ALDEBARAN α Tau *Palilicium 29*, 82, 135, 153, 157, *158*
ALDERAMIN α Cep *58*
ALDIB δ Dra *61*
ALFIRK β Cep *Alphirk 58*
ALGENIB γ Peg *Mirfak 117, 127*
ALGENIB α Per *Marfak, Mirfak, Mirzac 117, 129*
ALGENUBI ε Leo *Ras Elased Australis 82*
ALGIEBA γ Leo *82*
ALGOL β Per *Gorgona, the 'Demon Star' 48*, 49, 117, 129
ALGORES δ Crv *Algorab 78*
ALHAJOTH α Aur *see* Capella *137*
ALIOTH ε UMa *63*
AL KAFF AL JIDHMAH γ Cet *Kaffaljidhma 124*
ALKAID η UMa *see* Benetnasch
ALKALUROPS μ Boo *204m*
ALKES α Crt *79*
AL MA'AZ ε Aur *137*
ALMEISAN γ Gem *Alhena 148*
ALNAIR α Gru *208m*
AL NASL γ Sgr *Nushaba, Nash 108*
ALNILAM ε Ori *153*
ALNITAK ζ Ori *154*

ALPHARD α Hya *Alfard 79*, 80
ALPHECCA α CrB *Gnosia, Gemma 76*
ALPHERATZ α And *Sirrah* 117, *118*, 126, *127*
ALRAI γ Cep *see* Errai
ALRAMI α Sgr *see* Rukbat
AL RISCHA α Psc *Rescha, Alrisha, Okda, Kaitain 131*
ALRUCCABAH α UMi *see* Polaris
ALSHAIN β Aql *92*
ALSUHAIL λ Vel *209m*
ALTAIR α Aql 89, *92*, 93, 95, 104, 106, 107, 113
ALTARF β Cnc *139*
ALUDRA η CMa *143*
ALULA AUSTRALE ξ UMa *64*
ALULA BOREALE ν UMa *197m*, 205m
ALWAID β Dra *see* Rastaban
ALYA θ Ser *113*
ANCHA θ Aqr *121*
ANGETENAR τ² Eri *145*
ANSER α Vul *114*
ANTARES α Sco *Vespertilio 82*, 84, 91, 105, 109, *110*
ARCTURUS α Boo 36, 37, 71, 72, 75, 84, 85, 86, 101
ARICH γ Vir *see* Porrima
ARIDIF (ARIDED) α Cyg *see* Deneb
ARKAB, URKAB β¹, β² Sgr *Arkab Prior, Arkab Posterior 108*
ARNEB α Lep *150*
ARRAKIS μ Dra *197m*, *198m*
ASCELLA ζ Sgr *108*
ASELLUS AUSTRALIS δ Cnc *139*
ASELLUS BOREALIS γ Cnc *139*
ASTERION β CVn *see* Chara
ASTEROPE 21 Tau *Sterope 157, 160*
ATIKS o Per *195m*, *200m*
ATLAS 27 Tau *160*
AUVA δ Vir *87*
AZELFAFAGE π¹ Cyg *199m*

AZHA η Eri *145*
AZIMECH α Vir *see* Spica
AZMIDISKE ξ Pup *156*

BATEN KAITOS ζ Cet *Al Batnal Kaitos 124*
BEID o¹ Eri *145*
BELLATRIX γ Ori *153*
BENETNASCH (BENATNASCH) η UMa *Alcaid, Alkaid 64*
BETELGEUSE α Ori 135, 143, *153*
BOTEIN δ Ari *123*

CANICULA α CMa *see* Sirius
CANOPUS α Car *Suhel 165*, 166
CAPELLA α Aur *Alhajoth 89*, 91, 117, 128, 136, *137*, 138
CAPH β Cas *Kaff 56*
CAPUT TRIANGULI α Tri *Metallah, Mothallah 133*
CASTOR α Gem 19, 135, 146, *147–8*, 149
CEBALRAI β Oph *Kelb Alrai 105*
CEGINUS φ Boo *204m*
CELAENO 16 Tau 157, *160*
CHARA β CVn *Asterion 74*, 75
COR CAROLI α CVn *Chara 73*, 74, 75
COR HYDRAE α Hya *see* Alphard
COR SERPENTIS α Ser *see* Unukalhai
COXA θ Leo *82*
CURSA β Eri *145*
CYNOSURA α UMi *see* Polaris

DABIH MAJOR, DABIH MINOR β Cap *94*
DEMON STAR β Per *see* Algol
DENEB α Cyg *Aridif, Deneb Cygni 89*, 95, 96, 107, 113
DENEB ε Aql *92*
DENEB ζ Aql *92*
DENEB η Cet *Dheneb 125*
DENEB ALGEDI δ Cap *Algiedi, Scheddi 94*

DENEB KAITOS *1* Cet *125*
DENEB KAITOS *β* Cet *see Diphda*
DENEB OKAB *δ* Aql *92*
DENEBOLA *β* Leo *71, 73, 82, 85*
DHENIB *η* Cet *see Deneb*
DIADEM *α* Com *73–4*
DIPHDA *β* Cet *Deneb Kaitos 124*
DOG STAR *α* CMa *see Sirius*
DSCHUBBA *δ* Sco *110*
DUBHE *α* UMa *62–3*
DZIBAN *ψ* Dra *196m, 199m*

ELACRAB *β* Sco *see Graffias*
ELECTRA *17* Tau *157, 160*
ELGOMAISA *α* CMi *Procyon*
EL NATH *β* Tau *137, 158*
ELTAMIN *γ* Dra *Etamin, Rastaban 60*
ENIF *ε* Peg *128*
ERAKIS *μ* Cep *the 'Garnet Star' 59*
ERRAI *γ* Cep *Alrai 58*
ETA CARINAE *165–6*

FOMALHAUT (FUM AL HUT) *α* PsA *82, 117, 120, 132*
FUM AL SAMAKAH *β* Psc *131*
FURUD *ζ* CMa *143*

GARNET STAR *see Erakis*
GEMMA *α* CrB *see Alphecca*
GIANFAR *λ* Dra *61*
GIEDI *α* Cap *Gredi, Algedi, Dabih, Schedor 94*
GIENAH *γ* Crv *78*
GIENAH *ε* Cyg *96*
GNOSIA *α* CrB *see Alphecca*
GOMEISA *β* CMi *144*
GORGONA *β* Per *see Algol*
GRAFFIAS *β* Sco *Grappine, Acrab, Elacrab 110*
GREDI *α* Cap *see Giedi*
GRUMIUM *ξ* Dra *61*

HAMAL *α* Ari *122, 123*
HARIS *γ* Boo *see Seginus*
HASSALEH *ι* Aur *138*
HATYSA *ι* Ori *154*
HEKA *λ* Ori *154*
HEZE *ζ* Vir *87*
HOEDUS I *ζ* Aur *138*
HOEDUS II *η* Aur *138*
HOMAN *ζ* Peg *Homam 128*
HYADUM I *γ* Tau *Prima Hyadum 158*
HYADUM II *δ* Tau *158*

IZAR *ε* Boo *see Pulcherrima*

KAFFA *δ* UMa *see Megrez*
KAFFALJIDHMA *γ* Cet *see Al Kaff al Tidmah*
KAITAIN *α* Psc *see Al Rischa*
KAJAM *ω* Her *204m, 207m*
KALB *α* Leo *see Regulus*
KAUS AUSTRALIS *ε* Sgr *108*
KAUS BOREALIS *λ* Sgr *108*
KAUS MEDIUS *δ* Sgr *see Media*
KELB ALRAI *β* Oph *see Cebalrai*
KERB *τ* Peg *201m, 206m*
KIFFA AUSTRALIS *α* Lib *84*
KIFFA BOREALIS *β* Lib *84*
KITALPHA *α* Equ *99*
KOCHAB *β* UMi *66*
KORNEFOROS *β* Her *Kornephoros, Rutilicus 100*
KORNEPHOROS *β* Her *see Korneforos*
KRAZ *β* Crv *78*
KSORA *δ* Cas *see Ruchbah*
KUMA *ν* Dra *61*

LA SUPERBA Y CVn *75*
LESATH *ν* Sco *110*

MAASYM *λ* Her *207m*
MAIA *20* Tau *see Maya*
MARKAB *α* Peg *see Markeb, Menkib*
MARKEB *α* Peg *Markab, Menkib 117, 127*
MARKEB *κ* Pup *156*
MARSIK *κ* Her *100*
MATAR *η* Peg *128*
MAYA *20* Tau *Maia 157, 160*
MEBSUTA *ε* Gem *148*
MEDIA *δ* Sgr *Kaus Medius 108*
MEGREZ *δ* UMa *Kaffa 63*
MEKBUDA *ζ* Gem *148*
MENKAB *α* Cet *see Menkar*
MENKALINAN *β* Aur *Menkalina 137*
MENKAR *α* Cet *Mekab 124*
MENKHIB *ζ* Per *130*
MENKIB *β* Peg *see Markeb*
MERAK *β* UMa *63*
MEREZ *β* Boo *see Nakkar*
MEROPE *23* Tau *157, 160*
MESARTHIM *γ* Ari *Mesartim 123*
METALLAH *α* Tri *see Caput Trianguli*
MIAPLACIDUS *β* Car *209m*
MINELAUVA *δ* Vir *87*
MINKAR *ε* Crv *78*
MINTAKA *δ* Ori *153*
MIRA *ο* Cet *125*

MIRACH *β* And *118*
MIRAK *ε* Boo *see Pulcherrima*
MIRAM *η* Per *130*
MIRFAK *α* Per *see Algenib, Marfak*
MIRZAM *β* CMa *see Murzim*
MISAM *κ* Per *194m*
MIZAR *ζ* UMa *63*
MOTHALLAH *α* Tri *see Caput Trianguli*
MUFRID *η* Boo *see Muphrid*
MULIPHEIN *γ* CMa *see Muliphen*
MULIPHEN *γ* Oph *Muliphein 105*
MULIPHEN *γ* CMa *Muliphein, Mirza 143*
MUPHRID *η* Boo *Mufrid 72*
MURZIM *β* CMa *Mirzam 143*
MUSEIDA *π²* UMa *194m, 197m*

NAKKAR *β* Boo *Nekkar, Merez 72*
NAOS *ζ* Pup *156*
NASH *γ* Sgr *see Al Nasl*
NASHABA *γ* Sgr *see Al Nasl*
NASHIRA *γ* Cap *94*
(EL) NATH *β* Tau *137, 158*
NEKKAR *β* Boo *see Nakkar*
NIHAL *β* Lep *150*
NODUS I *ζ* Dra *61*
NODUS II *δ* Dra *61*
NUNKI *σ* Sgr *108*
NUSAKAN *β* CrB *76*
NUSHABA *γ* Sgr *see Al Nasl*

OCULUS BOREUS *ε* Tau *Ain 158*
OKDA *α* Psc *Al Rischa*

PALILICIUM *α* Tau *see Aldebaran*
PHAD (PHEKDA) *γ* UMa *63*
PHAKT *α* Col *209m*
PHERKAD *γ* UMi
PHERKAD *δ* UMi *see Yildun*
PLEIONE *28* Tau *160*
'POINTERS' *α, β* UMa *32, 41, 62*
POLARIS *α* UMi *Cynosura, Alruccabah 12, 32, 65–6, 101*
POLLUX *β* Gem *135, 138, 146, 147, 148*
PORRIMA *γ* Vir *Arich 86*
PRAESEPE (M44) *ε* Cnc *139–40*
PROCYON *α* CMi *Elgomaisa 71, 135, 143, 144*
PROPUS *η* Gem *Tejat Prior 148*
PROXIMA CENTAURI *see also α Centauri 165*
PULCHERRIMA *ε* Boo *Izar, Mirak 72*

RANA δ Eri *145*
RASALAS μ Leo *Ras Elased Borealis* 82
RAS ALGETHI α Her *100*
RAS ALHAGUE α Oph 104, *105*
RAS ELASED AUSTRALIS ε Leo see *Algenubi*
RAS ELASED BOREALIS μ Leo see *Rasalas*
RASTABAN β Dra *Alwaid* 60
REDA γ Aql see *Tarazed*
REGULUS α Leo *Kalb* 71, *81*, 85, 86
REṢCHA α Psc see *Al Rischa*
RIGEL β Ori 135, 144, 145, *153*
RIGEL KENT α Cen see *Toliman*
ROTANEV β Del *Rotaneb*
RUCHA δ Cas see *Ruchbah*
RUCHBAH δ Cas *Rucha, Ksora* 56
RUKBAT α Sgr *Alrami* 108
RUTILICUS β Her see *Korneforos*

SABIK η Oph *105*
SADACHBIA γ Aqr *Sadalachbia* 121
SADALACHBIA γ Aqr see *Sadachbia*
SA'D AL BARI λ Peg *128*
SADALMELIK α Aqr *121*
SADALSUD β Aqr see *Sadalsund*
SADALSUND β Aqr *Sadalsud* 121
SADOR γ Cyg see *Sadr*
SADR γ Cyg *Sador* 96
SAIPH η Ori *154*
SAIPH κ Ori *154*
SARIN δ Her *100*
SCEPTRUM 53 Eri (54 Eri), 200m, 203m
SCHEAT β Cap see *Deneb Algedi*

SCHEAT β Peg *Menkib* 117, *127*
SCHEDAR α Cas *Shadar, Schedir* 56
S DORADUS *167*
SEGIN ε Cas *56*
SEGINUS γ Boo *Haris* 72
SERTAN α Cnc see *Acubens*
SHAM(?) α Sge *107*
SHARATAN β Ari *Sheratan* 123
SHAULA λ Sco *110*
SHELIAK β Lyr *Shelyak, Shiliak* 102
'SHEPHERD'S STAR' α Aur see *Capella*
SHERATAN β Ari see *Sharatan*
SIRIUS α CMa *Canicula, Dog Star* 10, 34, 135, 141–3, 144, 146, 150, 153, 155, 165, 166
SIRRAH α And see *Alpheratz*
SITULA κ Aqr *121*
SKAT δ Aqr *121*
SPICA α Vir 71, 77, 85, 86
STEROPE I, II 21, 22 Tau see *Asterope*
SUBRA ο Leo 202m, 205m
SUHEL α Car see *Canopus*
SULAFAT γ Lyr *Sulaphat* 102
SVALOCIN(?) α Del *also Sualocin(?)* 98

TABIT π³ Ori 203m
TALITHA ι UMa 64
TANIA AUSTRALIS μ UMa 64
TANIA BOREALIS λ UMa 64
TARAZED γ Aql *Reda* 92
TAYGETE 19 Tau 157, *160*
TEGMINE ζ Cnc *Tegman* 139
TEJAT POSTERIOR μ Gem *148*
TEJAT PRIOR η Gem see *Propus*

THEEMIN υ² Eri 203m
THUBAN α Dra 60
TOLIMAN α Cen *Rigel Kent* 208m
TUREIS ι Car 209m
TYL ε Dra 61

UNUKALHAI α Ser *Unuk al hay, Unuk Elhaia, Cor Serpentis* 113

VEGA α Lyr *Wega* 75, 77, 89, 93, 95, 101, 104
VESPERTILIO α Sco see *Antares*
VINDEMIATRIX ε Vir *Almuredin* 87

WASAT δ Gem *Wesat* 148
WEGA α Lyr see *Vega*
WEZAN δ CMa 143

YAD δ Oph *Yed Prior* 105
YED POSTERIOR ε Oph 204m, 207m
YED PRIOR δ Oph *Yad* 105
YILDUN δ UMi *Pherkard* 66

ZARIJAN β Vir see *Zavijara*
ZAURAC γ Eri 145
ZAVIJAH β Vir see *Zavijara*
ZAVIJARA β Vir *Zarijan, Zavijah, Alaraph* 86
ZIBAL ζ Eri 200m, 203m
ZOSMA δ Leo *Duhr* 82
ZUBEN ELAKRAB γ Lib 84
ZUBEN ELAKRIBI δ Lib 84
ZUBEN ELGENUBI α Lib 84
ZUBEN ELSCHEMALI β Lib 84
ZUBEN HAKRABI ν Lib 204m

GENERAL INDEX

Figures in italics indicate the main reference.

Aaron 169
abbreviations and conventions 52, 53
Abel the Just 170
aborigines, Australian 24, 76, 141, 159, 165
Abraham 170
agriculture, association with stars 7, 11
Aiken, R. G. 125
Akkadian culture 11, 68

Alcock, G. E. D. 41, 77, 98, 112, 114–15, 171
Almagest 10
Al-Sufi 16, 129
Anderson, Dr Thomas 130, 138
Andromeda nebula (M31) 44, 117, 119
Andromedids, meteor shower 120
Apian, Peter 16
Aquarids, meteor shower 122

Aratus of Soli 10, 16, 20, 67, 83, 92, 99, 126, 128, 132, 140, 151, 158
Argelander, F. W. A. 20, 129
Aristotle 68
Armenia 13
artificial satellite 182–4
Asia Minor 13
asteroids 149, 175
astrology, 9, 10, 79, 108, 110, 121, 123, 157

Astronomical Ephemeris 176
Astronomical Telegrams,
  Central Bureau for (I.A.U.)
  171
Atlante Farnese globe 15, 166
Atlas Eclipticalis 177
aurora 50, 182
averted vision 45

Babylonians 11, 13, 120, 146
Backer, R.J. 20
Baltic Sea 164
Barnard, E.E. 115
Bartschius 55, 151, 152
Bathsheba 56
Bayer, Dr Johann 19, 20, 22,
  29, 78, 125, 140, 162, 164,
  166, 167, 168, 169, 170
Bede, the Venerable 22
Berlin Observatory 95
Bessel, W. 96, 142, 144
Biblical figures, representing
  constellations 22; *see also*
  Schiller
Biela's Comet 120
binoculars 37, 38, 39, 40, 41,
  42; field of view, 38, 41;
  numbers of stars visible with,
  27; performance, 52, 53
Birmingham, John 76
Blaeu, Willem 22
Blaze Star 76
Bode, Johann 31, 126
Borgian Globe 83
Bradley, James 60, 147
Brahe, Tycho 16, 17, 20, 57,
  80, 85, 92
British Association Catalogue
  29
Brunowski 106

Caelum Heraldicum 23
Cape Clouds *see* Magellanic
  Clouds
Cape of Good Hope 163, 165
Cape Town 168
Carlyle, Thomas 8
celestial co-ordinates 30
celestial equator 30
celestial poles 32, 34
celestial sphere 19
Cellarius 22
Ceres (minor planet) 175
Chaldeans 7, 11, 121
Charles II 75, 163
Chiltern hills 7
Chinese astronomy 24–5, 161

Chinese star maps 24
Christian saints, depicted in
  constellations 22; *see also*
  Schiller
chromatic aberration 39
circles, telescope setting 31
circumpolar stars 32, 34, 164
Clark, Alvan 142
clock time 34
clothing, for observation 46, 47
comet, 61, 86, 110, 120, 123,
  131, 171, 178–9, 182;
  Halley's 25, 148
comet hunting 77
constellations, boundaries of
  31, 151; origins of 9–25;
  origins of figures, 14, 16, 32
Air Pump *see* Antlia
Altar *see* Ara
American Goose (obsolete
  name) *see* Tucana
Andromeda 117, *118–20*,
  126, 128, 129, 131, 133
Anser (the Goose) *see*
  Vulpecula
Antinous (obsolete name) *see*
  Aquila
Antlia 166
Apis, the Bee (obsolete
  name) *see* Musca
Apus 166
Aquarius 11, 16, *120–2*
Aquila 67, 89, *91–3*, 97, 101,
  111, 112, 113, 114
Ara 67, 166
Archer, the *see* Sagittarius
Argo Navis (obsolete name)
  155, 165 *see* Carina, Vela,
  Puppis
Aries 11, 22, *122–3*, 124, 131,
  133
Arrow, the *see* Sagitta
Auriga 67, 72, 93, *136–8*,
  157, 158
Balance, the *see* Libra
Bear Driver, the *see* Boötes
Belt of Orion *see* Orion
Berenice's Hair *see* Coma
  Berenices
Bier, the *see* Ursa Major
Bird of Paradise, the *see* Apus
Boötes *71–3*, 74, 85, 89, 137
Bull, the *see* Taurus
Caelum *166*
Camelopardalis 55
Cancer 79, *138–41*
Canes Venatici 72, 73, *74–5*

Canis Major 67, 135, *141–3*,
  155
Canis Minor 135, *143–4*, 152
Capricornus 92, *93–5*, 120,
  139
Carina 67, 155, 165, *165–6*
Cassiopeia 16, *56–7*, 71, 91,
  117, 118, 128
Censor, the *see* Ara
Centaur, the *see* Centaurus
Centaurus 67, *164–5*, 166
Cepheus 45, *57–60*, 67, 118
Cetus 123–5
Chained Lady, the *see*
  Andromeda
Chamaeleon *166*
Chariot, the *see* Ursa Major
Charioteer, the *see* Auriga
Charles's Wain *see* Ursa
  Major
Chelae 84
Chemist's Furnace, the *see*
  Fornax
Circinus 67, 167
Columba 167
Coma Berenices *73–4*, 87
Corona Australis 167
Corona Borealis 71, *75–7*,
  89, 104, 112, 113
Corvus *77–8*, 85
Crab, the *see* Cancer
Crane, the *see* Grus
Crater *78–9*
Crow, the *see* Corvus
Crux 67, *163–4*, 167
Cup, the *see* Crater
Cygnus 23, 67, 89, 91, *95–7*,
  113, 117, 126
Delphinus *97–8*, 99
Dipper, Big *see* Ursa Major
Dolphin, the *see* Delphinus
Dorado 164, *167*
Draco *60–1*, 112, 136
Dragon, the *see* Draco
Eagle, the *see* Aquila
Engraving Tool, the *see*
  Caelum
Equuleus *99*
Equuleus Pictoris (obsolete
  name) *see* Pictor
Eridanus 124, *144–6*
Fishes, the *see* Pisces
Flying Fish, the *see* Volans
Foal, the *see* Equuleus
Fornax 167
Frederici Honores (obsolete
  name) 126

Gemini 11, 19, 67, 71, 135, 137, 143, 146–9, 151
Giraffe, the see Camelopardalis
Goat, the see Capricornus
Great Bear, the see Ursa Major
Greater Dog, the see Canis Major
Great Ship, the see Argo
Grus 168
Hare, the see Lepus
Harp, the see Lyra
Hercules 77, 89, 99–101
Herdsman, the see Boötes
Horologium 168
Hunter, the see Orion
Hunting Dogs, the see Canes Venatici
Hydra 78, 79–81, 143
Hydrus 168
Indian, the see Indus
Indus 168
Keel, the see Carina
Lacerta 67, 125–6
Lady in the Chair see Cassiopeia
Leo 11, 16, 71, 78, 79, 81–3, 138
Leo Minor 83
Lepus 150–1
Lesser Bear, the see Ursa Minor
Lesser Lion, the see Leo Minor
Libra 79, 84, 85, 109
Lion, the see Leo
Little Dog, the see Canis Minor
Little Fox, the see Vulpecula
Lizard, the see Lacerta
Lupus 67, 168
Lynx 137, 151
Lyra 22, 89, 99, 101–4
Lyre, the see Lyra
Malus (obsolete name) see Pyxis and Puppis
Mariner's Compass, the see Pyxis
Mast, the (Malus) (obsolete name) 155; see also Pyxis
Mensa 164, 168
Microscope, the see Microscopium
Microscopium 168
Monoceros 67, 152
Mons Mensae (obsolete

name) see Mensa
Musca 67, 168
Net, the see Reticulum
Noah's Dove see Columba
Norma 67, 168
Northern Cross, the see Cygnus
Northern Crown, the see Corona Borealis
Octans 163, 169
Octant, the see Octans
Ophiuchus 104–6, 109, 112
Orion 67, 124, 135, 141, 144, 150, 152, 153–4, 155
Painter's Easel, the see Pictor
Pair of Compasses, the see Circinus
Pavo 169
Peacock, the see Pavo
Pegasus 99, 117, 118, 126–8
Pendulum Clock, the see Horologium
Perseus 20, 67, 117, 118, 128–31, 133, 136
Phoenix 169
Pictor 169
Pisces 11, 122, 124, 131–2
Piscis Austrinus 117, 132–3
Piscis Volans (obsolete name) see Volans
Plough, the see Ursa Major
Poop, the see Puppis
Precursor Dog, the see Canis Minor
Puppis 67, 155–6, 165
Pyxis 67, 155, 169
Quadrans Muralis (obsolete name) 61
Ram, the see Aries
Reticulum 169
River, the see Eridanus
Robur Carolinum (obsolete name) 162–3
Sagitta 67, 106–7
Sagittarius 67, 91, 92, 93, 107–9, 111
Sails, the see Vela
Sceptre, the see Lacerta
Scorpion, the see Scorpio
Scorpio or Scorpius 10, 16, 24, 67, 91, 109–11, 163
Sculptor 169
Scutum 67, 111–12
Sea Serpent, the see Hydrus
Serpens 112–13
Serpens Caput, Serpens Cauda, Serpent see Serpens

Serpentarius, Serpent Bearer see Ophiuchus
Sextans 84–5
Sextant, the see Sextans
Snake, the see Hydra
Sobieski's Shield see Scutum
Southern Cross, the see Crux
Southern Crown, the see Corona Australis
Southern Fish, the see Piscis Austrinus
Southern Fly, the see Musca
Southern Triangle (old nickname) see Norma
Southern Triangle, the see Triangulum Australis
Square and Level, the see Norma
Stellio, the newt see Lacerta
Stern, the see Puppis
'String of Pearls' see Orion
Swan, the see Cygnus
Swordfish, the see Dorado
'Sword Hand of Perseus' 130
Table Mountain see Mensa
Taurus 11, 16, 22, 135, 144, 153, 157–61
Telescope, the see Telescopium
Telescopium 169
Telescopium Herschelii (obsolete name) 137, 169; see Auriga
Tiger, the see Lynx
Toucan, the see Tucana
Triangle, the see Triangulum
Triangulum 131, 133
Triangulum Australe 170
Triangulum Minor see Triangulum
Tucana 164, 170
Twins, the see Gemini
Unicorn, the see Monoceros
Ursa Major 23, 33, 35, 61–4, 65, 71, 72, 83, 91, 117, 136, 146, 151
Ursa Minor 65–6, 72
Vela 67, 155, 165, 170
Virgin, the see Virgo
Virgo 11, 16, 74, 79, 85–8
Volans 170
Vulpecula 67, 91, 113–15
Vulture, Ascending and Descending 101
Wagon, the see Ursa Major
Warrior King, the see Cepheus

Water Bearer, the see
Aquarius
Water Snake, the see Hydra
Whale, the see Cetus
Winged Horse, the see
Pegasus
Wolf, the see Lupus
Copernicus, Nicolas, 81
Crab Nebula (M1), 24, 106,
160–1

Dahlgren, Elis, 104
Dan, tribe of 110
dark adaptation 44, 45
Dawes, William Rutter 37
Dawes limit 37
'dazzle tints', double stars 87
Deborah 56
Declination 29, 30, 31
de la Hire, Philippe 20
Delporte, E. 31
Deltoton 133
Democritus 68
Demon's Head, the Bearer of
the 128
Dendera planisphere and
zodiac 15, 107, 110, 139
Denning, W. F. 77
Dog-days see Sirius
do's and don'ts 51
'double-double' (ε^1–ε^2 Lyr) 103
double stars, telescope and
binocular performances 52,
53
Draconids, meteor shower 61
Dumb-bell Nebula (M27) 114

Earth's axis 29
ecliptic 30, 131
Egyptian gods 15
Egyptians 7, 10, 11, 13, 24, 86
Ephemeris, for Algol 48
epoch, for star positions 31
equinoxes 30, 86, 122, 131,
146, 157, 159
Eratosthenes 106
Eudoxus of Cnidos 10, 15
Euphrates Valley 13, 92, 118,
127
Eve 168
extra-focal images 49, 50
eye, in observation 37, 44

False dawn see Zodiacal Light
Fasti (Ovid) 76, 77
field glasses, 38; see also
binoculars

'Field of Nebulae' 87
fireballs 50, 180–1
Flamsteed, John 20, 29, 82, 86,
114, 115
'flying saucers' 171
Frederick II, King of Prussia
126

Gabriel, Archangel 127
Galaxy 68; see also Milky Way
Galileo 37, 69, 140
Galle, J. G. 94
garden chair, for observation
42
gegenschein see Zodiacal Light
Geminids, meteor shower 149
Geminus, 99
Geruvigus planisphere 16, 20
globular cluster 45
Goodricke, John 59, 102, 129
Gould, Benjamin A. 86, 169
Greek alphabet 19, 20, 29
Greek astronomers 16
Greenwich meridian 30
'Guest stars' 24, 161

Habrecht, Isaak 169
Hadley, James 85, 169
Hadrian, Roman emperor 92
Halley, Edmund 20, 162, 165;
Halley's comet, 25, 148
Hathor, Temple of 60
Hell, Abbé 137, 169
Herbert, A. P. 23
Herodotus 11
Herschel, John 165
Herschel, William 82, 96, 137,
147, 148, 169
Hesiod 158
Hevelius, Johannes 20, 55, 74,
83, 85, 111, 114, 125, 126,
133, 151, 152
Hind, John Russell 87, 106, 115
Hind's Crimson Star (R Lep)
150–1
Hipparchus, 10, 16, 24, 34, 99
Histoire Celeste 115
Hond 22
Hooke, Robert 123
horoscopes 19
Houtmann, Friedrich, 20, 162
Humason, Milton, 115
Hyades, the 157

India 13, 24
International Astronomical
Union (I.A.U.) 31, 171

Isaac, 170
Isis, Temple of 15
Israelites 16

Jacob 170
Jacob's Staff, Rod or Rake see
Orion
Japanese astronomy 161
Jena University 23
Job 168
Jonah 124
Josephus 118
Jupiter 37, 83, 171, 176;
satellites 37, 176

Kalenburg 111
Kepler, Johannes 10, 17, 151,
152
Kepler's Star 106 '
Khons, Temple of 60
Kingsley, Charles 129
Kruger 60, double star 59

Lacaille, Nicholas de 163, 164,
165, 166, 167, 168, 169
Lagoon nebula (M8) 109
Lalande, J. J. L. de 29
Leipzig University 154
Lemonnier, Pierre C. 115
Leonids, 50, 83, 120
Le Verrier, Urbain 94
Lick telescope 125, 144
light grasp 37
limiting magnitude see
magnitude
Lion of Judah 81
Lockyer, Norman 141
Lode Star 65
Lowell Observatory 148
Lyrids 104

Magellan, Ferdinand 163, 167
Magellanic Clouds 163–4, 167,
168, 170
magnification 52
magnitude, effects of coating
lens 38, 39, 52
magnitude, limits for
binoculars and telescopes 52,
53
magnitude, scale 34
Mair, Alexander 19
Mars 17, 58, 175
Mary Magdalene 56
Mayan astronomy 24
Mayer, Christian 103
Megalithic 7

Mercury 174
meridian 30
Mesopotamians 7
Messier Catalogue 53
Metcalf, Joel 77
meteors, naked-eye
    observations 50, 83, 180
Meurisse 162
Milky Way 13, 67–9, 86, 93,
    95, 97, 106, 107, 112, 114,
    117, 128, 133, 145, 152, 163,
    164, 167, 168, 170
Montanari 129
Moon, magnitude 35
Morin 72
Mostlin 106
Mount Wilson Observatory
    115
Mullard Radio Observatory
    115
Mut, Temple of 60
Mythology:
    Aesculapius 104, 112
    Aetes, King of Colchis 122
    Alcmene 99
    Amalthea 93, 137
    Ambrosia 157
    Amphitryon 99
    Anubis 141
    Apis 157
    Apollo 77, 101, 104, 106
    Arcas 62, 65, 72
    Argo 123, 155
    Argonauts 57–8, 95, 101, 112,
    122, 155–6
    Argos 79
    Ariadne 71, 75, 76
    Arion 98
    Astraea 84
    Atlas 15, 157, 158
    Bacchus 76, 95
    Bellerophon 127
    Berenice's hair 73
    Caesar, Julius 84
    Callisto 62, 65
    Carmenta 86
    Castor 99
    Celeris 99
    Cecrops 121
    Cephalus 141
    Ceres 85
    Chimaera 127
    Chiron 104, 107
    Colchis 155
    Conon 73
    Coronis 157
    Crotus 108

Cupid 131
Cyclopes 106
Cycnus 95
Cysatus 154
Danaos 156
Dardanos 160
Deucalion 121
Diana 141, 153
Dodona 156
Dolphin 98
Eudora 157
Euergetes 73
Eurydice 101
Ganymede 92
Giants 92, 139
Gods 92
Golden Fleece 112, 122,
    155–6
Gorgons 127, 129
Hector 92
Helicon, Mt 127
Helle 122
Hercules 60, 79, 81, 99, 106,
    139
Hermes 101
Hesperides, garden of 60
Hippocrene 127
Hyas 157
Hyrieus 159
Icarus 144
Ilium 160
Ino, Queen 122
Isis 86
Jason 57, 123
Juno 60, 62, 79, 110, 118,
    139, 169
Jupiter 60, 62, 73, 93, 99,
    106, 127, 131, 133, 137, 141,
    145, 147
Justitia 85
Lacedaemon 160
Laomedon, King of Troy
    124
Latone 153
Leda 147
Lernaean serpent 79, 108, 139
Lesbos 98
Marduk 112
Mars 95, 110, 123
Mechus 84
Medusa 127, 129
Melissa 137
Melkarth 100
Menelaos 99
Mercury 99, 137
Minerva 131
Mithra 157

Moera 144
Mons Menalus 72
Muses, the 127
Myrtilus 137
Nemaeans 81
Neptune 56, 98, 118, 124, 127
Nereids 118
Noah 156
Nymphs 56
Oenomaus 137
Orion 110
Orpheus 95, 101
Osiris, the Boat of 150
Ovid 76, 77
Padus, River 95
Pan 72, 77, 93
Perseus 118
Phaethon 95, 145
Phaola 157
Phoenix 123
Phryxus 122
Pleione 157, 158
Polyxo 157
Poseidon 159
Procris 141
Prometheus 92, 106
Quetzalcoatl 121
Saturn 92, 107
Selkit 110
Serapis 157
Shawnee Indians 76
Theseus 76
Thessaly 121
Typhon 69, 77, 86, 93, 131
Valhalla 69
Venus 131; Temple of 73
Zeus 92, 121, 160

Naked-eye observation 48, 49,
    50
Napoleon *see* Orion
nebulae, visibility of 45
Nelson *see* Orion
Neptune 94, 177–8
neutron stars 115, 161
New General Catalogue
    (NGC) 53
Newton, Isaac 156
Newtonian reflecting telescope
    40
Nile, River 10, 81, 92, 93, 133,
    141–2, 144, 145
North America Nebula 97
North Pole 13
Nubecula Major 163–4, 167,
    168
Nubecula Minor 163–4, 170

observing book 50
observing techniques 44
Omega Nebula (M17) 109
opera glasses 37, 38; *see also* binoculars
Orion Nebula (M42) 45, 154

Pacific islands 24
Pallas, minor planet 175
Palomar Sky Atlas 25, 115
Pardies 22
Peltier, Leslie 104
Penicydes 75
Period/luminosity relationship (Cepheids) 59
Perseids 131
Persia 13
Phenomena 10, 146, 158; Anglo-Saxon version 20
Phoenicians 24, 62, 100, 127, 142
Picard, Jean 115
Pigott 92
planetary nebula, connection with novae 130
planet finding tables 186
planets *172–8*
planispheres 22, 165
Pleiades 136, 137, 141, 153, *157–8*
Pliny 86, 123
Pluto 148, 178
Pole Star, finding 32, 35
Pole Star, southern (σ Oct) 163, 169
Polynesian astronomy 24
Praesepe (M44, ε Cnc) *139–40*
precession 12
Ptolemy 10, 11, 16, 20, 129, 164, 166, 167
pulsar (M1) 24, 25; 115

Quadrantids 61

Rameses, Temple of 60
Raphael 168
Red Dwarfs 59
Reformation 22
Regent's Park Observatory 87, 106
resolution, telescopic 52
resolving power, optical 37; double stars 38
Riccioli 160
Richer 162
Right Ascension 29, 31, 122

Ring Nebula in Lyra (M57) 103–4
Rosse, Earl of 75
Royal Family of constellations 128
Royal stars 81–2
Royer, 22, 126, 167
Rudolphine Tables 17

St Helena 162
Saturn 176–7; satellites 177
Saturn Nebula 122
Scarborough, Sir Charles 75
Schaeberle 144
Schiller, Julius 22, 56, 100, 107, 118, 124, 127, 139, 150, 168, 169, 170
Schmidt, Julius 148
Secchi, Father 75
'seeing', astronomical 42; effect on different objects 43; influence of topography 43; relationship to sky transparency 42, 43
Seven Sisters *see* Pleiades
Seven Virgins *see* Pleiades
Sidereal Time 30
Sidereus Nuntius 69
Sidus Ludovicianum 63
Sky and Telescope 175, 185
Smiles, Samuel 36
Sobieski, John III, King of Poland 111
societies, national astronomical 185
Solomon 156
Sombrero Nebula (M104) 87, 88
South African Bushmen 165
Southern Pole Star *see* Pole Star
space probes 184
spectroscopic binary star, definition and explanation 63–4
Square of Pegasus 117, 120, 126, 127, 131
star designations 28
star, effect of colour differences in observation 49, 50
star magnitude 35
stars, numbers visible to naked eye 27
star sphere 32; apparent rotation of 32
star time 33
Steavenson, Dr 115
stellar triangle 95

Table Mountain 163, 168
Tears of St Lawrence *see* Perseids
telescope, invention of 37; performance 43, 52, 53; predictor 41; reflecting 40, 42; refracting 40, 42
Tempel, William 160
temples, orientated towards stars 7, 86, 110, 123, 137, 141, 157, 159, 167
Tennyson, Alfred, Lord 142
Theodorus, Petrus (Peter Dirckszoon Keyser) 20, 162, 169, 170
Three Kings *see* Orion
Three Magi 100
Three Patriarchs 170
Tombaugh, Clyde 148
Trapezium, the 154
Trifid Nebula (M20) 109
Tutankhamen 29
Tycho's Star 57

Universal Time 53
Uranometria, star atlas 19, 20, 22, 162
Uranometria Argentina 169
Uranus 82, 137, 148, 177

Valerius 78
variable star, method of estimating magnitude 48, 49; naked-eye list 215–16; observations 47, 48, 49, 50
Venus 171, 174–5; magnitude 34
Virgin's Spike *see* Spica
visual acuity 46
Vogel 129

Washington Observatory 92
Weigel, Erhard 23
Western Australia 20
Wolf, Max 148
Worcester, Battle of 163

Yuchi, Hoangti 24

zenith 30
zodiac 13, 15; origins of 13
Zodiac (star chart) 20, 93, 107, 108, 110, 157
zodiacal constellations, list 187
zodiacal light 181–2
zodiacal stars 13
zodiacal zone 13

224